Essentials ᴛʜᴅʀᴀᴡɴ

of **PSYCHOLOGICAL A** ... **S**

Everything you need to kno
and interpret the major psyc....

I'd like to order the following
ESSENTIALS OF PSYCHOLOGICAL ASSESSMENT:

All titles are
$34.95* each

- ❏ WAIS®-III Assessment / 0471-28295-2
- ❏ WISC-III® and WPPSI-R® Assessment / 0471-34501-6
- ❏ WJ III® Cognitive Abilities Assessment / 0471-34466-4
- ❏ Cross-Battery Assessment / 0471-38264-7
- ❏ Cognitive Assessment with KAIT & Other Kaufman Measures / 0471-38317-1
- ❏ Nonverbal Assessment / 0471-38318-X
- ❏ PAI® Assessment / 0471-08463-8
- ❏ CAS Assessment / 0471-29015-7
- ❏ MMPI-2™ Assessment / 0471-34533-4
- ❏ Myers-Briggs Type Indicator® Assessment / 0471-33239-9
- ❏ Rorschach® Assessment / 0471-33146-5
- ❏ Millon™ Inventories Assessment, Second Edition / 0471-21891-X
- ❏ TAT and Other Storytelling Techniques / 0471-39469-6
- ❏ MMPI-A™ Assessment / 0471-39815-2
- ❏ NEPSY® Assessment / 0471-32690-9
- ❏ Neuropsychological Assessment / 0471-40522-1
- ❏ WJ III® Tests of Achievement Assessment / 0471-33059-0
- ❏ Individual Achievement Assessment / 0471-32432-9
- ❏ WMS®-III Assessment / 0471-38080-6
- ❏ Behavioral Assessment / 0471-35367-1
- ❏ Forensic Assessment / 0471-33186-4
- ❏ Bayley Scales of Infant Development—II Assessment / 0471-32651-8
- ❏ Career Interest Assessment / 0471-35365-5
- ❏ WPPSI™-III Assessment / 0471-28895-0
- ❏ 16PF® Assessment / 0471-23424-9

Please complete the order form on the back

TO ORDER BY PHONE, CALL TOLL FREE 1-877-762-2974
To order online: www.wiley.com/essentials
To order by mail refer to order form on next page

Ⓦ **WILEY**

Essentials

of **PSYCHOLOGICAL ASSESSMENT** Series

Order Form

Please send this order form with your payment (credit card or check) to:
John Wiley & Sons, Inc.
Attn: J. Knott
111 River Street
Hoboken, NJ 07030

Name _____

Affiliation _____

Address _____

City/State/Zip _____

Phone _____

E-mail _____

❑ Please add me to your e-mailing list

Quantity of Book(s) ordered _____ x $34.95* each

Shipping charges:	Surface	2-Day	1-Day	
First Item	$5.00	$10.50	$17.50	
Each additional item	$3.00	$3.00	$4.00	**Total $_____**

For orders greater than 15 items, please contact Customer Care at 1-877-762-2974.

Payment Method: ❑ Check ❑ Credit Card (*All orders subject to credit approval*)
❑ MasterCard ❑ Visa ❑ American Express

Card Number _____ Exp. Date_____

Signature _____

* Prices subject to change.

TO ORDER BY PHONE, CALL TOLL FREE 1-877-762-2974
To order online: www.wiley.com/essentials

Essentials of 16PF® Assessment

Essentials of Psychological Assessment Series

Series Editors, Alan S. Kaufman and Nadeen L. Kaufman

Essentials

of 16PF® Assessment

Heather E. P. Cattell
James M. Schuerger

John Wiley & Sons, Inc.

Library of Congress Cataloging-in-Publication Data:

Cattell, Heather E.P.
Essentials of 16PF assessment / Heather Cattell, James M. Schuerger.
p. cm. — (Essentials of psychological assessment series)
Includes bibliographical references and index.
ISBN 0-471-23424-9 (pbk.)
1. Sixteen Personality Factor Questionnaire. I. Schuerger, James M. II. Title. III. Series.

BF698.8.S5C265 2003
155.2'83—dc2

2003045081

Printed in the United States of America.

10 9 8 7 6 5 4

The authors wish to dedicate this book to the memory of

Alberta Karen Cattell

(1916-1996)

Although she was first a gifted and enthusiastic mathematician, Karen gradually became the worlds' foremost 16PF supporter. No one knew it better than she did—from item content to factor structure to early research in Czechoslovakia. Her enthusiasm was contagious, and she was generous in sharing her knowledge and in her encouragement of others. She enjoyed giving in-depth 16PF profile interpretations to those who showed a personal interest. As a friend, mentor, and colleague, she was kind, tactful, considerate, affirmative, and loyal. She drew people out, empowering them to give their best, even in difficult times. She passionately supported the people around her and their feelings and interests.
She is greatly missed.

CONTENTS

SERIES PREFACE

In the *Essentials of Psychological Assessment* series, we have attempted to provide the reader with books that will deliver key practical information in the most efficient and accessible style. The series features instruments in a variety of domains, such as cognition, personality, education, and neuropsychology. For the experienced clinician, books in the series will offer a concise, yet thorough way to master utilization of the continuously evolving supply of new and revised instruments, as well as a convenient method for keeping up to date on the tried-and-true measures. The novice will find here a prioritized assembly of all the information and techniques that must be at one's fingertips to begin the complicated process of individual psychological assessment.

Wherever feasible, visual shortcuts to highlight key points are utilized alongside systematic, step-by-step guidelines. Chapters are focused and succinct. Topics are targeted for an easy understanding of the essentials of administration, scoring, interpretation, and clinical application. Theory and research are continually woven into the fabric of each book, but always to enhance clinical interference, never to sidetrack or overwhelm. We have long been advocates of "intelligent" testing — the notion that a profile of test scores is meaningless unless it is brought to life by the clinical observations and astute detective work of knowledgeable examiners. Test profiles must be used to make a difference in a child's or adult's life, or why bother to test? We want this series to help our readers become the best intelligent testers they can be.

In *Essentials of 16PF® Assessment,* the authors present a foundation of basic information for beginners as well as in-depth information for the experienced practitioner. The goal in writing this text was always to provide sufficient explanation so that a person with no 16PF experience could, after careful study, make sense of a set of scores. The text draws upon the authors' own considerable research, teaching, and applied experience with the test, as well as that of many other authors. Detailed information is provided on all of the scales measured by the 16PF Questionnaire, as well as some information about scale interactions, a range of case studies, and information about how to use the test in career counseling, employee selection and development, and clinical and counseling applications.

Alan S. Kaufman, PhD, and Nadeen L. Kaufman, EdD, Series Editors
Yale University School of Medicine

One

HISTORY AND DEVELOPMENT

The 16 Personality Factor Questionnaire (16PF®) is a comprehensive measure of normal-range personality that is widely used in settings in which an in-depth, integrated picture of the whole person is needed. Key information about the test is provided in Rapid Reference 1.1. The history of the development of the 16PF Questionnaire spans almost the entire history of objective personality measurement. Instead of being developed to measure preconceived dimensions of interest to a particular author for a particular purpose, the 16PF Questionnaire originated from the unique perspective of an empirical quest to try to discover the basic structural elements of personality via scientific research sampling of the whole domain of human personality. In addition to leading to the discovery of the 16 personality factors for which the test is named, the research identified the broad dimensions currently called the Big Five factors of personality. Because of its scientific origin, the test has a long history of empirical research, is embedded in a well-established theory of individual differences, and has proven useful in understanding a wide variety of important behaviors. These features provide a rich source of interpretation for the test user.

That the 16PF Questionnaire originated from scientific inquiry was no accident; its author, Raymond B. Cattell, was the product of a strong scientific and analytical background. His grandfather, father, and brother were inventors and engineers. As a young man, he witnessed the astounding results of pioneering scientific research—electricity, radios, telephones, automobiles, and airplanes. These influences inspired his decision to pursue undergraduate and master's degrees in the physical sciences at the University of London in the 1920s.

At that time, the field of scientific psychology was quite limited in scope. Cattell studied the work of physiological and experimental psychologists (e.g., Pavlov, Thorndike, and Wundt) who used the scientific method to examine very particular areas of human functioning such as sensation and learning. He found that personality theory originated in the postulations of philosophers such as Aristotle, Locke, and Nietzsche, whereas modern developments were largely generated by medically trained professionals such as Sigmund Freud and Carl Jung, who studied the symptoms and problems of troubled patients. These professionals drew their ideas primarily from clinical experience and relied on intuition for reconstruction of what was going on inside people,

≣*Rapid Reference 1.1*

Key Features of the 16PF Fifth Edition Questionnaire

1. Result of scientific research into the basic elements of human personality
2. Multitiered trait structure that provides rich, integrated picture of the whole person, including global (Big Five) traits
3. Comprehensive, integrated measure of normal-range personality
4. Extensive research available from a range of applied settings
5. Useful in a wide variety of applied settings: clinical, counseling, career development, employee selection, educational settings, and basic research
6. Available in more than 30 languages worldwide, with many languages available online

often scorning the rigor and precision of science. Thus, Cattell discovered that experimental psychologists seemed to have little to say about the larger issues of human personality and that personality theorists showed little inclination to use a scientific approach.

Cattell was influenced by his studies and by the social and political ferment of post-World War I London, where he regularly was exposed to people like George Bernard Shaw, Aldous Huxley, H. G. Wells, and Bertram Russell. This experience led Cattell to believe that the biggest problems in the world were often the result of human temperament and motivation. He speculated that there must be some way to apply the powerful tools of science to understanding human personality.

At the University of London, Cattell worked with Charles Spearman, who was developing the methods of factor analysis to try to identify and organize the basic elements of human ability. Cattell's involvement in this study sparked his conviction that factor analysis, a powerful tool for discovering the basic underlying dimensions behind complex phenomena, could also be applied productively to personality. He reasoned that human personality must have basic structural elements in the same way that the physical world has basic building blocks (e.g., oxygen and hydrogen). If the basic building blocks of personality were discovered and the structure of personality was indeed measurable, then human behavior would—to some extent—become understandable and predictable. For example, complex behavioral criteria such as leadership, self-esteem, and creativity could be predicted from these basic structural elements of personality.

Thus, Cattell's goal in creating the 16PF Questionnaire was to provide a thorough, research-based map of normal personality. However, the development of the 16PF represented only one part of a much larger research effort. Cattell believed in examining the broadest possible range of personality phenomena, including roles and states, thoughts and actions, verbal and nonverbal behavior, normal and abnormal personality, and ability and interest variables. He believed that for psychology to advance as a science, psychologists needed scientific measurement procedures for three distinct domains of human characteristics: personality, ability, and motivation (with the latter defined as dynamic drives such as a need for power, achievement, or security). By sampling each of these domains and applying factor-analytic methods, Cattell sought to discover the number and nature of the variables that comprised the meaning of each.

In addition, Cattell posited three types of information or data sources that need to be sampled in exploring each of the three domains. Life record or life observation (L-data) involves observing and recording information about a person from natural, real life settings—actual in situ behavior from everyday life. These data range from historical or biographical facts to behavior counts to observer ratings by those who know the person well. Questionnaire data (Q-data) are obtained from the person's self-description in response to multiple-choice or open-ended questions. This type of conscious self-disclosure provides the mental interior to the external record provided by the L-data, but it is still just another piece of behavior whose actual meaning is discerned through further research. Objective tests (T-data), on the other hand, involve objective measurement of behavior through standardized, contrived tests or laboratory situations that do not require the individual to conduct any self-examination. T-data instruments range from paper-and-pencil tests, such as ability or projective tests, to behavioral measures in experimental situations. Cattell sought to identify the basic traits of personality from factor-analytic studies covering information from L-, Q-, and T-data sources, assuming that traits that emerged in all three media would represent true functional unities.

Cattell and his colleagues embarked on a comprehensive program of research to identify and map the underlying dimensions of personality. Because a critical determinant of the outcome of a factor analysis is the range of data that is used, Cattell stressed the importance of adequately sampling the whole domain of personality. Thus, the researchers began their search with an exhaustive listing of personality descriptors—based on the belief that "all aspects of human personality which are or have been of importance, interest, or utility have already become recorded in the substance of language" (Cattell, 1943, p. 483). Starting with a compilation of all known personality descriptors in the English language (Allport & Odbert, 1936), they tried to discover the factors underlying the traits by analyzing the patterns among them in actual peer ratings, self-report questionnaires, and objective behavioral measures. An extensive description of this research process is included in Cattell's *Personality and Mood by Questionnaire* (1973).

After years of factor-analytic work, Cattell and his colleagues around the world determined a list of the fundamental building blocks of personality that were termed *primary traits*. These traits, the dimensions measured by the 16PF Questionnaire, are presented in Rapid Reference 1.2. The traits were developed using data from all three research media (peer ratings, self-report tests, and objective behavioral measures) and in a wide range of populations (e.g., undergraduates, military personnel, working adults), which has contributed to the robustness of the 16PF scales and their predictive utility in many kinds of settings. Lengthier descriptions of the scales appear in chapter 3.

Rapid Reference 1.2

16PF Scale Names and Descriptors

Descriptors of Low Range	Primary Scales	Descriptors of High Range
Reserved, impersonal, distant	**Warmth (A)**	Warm, participating, attentive to others
Concrete, lower mental capacity	**Reasoning (B)**	Abstract, bright, fast-learner
Reactive, affected by feelings	**Emotional Stability (C)**	Emotionally stable, adaptive, mature
Deferential, cooperative, avoids conflict	**Dominance (E)**	Dominant, forceful, assertive
Serious, restrained, careful	**Liveliness (F)**	Enthusiastic, animated, spontaneous
Expedient, nonconforming	**Rule-Consciousness (G)**	Rule conscious, dutiful
Shy, timid, threat sensitive	**Social Boldness (H)**	Socially bold, venturesome, thick-skinned
Tough, objective, unsentimental	**Sensitivity (I)**	Sensitive, aesthetic, tender–minded
Trusting, unsuspecting, accepting	**Vigilance (L)**	Vigilant, suspicious, skeptical, wary
Practical, grounded, down-to-earth	**Abstractedness (M)**	Abstracted, imaginative, idea oriented
Forthright, genuine, artless	**Privateness (N)**	Private, discreet, nondisclosing
Self-assured, unworried, complacent	**Apprehension (O)**	Apprehensive, self-doubting, worried
Traditional, attached to familiar	**Openness to Change (Q1)**	Open to change, experimenting
Group-oriented, affiliative	**Self-Reliance (Q2)**	Self-reliant, solitary, individualistic
Tolerates disorder, unexacting, flexible	**Perfectionism (Q3)**	Perfectionistic, organized, self-disciplined
Relaxed, placid, patient	**Tension (Q4)**	Tense, high energy, driven

(continued)

Descriptors of Low Range	Global Scales	Descriptors of High Range
Introverted, socially inhibited	**Extraversion**	Extraverted, socially participating
Low anxiety, imperturbable	**Anxiety**	High anxiety, perturbable
Receptive, open-minded, intuitive	**Tough-Mindedness**	Tough-minded, resolute, unempathic
Accommodating, agreeable, selfless	**Independence**	Independent, persuasive, willful
Unrestrained, follows urges	**Self-Control**	Self-controlled, inhibits urges

Note. Adapted with permission from Conn, S. R., & Rieke, M. L. (1994). *16PF Fifth Edition technical manual.* Champaign, IL: Institute for Personality and Ability Testing, Inc.

Some letters are missing from the alphabetic designations of the 16PF primary scales (D, J, K, or P); these scales turned up only inconsistently in early factor analyses and therefore were dropped.

THE 16PF STRUCTURE AND THE ORIGINAL BIG FIVE

From the beginning, Cattell conceptualized personality in terms of a hierarchical, multilevel structure (Cattell, 1946). He found that when the primary traits themselves were factor analyzed, a smaller number of broad, underlying influences among the primaries emerged; Cattell called these "second-order" or "global" traits (see Rapid Reference 1.2). Thus, the global traits were constructed from the primary traits, which define the global traits, and the two levels of personality structure are fundamentally interrelated. Although Cattell continued to search for more than five global factors, only five have remained clearly and consistently identifiable, and these factors have been scored from the test for the last 30 years.

Figure 1.1 highlights the significance and usefulness of the multilevel 16PF factor structure. The five global scales give an overview of an individual's personality makeup at a broad level of functioning while the more specific primary scales (from which the globals were constructed) provide an in-depth picture of the individual's unique personality dynamics.

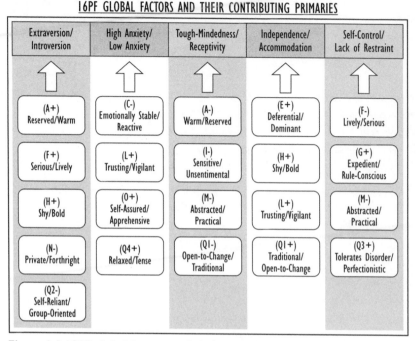

Figure 1.1 16PF global factors and their contributing primaries.

For example, global scale Extraversion/Introversion emerged as a combination of five primary scales, each representing a unique motivation for moving toward versus away from other people. Thus, two people who are each at the 80th percentile on Extraversion may spend equal amounts of time around other people but for very different reasons. One person, for example, might move toward others because he is caring and warm (high on Warmth-A), feels a need for companionship and support (low on Self-Reliance-Q2), but is shy and modest (low on Social Boldness-H). Another person at the 80th percentile on Extraversion might be talkative and high-spirited (high on Liveliness-F), bold and thick-skinned (high on Social Boldness-H), but detached and objective (low on Warmth-A). This second extravert may be perceived as less sincere and shallower than the first; therefore, people would respond very differently to the two. Overall, these two extraverts contrast greatly in their empathy for others and would be quite dissimilar to live with, to work for, or to supervise.

As the preceding example illustrates, the 16PF structure allows the professional to view an individual's personality at various levels of organization and to understand deeper motivations. Note that all the scales have distinct definitions for both ends or poles (i.e., are bipolar) and that the high ends are not "good" and the low ends are not "bad"—that is, both high and low scores have both strengths and weaknesses depending on the situation. Primary scales may contribute to a particular global scale in either a positive or negative direction (either the high or low end of the scale), depending on how the factor analysis defined a given global scale.

Test users frequently focus on the 16PF primary-level traits because they offer a more fine-grained definition of an individual's unique dynamics and because they have been proven more powerful predictors of actual behavior (Ashton, 1998; Ashton, Jackson, Paunonen, Helmes, & Rothstein, 1995; Goldberg, 1972, in press; Mershon & Gorsuch, 1988; Paunonen, 1993). However, the five global scales create a basic conceptual organizing structure among the primaries—that is, they help to give meaning to the primaries and contribute to the interpretation and understanding of individual scores.

These five global scales represent the original traits now commonly referred to as the Big Five (Cattell, 1957). In fact, the development of the recent Big Five theories was heavily influenced by the use of Cattell's original scales (e.g., Digman, 1990; Goldberg, 1993; Norman, 1963; Tupes & Christal, 1961). For example, the authors of the NEO describe its development as beginning with cluster analyses of the 16PF scales (Costa & McCrae, 1976, 1985). Comparisons between the five 16PF global scales and other Big Five scales (such as those from the NEO) show a high level of alignment. Research has found that the average correlation between the NEO five factors and the 16PF globals is just as high as the average correlation between the NEO five factors and Goldberg's Big Five factors (Cattell, H. E. P., 1996; Pipher, 2002). Rapid Reference 1.3 indicates the alignments between the factors in the three major systems.

Although the fit across the various representatives of the model is close, the 16PF global scales have an important advantage over the other five-factor models. They have this advantage because the method used in the 16PF development allowed the data itself to determine the factors, whereas the other Big Five systems were developed based on methods that forced their factors to be uncorrelated, thus affecting their definitions. Technically, the

≡Rapid Reference 1.3

Alignments Among the Three Main Five-Factor Models

16PF (Cattell)	NEO-PI-R (Costa & McCrae)	Big-Five (Goldberg)
Extraversion/Introversion	Extraversion	Surgency
Low Anxiety/High Anxiety	Neuroticism	Emotional Stability
Tough-Mindedness/Receptivity	Openness	Intellect or Culture
Independence/Accommodation	Agreeableness	Agreeableness
Self-Control/Lack of Restraint	Conscientiousness	Conscientiousness or Dependability

16PF global scales emerged in a factor analysis that allowed oblique rotations; in contrast, the other systems used orthogonal rotations, despite the fact that the scales in these systems have repeatedly been found to be significantly correlated (not orthogonal). Thus, the 16PF global scales are the only Big Five scales developed without their definitions' being constricted by methods of statistical convenience.

USES OF THE 16PF QUESTIONNAIRE

Although the 16PF Questionnaire measures normal-range traits (not psychopathology), it has been used extensively in counseling and clinical settings because of its ability to give an in-depth, integrated picture of the whole person, including strengths and weaknesses. In addition, it can facilitate dialogue between the clinician and client by promoting understanding, empathy, and rapport from the very first session. Furthermore, because 16PF scale meanings represent common areas of everyday experience, the professional can share test results openly with clients, thus facilitating discussion, increasing self-awareness, and enabling clients to feel a sense of partnership in the assessment and planning processes.

The test can provide information on issues relevant to the counseling process, such as the individual's capacity for insight, self-esteem, cognitive style, internalization of standards, openness to change, capacity for empathy, level of interpersonal trust, quality of attachments, interpersonal needs, attitude toward authority, power dynamics, frustration tolerance, and coping style. Additionally, test results can suggest effective strategies for establishing a working alliance, developing a therapeutic plan, and selecting effective therapeutic interventions or modes of treatment. 16PF scores can be particularly useful in time-limited or managed-care environments, where the clinician needs to quickly develop a picture of the whole person as a context in which to place presenting problems and then develop a therapeutic plan to suit the client's individual needs.

The 16PF Questionnaire also provides an objective, comprehensive, and efficient source of information in employment and career settings. Its relevance for world-of-work issues has led to its wide use in employment settings, including the areas of career development and career counseling; employee selection, promotion, and outplacement; and employee development, training, and coaching. Research has generated a wide range of occupational profiles, such as for executives and managers, salespeople and customer service people, law enforcement officers and security personnel, social workers and teachers, scientists and engineers, and writers and artists (see chapter 6). Comparisons with these occupational profiles are often useful in interpreting individual profiles. Decades of use in industrial settings has led to prediction equations for a variety of criteria, such as problem-solving style, creativity, leadership, social skills, stress tolerance, conscientiousness, initiative taking, learning style, and the Holland occupational types.

The 16PF Questionnaire is used in a wide range of other settings, including basic research, education, sports psychology, medical treatment, and military training. For example, it has been used to study the effects of birth order on personality (Beer, 2001), investigate effects of aging (Long, 2000), understand differences in learning styles (Macgregor, 2000), study equivalence of cross-cultural test translations (Budd, 1998), investigate the effects of social desirability on tests (Ellington, Smith, & Sackett, 2001), understand issues of sexual orientation (Cabrera, 2001), and improve selection and training of military pilots (Bartram, 1995).

VERSIONS OF THE 16PF QUESTIONNAIRE

Since the 16PF Questionnaire was first published in 1949, research and refinement have continued, resulting in new editions published in 1956, 1962, and 1968 and in the 16PF Fifth Edition Questionnaire in 1993. (See Rapid Reference 1.4 for a brief history of 16PF development and Rapid Reference 1.6 for basic information about the test.) In 2001, the 16PF Questionnaire was restandardized on a stratified random sample of over 10,000 individuals, which reflects the 2000 U.S. Census figures for sex, race, and age.

The personality structure of younger age ranges was also studied, resulting in parallel 16PF testing forms for children and teens. These forms include the High School Personality Questionnaire (HSPQ) for ages 12 to 18 (Cattell, M. Cattell, & Johns, 1984), the Children's Personality Questionnaire (CPQ) for ages 8 to12 (Porter & Cattell, 1975), and the Early School Personality Questionnaire (ESPQ) for ages 6 to 8 (Cattell & R. W. Coan, 1976). The HSPQ has been updated and renamed the 16PF Adolescent Personality Questionnaire (Schuerger, 2001a); this test includes new sections of career interest questions and a section asking directly about problems in living. A revision of the CPQ is in progress.

A shortened version of the test, called the 16PF Select Questionnaire (R. B. Cattell, H. E. P. Cattell, A. K. Cattell, & Kelly, 1999), is available for selection settings. It allows the professional to define the personality characteristics that are most important for effective job performance, and provides objective feedback comparing an applicant's personality characteristics to the desired personality dimensions for the job.

Because of the international nature of Cattell's research, the 16PF Questionnaire was quickly translated and adapted into many other languages. Since its first publication in 1949, the test has been adapted into more than 35 languages and dialects. The introduction of 16PFworld.com in 1999 enabled multinational users to access the test in many different languages for Internet administration, scoring, and computer interpretive reports. Ongoing adaptation and improvement of the 16PF test continues at the Institute for Personality & Ability Testing (IPAT), the publisher, in conjunction with scientists and practitioners throughout the world.

≡Rapid Reference 1.4

History and Development of the 16PF Questionnaire

- 1930s—Cattell works with Charles Spearman in the development of factor-analytic methods to study the structure of human abilities.
- 1940s—Cattell begins comprehensive program of research, applying factor analysis to identify the basic elements of personality structure.
- 1949—First publication of the 16PF Questionnaire in the United States.
- 1952—First publication of the 16PF Questionnaire in Great Britain.
- 1953—First publication of the High School Personality Questionnaire (HSPQ).
- 1956—Publication of the 16PF Second Edition.
- 1959—First publication of the Children's Personality Questionnaire (CPQ).
- 1962—Publication of the 16PF Third Edition.
- 1965—Introduction of computer scoring by mail.
- 1968—Publication of the 16PF Fourth Edition.
- 1972—Publication of first computerized interpretive report.
- 1980—Test translations exceed 35 languages worldwide.
- 1992—Computer scoring by OnSite software.
- 1993—Publication of the 16PF Fifth Edition.
- 1999—Online administration and scoring and computerized interpretive reports (NetAssess) were introduced.
- 1999—Publication of the 16PF Select Questionnaire.
- 2000—Restandardization of the 16PF Fifth Edition with over 10,000 people.
- 2001—Online administration and scoring and computerized interpretive reports became available in multiple international languages (16PF world.com).
- 2001—Publication of the 16PF Adolescent Personality Questionnaire (APQ, a revision of the HSPQ).

TEST DESCRIPTION, RELIABILITY, AND VALIDITY

Description

Since its first publication in 1949, the test has undergone four major revisions. The latest edition, the 16PF Fifth Edition Questionnaire (1993), is the main subject of this book. In contrast to previous editions, the 16PF Fifth

Edition Questionnaire features simpler, updated language; a lower reading level; improved psychometric characteristics; new response-style indices; easier hand scoring; and updated norms. It was reviewed for compliance with the Americans with Disabilities Act, and for gender, cultural, and racial biases. Special attention was given to cross-cultural translatability of items since previous editions had been translated into over 35 languages. In 2001, the test was restandardized on a stratified random sample of more than 10,000 individuals, which reflects the 2000 U.S. Census figures for sex, race, and age.

The 16PF Fifth Edition contains 185 multiple-choice items that are written at a fifth-grade reading level. It provides scores on 16 primary personality scales (one of which is a short reasoning-ability scale, positioned by itself at the end of the test) and five global (Big Five) scales. Three response-style scales are also included to help in identifying unusual response patterns that may affect the validity of scores. Each primary scale contains 10–15 items, and each item has a three-choice answer format, with the middle choice being a question mark (?).

A distinguishing characteristic of 16PF items is that they tend to sample a broad range of normal behavior by asking test takers about their behavior in specific situations (rather than merely asking how they would rate themselves on personality traits, as is the practice of many other tests). The test includes a wide range of item types, including items that ask about actual behavior:

- When I find myself in a boring situation, I usually "tune out" and daydream about other things. (*a. true; b. ?; c. false*)
- In talking to a friend, I tend to: (*a. let my feelings show; b. ?; c. keep my feelings to myself*)
- I hardly ever feel hurried or rushed as I go about my daily tasks. (*a. true: I don't; b. ?; c. false: I often feel rushed.*)

Reliability

Reliabilities for the 16PF Fifth Edition's primary and global scales are comparable to those of other personality measures even though the scales are fairly short (10–15 items). These reliabilities are summarized in Rapid Reference 1.5. Internal consistency reliabilities (how highly the items in a scale correlate with each other) for the primary scales average .76 (ranging from

.68 to .87 over the 16 scales) in the normative sample of 10,261 individuals. Test-retest reliabilities (or estimates of the consistency of scores over time) for a 2-week interval ranged from .69 to .87 with a median of .80. Two-month test-retest reliabilities ranged from .56 to .79 with a median of .69. The 16PF global scales have even higher reliabilities; 2-week test-retest estimates ranged from .84 to .91 with a mean of .87, and 2-month test-retest estimates ranged from .70 to .82 with a median of .80. Further information can be found in the *16PF Fifth Edition Technical Manual* (Conn & Rieke, 1994).

≡Rapid Reference 1.5

Reliability Estimates for 16PF Fifth Edition Scales

| | Internal Consistency[a] | Test-Retest Interval | |
| | (Cronbach's alpha) | 2-week | 2-month |
Primary Scales	(N = 10,261)	(N = 204)	(N = 159)
A Warmth	.69	.83	.77
B Reasoning	.75	.69	.65
C Emotional Stability	.79	.75	.67
E Dominance	.68	.77	.69
F Liveliness	.73	.82	.69
G Rule-Consciousness	.77	.80	.76
H Social Boldness	.87	.87	.79
I Sensitivity	.79	.82	.76
L Vigilance	.73	.76	.56
M Abstractedness	.78	.84	.67
N Privateness	.77	.77	.70
O Apprehension	.80	.79	.64
Q1 Openness to Change	.68	.83	.70
Q2 Self-Reliance	.79	.86	.69
Q3 Perfectionism	.74	.80	.77
Q4 Tension	.79	.78	.68
Mean	.76	.80	.70

(continued)

Primary Scales	Internal Consistency[a] (Cronbach's alpha) (N = 10,261)	Test-Retest Interval	
		2-week (N = 204)	2-month (N = 159)
Global Scales			
Extraversion		.91	.80
Anxiety		.84	.70
Tough-Mindedness		.87	.82
Independence		.84	.81
Self-Control		.87	.79
Mean		.87	.78

Note. Adapted with permission from *16PF Fifth Edition norm supplement, release 2002* by C. C. Maraist and M. T. Russell, 2002; and from "Reliability and Equivalency" by S. R. Conn, 1994, in S. R. Conn & M. L. Rieke (Eds.), *The 16PF Fifth Edition technical manual.* Champaign, IL: Institute for Personality and Ability Testing, Inc.

[a]Internal consistency values are not available for the global factor scales because their scores are derived from combinations of the 16 primary scales.

Validity

Because the 16PF dimensions were developed through factor analysis, construct validity is provided by studies confirming its factor structure (e.g., Chernyshenko, Stark, & Chan, 2001; Conn & Rieke, 1994; Cattell & Krug, 1986; Gerbing & Tuley, 1991; Hofer, Horn, & Eber, 1997). Additionally, the factor structure has been confirmed in a range of languages (e.g., *Italian:* Barbaranelli & Caprara, 1996; *French:* Mogenet & Rolland, 1995; *Japanese:* Motegi, 1982; *Spanish:* Prieto, Gouveia, & Fernandez, 1996; and *German:* Schneewind & Graf, 1998).

An extensive body of research dating back a half century provides evidence of the test's applied validity—its utility in counseling, clinical, career development, personnel selection and development, educational, and research settings. Profiles and prediction equations exist for a wide range of criteria such as leadership, creativity, academic achievement, conscientiousness, social skills, empathy, self-esteem, marital adjustment, power dynamics, coping patterns, cognitive processing style, and dozens of occupational profiles (Cattell, Eber, & Tatsuoka, 1992; Conn & Rieke, 1994; Guastello & Rieke, 1993; Kelly, 1999; Krug & Johns, 1990; Russell & Karol, 2002; Schuerger & Watterson, 1998).

By the 1980s, the 16PF Questionnaire was ranked among the highest in number of research articles (Graham & Lilly, 1984, p. 234), and a recent estimate places the number of references since 1974 at more than 2,000 publications (Hofer & Eber, 2002). Since the 1960s, the test has been noted as a significant instrument in professional practice. For example, a study by Piotrowski and Keller (1989) found the 16PF Questionnaire to be the most recommended of general personality questionnaires. Research also suggests

---

≡ Rapid Reference 1.6

Basics of the 16PF Fifth Edition Questionnaire

Authors: Raymond B. Cattell, A. Karen S. Cattell, and Heather E. P. Cattell

Publication date: 1993

What the test measures: Full range of normal personality—16 primary scales, 5 global scales, and 3 response style indices

Reading level: Fifth grade

Age range: 16 years and older

International usage: Special editions exist for use in Argentina, Australia, Brazil, Canada, Croatia, Czech Republic, Denmark, France, Finland, Germany, Greece, Italy, Japan, Norway, Philippines, Portugal, Romania, Slovak Republic, South Africa, Spain, Sweden, Turkey, and United Kingdom

Qualifications of examiners: Graduate or professional-level training in psychological assessment

Publisher: Institute for Personality & Ability Testing, Inc. (IPAT)

P.O. Box 1188
Champaign, IL 61824-1188
800-225-4728; 217-352-4739
http://www.ipat.com
custserv@ipat.com

that the test is somewhat more powerful than other major questionnaires in predicting real-life behavior. A recent study (Goldberg, in press) compared many popular personality questionnaires in their ability to predict six behavioral clusters and found that the 16PF dimensions had the highest predictive validity.

🪓 TEST YOURSELF 🪓

1. **The 16PF Questionnaire, unlike many psychological measures, did NOT emerge out of applied clinical needs. What was the main influence on its development?**

   (a) Studies into the structure of human abilities

   (b) Theory about the basic dimensions of personality

   (c) Scientific research into the basic structural elements of personality

   (d) Development of modern projective techniques

2. **What is the name given to the statistical method that Cattell used to identify his 16 primary scales and 5 global scales?**

   (a) Orthogonal rotation

   (b) Correlation coefficient

   (c) Multivariate analysis

   (d) Factor analysis

3. **Cattell's research was based on data from which of the following domains?**

   (a) peer ratings

   (b) self-report questionnaires

   (c) observable behavioral ratings

   (d) all of the above

4. **How much of the personality domain was the test constructed to cover?**

   (a) The Big Five traits

   (b) The abnormal range of personality

   (c) The entire domain of normal personality

   (d) Traits in which the author was interested

(continued)

5. When was the test first published?

(a) 1949

(b) 1957

(c) 1968

(d) 1993

6. The five global scales that measure broad organizing influences in personality, align fairly well with other Big-Five measures (and were discovered 30 years earlier). True or False?

7. The test is appropriate for ages 16 and above, is written at a fifth grade reading level, and takes about 45 minutes to complete. True or False?

8. Which of these is NOT a possible method of 16PF administration and scoring?

(a) Paper and pencil

(b) OnSite computer software

(c) NetAssess

(d) 16PFworld.com

(e) OnFax

9. To what areas of practical use has the 16PF been applied?

(a) Employee selection and development

(b) Clinical and counseling

(c) Basic research

(d) Educational research

(e) All of the above

Answers: 1. c; 2. d; 3. d; 4. c; 5. a; 6. True; 7. True; 8. e; 9. e.

Two

HOW TO ADMINISTER AND SCORE THE 16PF QUESTIONNAIRE

ADMINISTRATION

The 16PF Questionnaire is appropriate for a wide range of clients, including most adults aged 16 years or older with reading skills at the fifth-grade level or higher (as noted in Rapid Reference 2.1). Whether the test is appropriate for a particular individual's age or reading level is a decision that should be based on professional consideration of the client's maturity level. A careful assessment of reading ability may be necessary for individuals with limited reading or English skills or for those with visual disabilities. The test can be administered individually or in groups and in paper-and-pencil or computer format.

The test is composed of nonthreatening items that ask about personal preferences, interests, behaviors, and opinions. Personality items have three response choices, and the middle response is always a question mark. The test concludes with a short section consisting of ability items.

The test is untimed. Most people complete the paper-and-pencil format in 35–50 minutes, and under ordinary conditions, about 80% of test takers finish in 40 minutes. Computerized administration takes less time, generally about 25–35 minutes.

Paper-and-Pencil Administration

The materials needed to administer the paper-and-pencil format of the 16PF test are minimal: a test booklet, an answer sheet, and a number-two pencil. Use of a pencil is necessary if the answer sheet is to be computer scored,

◢Rapid Reference 2.1

Keynotes of Administration and Scoring

- Easily administered, nonthreatening, multiple-choice format
- Untimed administration, averaging 35–50 minutes for paper-and-pencil and 25–35 minutes for computer administration
- Appropriate for ages 16 and older
- Fifth-grade reading level
- Administration and scoring available by both traditional (paper and pencil, scoring keys) and modern (Internet and computer software) modes
- Score reporting on a sten scale, a 10-point standard-score scale
- Wide range of computer-generated narrative interpretive reports for various settings
- Restandardized in 2001 with a representative sample of more than 10,000 people

either by mailing to the test publisher or on a local optical scanner. Additionally, a pencil is preferable so that the test taker can change his or her answers if necessary.

Paper-and-pencil administration of the 16PF test involves little active supervision. Simple, concise instructions are printed in the test booklet. Administrators may choose to read the instructions aloud, or they may ask test takers to read the instructions silently, responding to any questions as necessary. During testing, administrators should ensure that test takers are marking responses appropriately and not skipping items.

Computer Administration

The 16PF Questionnaire can be administered on a personal computer, either by connection to the Internet or via software available from the test publisher. Both formats can immediately score tests and produce reports. Client-friendly features include practice questions, item-by-item administration, a routine that allows test takers to change their previous answer, and a "test interrupt and resume" option.

≡Rapid Reference 2.2

Creating Rapport With the Test Taker

- Ensure that the testing environment is comfortable for the test taker (e.g., seating, lighting, temperature).
- Establish a procedure for taking a break (if appropriate), and inform the test taker about the location of restrooms and drinking water.
- Understand the test taker's attitude toward the testing process.
- Explain to the test taker the purpose and objectives of the testing, by whom the results will be reviewed, and what benefits to expect from the testing.
- Explain to the test taker the nature of the test materials, how to take the test, and the anticipated time for completing the test.

The Testing Environment

Rapport with the test taker is always important in personality testing. Rapid Reference 2.2 presents suggestions that may encourage the test taker to adopt a favorable disposition toward the testing. Creating rapport is also a means for enhancing the likelihood of obtaining valid and useful results.

DON'T FORGET

Elements That Can Affect Test Taker Responses

The degree to which a test taker presents candid and realistic answers to 16PF items can be influenced by a number of elements beyond the personality characteristics being measured, including the test taker's:

- Reading ability
- Facility with the English language (or the language in which the test is administered)
- Attitude toward the testing
- Physical comfort
- Psychological comfort with the testing
- General psychological condition, such as severe depression or anxiety
- Attitude toward what is at stake as a consequence of the testing

Rapid Reference 2.3

Talking to Test Takers About the Test and Its Format

- Most of the questions on the test ask about your feelings, attitudes, or behavior; there are no right and wrong answers.
- Many people say that they learned a lot about themselves by answering these questions and having their answers compared to those of others.
- It works best if you just give the answer that comes to you first, without a lot of thought or second-guessing yourself.
- Try to avoid the middle, *(b)* answer and stay with the *(a)* or *(c)* answers if you can because doing so gives a clearer picture of your qualities, but don't take a lot of time trying to decide; if you really can't decide, just choose *(b)*.
- There are no right or wrong answers, except for 15 special questions at the end that are set off from the others and do have correct answers.
- (In an assessment context) Try to be candid about your own favorable qualities and about some that may not be so favorable. If you exaggerate or minimize very much, it can show up in the results and make them hard to explain.

A few moments spent talking about the testing experience can make a difference in the client's approach to the test. In such situations, wording can be important. Based on practitioner experience, Rapid Reference 2.3 provides some comments on the test and suggestions to test takers that may help to reduce their uncertainties and encourage them to give maximally useful results.

SCORING

Hand Scoring

Hand scoring the test is a quick and simple procedure. The materials needed to hand score include a set of four scoring keys, a norm table, and an Individual Record Form. Before scoring, each answer sheet should be checked to ensure that the test taker answered all items and gave only one response per item. Raw scores are obtained by placing each scoring key over the answer sheet and counting the items that are marked for each scale if they appear through holes in the keys. The raw scores are then transformed to standard scores through the use of the norm table. For an experienced scorer, the whole process takes only 6 or 7 minutes. Detailed hand-scoring instructions are provided in the test administrator's manual.

Computer Scoring

Answer sheets may be mailed or faxed to the test publisher for computer scoring, or they may be scored on a personal computer via the Internet or software. Computer scoring adds the ability to obtain a range of computer-generated interpretive reports that include additional scores and information that enrich test interpretation. The test publisher offers a number of interpretive reports that can be generated from the 16PF Fifth Edition Questionnaire. Some reports are suitable for use in a variety of applications, whereas others are more focused in their purpose (e.g., industrial-organizational, career development, personal development, leadership development, and clinical and counseling applications). These reports are described in the appendix.

Online administration and scoring are available on the Internet via NetAssess. Clients access the test using a pass code. On its completion, the test is scored, and reports are transmitted to the professional via e-mail. Internet multilingual testing is available using 16PFworld.com, which can administer the test in more than a dozen different languages, score the test with appropriate national norms, and produce a narrative report in any of the languages.

Score Reporting On the Sten Scale

Scores on the test are presented on a 10-point scale called a "sten" or standard-ten scale, with a mean of 5.5 and a standard deviation of 2. Scores are based on representative and up-to-date norms. The current standardization sample was released in 2002 and has data on over 10,000 persons who are representative of the 2000 U.S. census for sex, race, and age.

As illustrated by Figure 2.1, a person scoring 4 is at the 23rd percentile, and one scoring 7 is at the 77th percentile. Traditionally, in interpreting scores for individuals, scores below 4 are considered low and scores above 7 are considered high. In addition, some professionals refer to scores of 4 as low

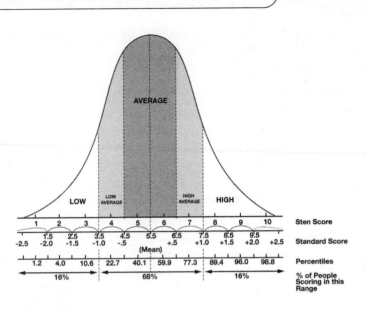

Figure 2.1. Sten distribution

Figure adapted from the *16PF Fifth Edition administrator's manual* by Mary Russell and Darcie Karol, 2002; and from the *Handbook for the Sixteen Personality Factor Questionnaire (16PF)* by Raymond B. Cattell, Herbert W. Eber, and Maurice M. Tatsuoka, 1992. Champaign, IL: Institute for Personality and Ability Testing.

average and scores of 7 as high average. The scales are bipolar, and even though they are designated high or low, a high score should not be considered good and a low score should not be regarded as bad.

A preferred way to indicate whether a score is high or low is to insert a plus or minus sign after the scale letter. Thus, for a high score on a particular scale, the scale letter would be followed by a plus sign (e.g., A+). Similarly, for a low score, the scale letter would be followed by a minus sign (e.g., A-).

If two scores together have particular significance, as is true of a number of score combinations, they are indicated by the letters for the scales, each followed by a plus sign or a minus sign as appropriate. For example, a common pattern is that in which the client has a high score on Warmth (A) and a low score on Self-Reliance (Q2). This pattern may be indicated as A+, Q2-.

✍ TEST YOURSELF ✍

1. **How long does it take to administer the 16PF Fifth Edition Questionnaire?**

2. **A "sten" score is a ten-point standard score with mean of 5.5 and standard deviation of 2.** True or False?

3. **About what percent of persons fall at or below a sten score of 3?**
   (a) 16%
   (b) 23%
   (c) 50%
   (d) 68%

4. **What score on the 16PF Questionnaire is considered a "high" score?**
   (a) above 4
   (b) above 5
   (c) above 6
   (d) above 7

5. **How recently was the test restandardized?**
   (a) 1970
   (b) 1985
   (c) 1994
   (d) 2001

Answers: 1. 35-50 minutes; 2. True; 3. a; 4. d; 5. d

Three

THE 16PF QUESTIONNAIRE SCALES

Before proceeding with the interpretation of a client's profile, the professional needs to understand the meanings of the 16PF scales. This chapter provides descriptions of the following scales:

1. 5 global scales
2. 16 primary scales
3. Interactions among the scales
4. Response style or validity indexes

The scale descriptions are based on the clinical, consulting, and research experience of the authors, and they also incorporate information from other 16PF resources and authors. For example in their 1976 book, *A Guide to the Clinical Use of the 16PF*, Samuel Karson and Jerry O'Dell described the 16PF scales in terms of their clinical importance. In 1997, Dr. Michael Karson wrote an expanded, updated guide with these same authors: *16PF Interpretation in Clinical Practice: A Guide to the Fifth Edition*.

Another example is the work of Dr. Heather Birkett Cattell, author of *The 16PF: Personality in Depth* (1989). On the basis of more than 10 years of research conducted with three databases in her clinical practice, Cattell identified certain patterns of thinking, feeling, and behaving associated with individual scale scores and certain score combinations. She recorded mental status exams, clinical assessments, psychosocial histories, client insights and self-disclosures, and client behavior including their interactions with family, coworkers, and group therapy members.

These two works and many others have provided valuable insights for the present authors in their attempts to describe the various scales and their interpretations. The basic 16PF resource books that are cited most consistently throughout these scale descriptions are presented in Rapid Reference 3.1. There

Rapid Reference 3.1

Reference Book Sources of Scale Descriptions Cited in Chapter 3

- *Handbook for the 16PF* (Cattell et al., 1992)
- *The 16PF: Personality in Depth* (H. B. Cattell, 1989)
- *The 16PF Fifth Edition Administrator's Manual* (Russell & Karol, 2002)
- *The 16PF Fifth Edition Technical Manual* (Conn & Rieke, 1994)
- *16PF Interpretation in Clinical Practice* (Karson et al., 1997)
- *Personality in Practice* (Lord, 1997)
- *The 16PF Cattell Comprehensive Personality Interpretation* (H. B. Cattell & H. E. P. Cattell, 1997)
- *Occupational Interpretation of the 16 Personality Factor Questionnaire* (Schuerger & Watterson, 1998)
- *Overcoming Obstacles to Interpretation* (Lord, 1999)
- *16PF Personal Career Development Profile Technical and Interpretive Manual* (Walter, 2000)

are many other interpretive books that describe the 16PF scales (e.g., Lowman, 1991; Meyer, 1989); however, they discuss a complex combination of other measures and so are not included in this basic list. As with all interpretations of test scores, the following interpretations should be considered as hypotheses to be tested against other sources of information about an individual.

GENERAL CHARACTERISTICS OF THE SCALES

All of the 16PF personality scales are bipolar—that is, each end of each scale has a distinct definition and meaning. Scores on the 16PF personality scales are given in "standard-ten" or sten scores, which range from 1 to 10, with a mean of 5.5 and a standard deviation of 2. The sten-score ranges for the 16PF scales are shown in Rapid Reference 3.2. A high score on a scale is not regarded as good, and a low score is not viewed as bad. Rather, a score toward either end of the scale increases the likelihood that the trait defined by the pole will be apparent and distinctive in the client's behavior. Whether that trait is determined to have positive or negative effects depends on the particular situation.

≡Rapid Reference 3.2

Sten-Score Ranges for the 16PF Questionnaire

Sten Score	Percentile	Range
1–3	16%	low
4	15%	low average
5–6	38%	average
7	15%	high average
8–10	16%	high

Although the primary scales were originally labeled with letters (e.g., Scale A, B, C, . . . Q4), they also have common-language or trait-descriptive names such as Warmth and Dominance. Whenever possible, both the letter and the name are used when referring to a primary scale. A high score on a primary scale is indicated by a plus (+) sign; a low score is indicated by a minus (-) sign. For example, A+ indicates a high score on the primary scale Warmth (A), and C- indicates a low score on the primary scale Emotional Stability (C). Additionally, note that because the global scales were developed through factor analysis of the primary scales, the primary scales may contribute to global scales in either a positive or a negative direction. For example, Warmth (A) contributes to global Extraversion in a positive direction (A+) but to global Tough-Mindedness in a negative direction (A-).

THE GLOBAL (Big-Five) SCALES

Chapter 1 presents Raymond B. Cattell's theory that the basic elements of personality, the primary scales, could themselves be factor analyzed to reveal a smaller number of underlying, organizing influences among the primary factors. The global scales that emerged from this factor analysis (originally called second-order factors) are broad, overarching traits; each is made up of four or five of the more specific primary traits. Because these global scales were created by factor analysis of the primary scales, they are defined by the primary traits that make them up. Figure 1.2 and Rapid Reference 4.3 present the global scales and their contributing primary scales.

Developed in the 1950s and 1960s, the global scales represent the original Big Five traits. Because they provide the interpreter with a brief summary of an individual's overall personality style, they serve as the framework for organizing the more specific information provided by the primary scales. An advantage of the global scales is that they are based on many more items (40–50) than are the primary scales. Because the globals are more reliable and robust than the primaries, more confidence can be placed in their accuracy. A limitation of the global scales is that because they are quite broad in meaning, they do not convey detailed information about important nuances of an individual's unique personality. If the primary scores within a global score are all in the same direction, then the global score is a good indicator of personality; however, if the global score is an average of diverse or opposite primary scores, then it may disguise important aspects of personality.

The relationship of the global scales to the primary scales is analogous to that between a map of a major city and a map of a specific neighborhood. Just as the specific neighborhood map provides more detailed information than does the larger map, so do the primary scales provide more detailed information than do the global scales. Of course, when one needs the big picture, the city map is preferable to the neighborhood map. In a similar way, the five global scales provide a big picture of a client's personality in a single glance. The professional is able to form impressions of the interaction of personality elements quickly and from a viewpoint that is not possible with just the 16 primary scales alone.

The descriptions of the global scales that follow are brief, consistent with their role as broad personality descriptors, and include the following elements:

- Its defining primary scales
- Significant correlations with scales from other personality measures (see Rapid Reference 3.3)
- Descriptions of high scorers and low scorers (see Rapid Reference 3.1 for reference sources)
- Occupational implications of high and low scorers as they relate to Holland's occupational types (Holland, 1997)—Realistic, Investigative, Artistic, Social, Enterprising, and Conventional (see Rapid Reference 3.4)

=≡*Rapid Reference 3.3*

Correlations Between the 16PF Scales and Other Personality Measures

Significant correlations between the 16PF scales and the scales of the following personality measures are discussed in this chapter. A complete description of this research is presented in *The 16PF Fifth Edition Administrator's Manual* (Russell & Karol, 2002) and *The 16PF Fifth Edition Technical Manual* (Conn & Rieke, 1994).

- *MBTI:* The Myers-Briggs Type Indicator (Myers, McCaulley, Quenk, & Hammer, 1998; Quenk, 2000) is a measure of personality type based on the theories of Carl Jung. It generates the types by measuring four preferences: Extraversion versus Introversion, Sensing versus Intuition, Thinking versus Feeling, and Judging versus Perceiving.

- *NEO:* The NEO Personality Inventory–Revised (Costa & McCrae, 1992) is a measure of the Big Five personality characteristics—Extraversion, Neuroticism, Openness, Agreeableness, and Conscientiousness—each of which has six facet subscores.

- *PRF:* The Personality Research Form (Jackson, 1997) measures 22 scales based to a large extent on Murray's work on human needs, such as the need for Achievement and the need for Dominance.

- *CPI:* The California Psychological Inventory (Gough, 1987) measures almost 50 scales, most of which are based on "folk concepts" of human personality.

- *SEI:* The Coopersmith Self-Esteem Inventory (Coopersmith, 1981) is a measure of self-esteem, which the author defines as "the extent to which a person believes him- or herself competent, successful, significant, and worthy" (Coopersmith, 1981, p. 5).

Extraversion/Introversion

The global scale Extraversion is defined by the primary scales Warmth (A+), Liveliness (F+), Social Boldness (H+), Privateness (N-), and Self-Reliance (Q2-), with the latter two being in the negative direction. A consistently high pattern on Extraversion indicates a person who is warm (A+), animated (F+), boldly outgoing (H+), self-disclosing (N-), and group oriented (Q2-). This scale is included in most descriptions of the Big Five traits (Goldberg, 1990); however, other Big Five measures tend to include dominance in their Extraversion scales unlike the 16PF model, which identifies dominance as part of a separate scale (Independence vs. Accommodation).

≡≡*Rapid Reference 3.4*

Sources of Occupational Information About the 16PF Scales

- *Handbook for the 16PF* (Cattell et al., 1992)
- *The 16PF Fifth Edition Administrator's Manual* (Russell & Karol, 2002)
- *The 16PF Fifth Edition Technical Manual* (Conn & Rieke, 1994)
- *Occupational Interpretation of the 16 Personality Factor Questionnaire* (Schuerger & Watterson, 1998)
- *16PF Personal Career Development Profile Technical and Interpretive Manual* (Walter, 2000)
- *16PF Leadership Coaching Report Manual* (Watterson, 2002)
- A large databank collected by J. M. Schuerger and his graduate students consisting of mean profiles for more than 230 occupational groups.

Correlations with scales from other personality tests are strongly supportive of Extraversion as a measure of motivation to be with other people. Its highest correlation is with the Myers-Briggs Type Indicator's (MBTI's) Extraversion (positively) and Introversion (negatively) scales. It also correlates strongly with the Personality Research Form's (PRF's) need for Affiliation, Exhibition, Nurturance, and Succorance scales; with the California Personality Inventory's (CPI's) Sociability, Social Presence, Empathy, Capacity for Status, and Self-Acceptance scales; and with all of the NEO's Extraversion scales. Extraversion also correlates strongly with measures of social desirability, including the 16PF Impression Management scale.

Jung first recognized extraversion as a concept for understanding personality (Jung, 1928). High scorers tend to be people-oriented and to seek interaction with others. Lord (1997) describes Extraversion scores as indicating the degree to which people like to be with or around others, want to be noticed by others, and want to devote energy to initiating and maintaining social relationships. In contrast to high scorers, low scorers tend to be less outgoing and sociable, preferring to spend more time alone than in the company of others. They often exhibit independence of thought and self-restraint, and they tend to think things through deliberately and objectively.

Extraversion can be conceptualized as a set of distinct motivations for moving either toward or away from others as is demonstrated by its contributing primary scales. Warm (A+) individuals tend to care genuinely for others and to seek connections and close relationships with them, although they may be quiet rather than talkative or outgoing. Lively (F+) people are inclined to bring a lot of carefree energy and high spirits to interactions but do not necessarily seek close relationships. Socially bold (H+) individuals are quite out-going but often seek stimulation or attention rather than closeness. Private (N+) individuals tend to avoid revealing personal information. Self-reliant (Q2+) individuals prefer to work and make decisions independently without suggestions or interference from others, whereas low scorers seek the company and support of others. Thus, scores on Extraversion's primary scales can help the professional identify an individual's complex social makeup.

Scores on Extraversion strongly influence how other traits may be expressed. For example, high scores on Warmth (A+) may soften the expression of traits like Dominance (E+) or Vigilance (L+). Karson et al. (1997) describe how extremely high and low scores on Extraversion can also have drawbacks. For example, they observe that extremely low scores may indicate social indifference or withdrawal and that extremely high scores may

. . . suggest an identity organized around interpersonal relationships. . . . Those who manage feelings of unlovability by defining a perfectionistic ideal of social acceptance and trying to achieve it will score very high on Extraversion. On the other hand, those who are socially successful, fun-loving, and generous will score very high, too. (p. 72)

Thus, extreme scores in the Extraverted direction may be related to discomfort in functioning alone, strong needs for interpersonal contact and support, a tendency to trust others, or a tendency to seek attention.

High scorers tend to possess any of a range of social skills. Thus, high scores are found particularly in Holland's Social occupations or other helping occupations such as teacher, counselor, and physical therapist, as well as in Enterprising or business occupations such as manager, salesperson, and attorney. Low scores are found among Investigative occupations such as scientist and computer programmer as well as in some Artistic occupations and in many Mechanical occupations.

Anxiety

The global scale Anxiety includes the primary scales of Emotional Stability (C-) in the negative direction, Vigilance (L+), Apprehension (O+), and Tension (Q4+). A consistently high pattern on the Anxiety scale shows a client who is emotionally reactive (C-), suspicious of others' motives (L+), worried and insecure (O+), and tense (Q4+). This scale generally indicates a person's internal level of emotional comfort or discomfort.

Correlations with other measures of personality consistently support Anxiety as a general measure of a person's psychological discomfort. It correlates most strongly with the Coopersmith Self-Esteem Inventory, with all of the NEO's Neuroticism facets, and with the PRF's Defendence and Aggression scales. It correlates negatively with the CPI's Well-Being, Psychological-Mindedness, Intellectual Efficiency, Social Presence, Capacity for Status, Empathy, and Good Impression scales. These correlations indicate that in addition to having subjective feelings of discomfort, high scorers may make a poor social impression—for example, because they lack confidence or assertiveness. The correlations also suggest that when people are anxious, they tend to have pent-up feelings that hinder their ability to view themselves or others clearly and objectively. Anxiety also correlates strongly with measures of social desirability, including the 16PF Impression Management scale.

Anxiety has a long history as a topic of inquiry in psychology, and is currently one of the Big Five dimensions of personality (Goldberg, 1993). The high pole of the global Anxiety scale corresponds to the commonly understood meaning of the term *anxiety*. High scorers may feel worried, tense, self-critical, distressed, alienated from others, or overwhelmed. High Anxiety may be a characteristic trait (i.e., experienced when nothing particularly stressful is occurring) or a state provoked by some current event or experience, such as a series of increased demands. Russell and Karol (2002) state that "Anxiety can be aroused in response to external events, or it can be internally generated. Since anxious people often experience more negative affect, they may have difficulty controlling their emotions or reactions and may act in counterproductive ways." (p. 31)

Low scorers tend to be calm, confident, at ease, and relaxed. Although this laid-back style may seem to be a highly desirable state, it may indicate a tendency to underestimate negative feelings, experiences, or circumstances. Extremely low scorers may be self-satisfied or complacent, or they may deny their stress or problems. Their level of comfort also may lead to a lack of motivation, especially for difficult tasks. In fact, very low anxiety generally is related to low levels of achievement.

Karson et al. (1997) advise that careful attention should be paid to high Anxiety scores because they involve openly admitting to a great deal of distress and may represent a conscious or unconscious plea for help. The authors further note that when elevated Anxiety scores mainly result from high Apprehension (O+) and high Tension (Q4+) scores, then distress is more likely to be situational and transitory:

> Indeed, in a therapy assessment, some degree of Apprehension (O+) and Tension (Q4+) is expected and even desirable. This indicates that the individual is bothered by the situation compelling the therapy and is motivated by discomfort to engage in therapeutic tasks. (p. 74)

Karson et al. also describe how scores on Anxiety can mediate the expression of other extreme scores. For example, the expression of extreme high or low scores on Dominance (E) is likely to be more modulated when the individual shows low scores on Anxiety.

This global scale and its contributing primary scales are the most highly correlated with the Impression Management scale and therefore can be affected by socially desirable responding. Very low scores may be the result of trying to present a positive impression on the test. People may consciously or unconsciously deny that they have any problems. Alternatively, high scorers may attempt to present a negative impression for some reason, such as in a disability evaluation.

Generally, low Anxiety scorers are found in Holland's Enterprising occupations such as manager, executive, and salesperson as well as in Realistic occupations such as engineer, mechanic, and firefighter. Low scorers also may be found in some Social occupations such as nurse or psychologist.

Tough-Mindedness/Receptivity

The global scale Tough-Mindedness includes the primary scales of Warmth (A-), Sensitivity (I-), Abstractedness (M-), and Openness to Change (Q1-), all in the negative direction. A consistently high pattern on Tough-Mindedness typifies a client who is somewhat disinterested in people (A-), has a factual and unsentimental approach to life (I-), is practical and concrete in focus (M-), and is set in his or her ways (Q1-). Low scorers, those at the Receptive end of the scale, tend to be both interpersonally and artistically sensitive and intuitive as well as interested in new ideas and experiences.

Correlations with other personality tests are consistent with this scale's being a measure of unemotional focus, logical thought, and resistance to change as opposed to showing an openness to feelings and fantasy, aesthetic values, and new ideas. In relation to the MBTI's scales, Tough-Mindedness correlates strongly with Sensing, to a lesser extent with Thinking, and negatively with Intuitive and Feeling. It also correlates negatively with the NEO's Openness facets, particularly Aesthetics, Fantasy, Feelings, and Values. Tough-Mindedness also correlates negatively with the PRF's Need for Change, Understanding, Sentience, and Nurturance scales and with the CPI's Flexibility, Empathy, Self-Acceptance, and Achievement via Independence scales.

Tough-Mindedness frequently provides information about an individual's way of experiencing the world, or what is often called an information processing style. Evidence for the latter is reflected in the scale's strong correlations with the MBTI dimensions. People who score high on Tough-Mindedness tend to experience the world in concrete, logical, unsentimental terms. They are inclined to be hardheaded and are not very interested in feelings, theoretical issues, or new ideas. They pay attention to practical aspects of situations and value realistic and traditional solutions. Russell and Karol (2002) state that

> In addition to operating at a dry, cognitive level, extremely Tough-Minded people may portray a sense of being "established," possibly to the degree of being set or fixed. That is, they may not be open to other points of view, to unusual people, or to new experiences. (p. 32)

Such a cool, factual focus is very useful in situations that require alertness to facts and attention to objective issues. For example, air traffic controllers and surgeons tend to have high scores on this scale. On the other hand, this rational approach has disadvantages in situations that involve solving problems related to people, attending to feelings, or thinking beyond a concrete situation to develop new ideas and solutions. Extremely high scorers may seem inflexible or entrenched in their lack of openness to new viewpoints.

The Receptive end of this scale is similar to the Openness dimension in the Big Five factors. The first author conceptualizes low scores on this scale as representing openness to people (A+), openness to feelings (I+), openness to imagination and fantasy (M+), and openness to change (Q1+). Receptive individuals tend to welcome rich and varied experiences. They pay attention to emotions, intuition, artistic values, and other subjective aspects of experience. They are interested in aesthetics, ideas, theories, and new approaches. However, very low scorers may be easily swayed by emotions or have difficulty distancing themselves from their feelings. Thus, they may overlook the need to be practical, objective, or realistic in some situations.

The Tough-Mindedness score may be helpful to professionals in understanding the internal experience of the people they work with. H. B. Cattell (1989) points out that it also may be helpful in identifying productive ways of working with individuals. For example, high scorers on Tough-Mindedness may respond best when they are presented with established facts and practical solutions. In contrast, people who score at the low Receptive end may respond better to a sympathetic and imaginative approach that acknowledges their feelings and that appeals to their intuitive understanding.

Tough-Mindedness is a powerful discriminator among occupational groups. Low or receptive scores are consistently found among Artistic occupations such as writer, musician, and designer as well as among many Social occupations such as social worker, elementary school teacher, and minister. Persons with high scores on Tough-Mindedness tend toward Conventional types of occupations such as bookkeeper, retail store manager, and insurance agent. High scorers also are found in Realistic occupations such as firefighter, police or military officer, and the mechanical and technical trades.

Independence/Accommodation

The global scale Independence includes the primary scales of Dominance (E+), Social Boldness (H+), Vigilance (L+) and Openness to Change (Q1+), all in the positive direction. A consistently high pattern on the Independence scale indicates a person who is assertive and interested in influencing people (E+), is adventurous and fearless in approaching new people and situations (H+), is wary and thinks strategically about others' motives (L+), and has original and innovative ideas (Q1+). Such persons tend to be self-directed, even to the point of attempting to change the world to suit themselves rather than trying to adjust to others. Low scorers, those at the Accommodating end of the scale, tend to prefer taking a back seat and letting others be in charge.

Thus, it is not too surprising that the low Accommodating end corresponds to the Big-Five Agreeableness trait and the Independence end equates to the Disagreeable pole.

Correlations with other personality tests are consistent with this scale's being a measure of social assertiveness, independence, and self-confidence. It correlates strongly with the CPI's Dominance, Independence, Self-Acceptance, Social Presence, and Capacity for Status scales and with the PRF's Dominance, Exhibition, Aggression, Change, and (negatively) Abasement scales. In relation to the NEO, Independence correlates strongly in a positive direction with the Assertiveness and Openness to Ideas and Actions facets and in a negative direction with the Compliance, Modesty, and Self-Consciousness facets.

High scorers are take-charge people who have an active stance on life. Rather than accommodate to the influence of others, they significantly impact their environments. Not surprisingly, the Dominance (E+) primary scale is the strongest contributor to global Independence. High scorers on Independence tend to be assertive, competitive, and successful at meeting challenges. They also tend to be bold and fearless adventurers and to think in original, nontraditional ways. They are interested in trying new things, show intellectual curiosity, and form their own opinions. They are often seen as a force unto themselves because they have their own ideas and pursue them boldly and strategically. They tend to persist against opposition and setbacks in achieving their goals. High scorers tend to be actively self-determined in their thinking and actions and to take the initiative in getting the things they want in life—a characteristic that some authors conceptualize as similar to external versus internal control.

However, people with extremely high scores can be seen as disagreeable by others who feel that they are aggressive or forceful in wanting to do things their own way—hence the naming of the other end as Agreeableness in the Big Five system. Indeed, extremely high scorers may be difficult to get along with because they tend to challenge the status quo and may be oppositional or argumentative. Some people may feel controlled or dominated by extremely high scorers. High scorers may also be suspicious of others and their motives, and they may have difficulty accommodating others when it is important to do so. It is useful to note that global Independence includes almost all of the 16PF scales that involve extrapunitive versus intropunitive tendencies. Russell and Karol (2002) state that

> Extreme Independence—especially when not tempered with Self-Control or the sociability of Extraversion or the sensitivity of Receptivity—can assume a certain amount of disagreeableness. . . . Independent people may be uncomfortable or ineffective in situations that involve accommodating other people. (p. 34)

In its low Accommodating direction, this scale is aligned with the Big Five trait Agreeableness. Low scorers tend to be cooperative, deferential, and trusting. Generally, they are easy to get along with and value accommodation rather than self-determination. In social situations they often are shy, unassertive, and easily influenced by other people. They tend to avoid questioning other people's preferences or established ways of doing things; however, their proclivity to accommodate others may be viewed as a weakness and may alienate people who prefer mutual decision-making. Russell and Karol (2002) state

> External situations and other people tend to influence them, both in terms of forming opinions and shaping behavior. They may be very uncomfortable or ineffective in situations that call for self-expression, assertiveness, or persuasion. (p. 34)

Additionally, H. B. Cattell (1989) points out that low scorers may have a need for external structure or guidelines. They may prefer to have a fair amount of interpersonal support or outside feedback in various areas of their lives. Cattell notes that in clinical situations, low scorers usually respond well to directions and may feel most confident with therapists and counselors who are active or even somewhat authoritarian.

High scores on Independence are found particularly among the Holland's Enterprising occupational type, such as marketing director, executive, lawyer, and realtor. High scores also are found among some Artistic occupations such as writer and architect, some Social occupations such as psychologist and school principal, and Investigative occupations such as scientist and dentist. Low, accommodating scores may be found in some Conventional occupations such as secretary, clerical worker, and data entry worker; some Realistic occupations such as janitor, carpenter, and forest worker; and some Social occupations like nurse, nun, and child care worker.

Self-Control

The global scale Self-Control includes most centrally the primary scales of Rule-Consciousness (G+) and Perfectionism (Q3+) in the positive direction and to a lesser degree, Liveliness (F-) and Abstractedness (M-) in the negative direction. A consistently high pattern on the Self-Control scale defines a person who is concerned about following accepted rules (G+), evinces self-discipline and organizational skills (Q3+), is cautious rather than fun-loving (F-), and can remain focused on practical issues (M-). Low scorers, those at the Unrestrained end of the scale, tend to be nonconforming, casual about rules and standards, spontaneous, and unreliable. High scores tend to be related to social desirability.

Correlations with other personality tests are consistent with this scale's being a measure of self-control and orientation to structure and rules. Self-Control correlates positively with all of the NEO's Conscientiousness facets and negatively with its three Openness facets; positively with the CPI's Self-Control, Socialization, Responsibility, and Achievement via Conformance scales; and negatively with the PRI's need for Play, Impulsivity, Change, and Autonomy scales. Self-Control also correlates positively with the MBTI's Judging and Sensing scales and negatively with its Perceptive and Intuitive scales.

Global Self-Control is aligned with the Big Five factor Conscientiousness. The contributing primary scales represent basic human resources for restraining urges and impulses. High scorers are attentive to rules and mainstream moral standards, and they tend to have a strong internalized sense of right and wrong. High scorers also can be described as self-disciplined in the sense of organizing, planning, and persevering in order to accomplish their goals. They tend to consider carefully the consequences of their actions and to live in an orderly fashion. They typically are able to focus their attention on concrete, immediate things, and they tend to be less high-spirited, spontaneous, and impulsive than low scorers. Generally, high scorers tend to be well socialized and conventional in their behavior. They are often seen as having willpower and persistence. The latter qualities may be so overdeveloped by extremely high scorers that their behavior may be viewed as rigid or over-controlled. Extremely high scorers may seem to be so concerned with rules, duties, tasks, or details that they may lack flexibility or spontaneity and may appear to have little fun in their lives.

People with scores at the low Unrestrained end of the scale tend to follow their own urges. They dislike having their lives too organized or planned. Instead, they tend to be carefree and spontaneous, going with the flow in many situations. They also tend to be nonconforming and to pay less atten-tion to rules and regulations. H. B. Cattell (1989) points out that some low scorers may have strongly developed but unconventional moral standards and thus they may "march to a different drummer." However, most extremely low scorers may be seen as undercontrolled or capricious. Russell and Karol (2002) state

> Unrestrained people may be flexible in their responses; however, in situations that call for self-control, they may find it difficult to restrain themselves. They may be perceived as self-indulgent, disorganized, irre-pressible, or irresponsible, depending on whether they can muster resources for self-control when doing so is important. (p. 35)

Several authors suggest consulting an individual's score on Emotional Stability (C) before concluding that his or her resources for self-control are lacking. Karson et al. (1997) note that Emotional Stability may indicate the "ability to defer needs and to behave under the influence of long-term con-sequences" (p. 80), which also may curb impulses.

High scores can be found in almost all occupations, but particularly in Holland's Conventional type, including positions such as clerk, accountant, and bank examiner. High scores also can be found in some Realistic occupa-tions such as mechanic, carpenter, and naval cadet; in Enterprising occupa-tions such as technical manager, salesperson, and realtor; and in some Social occupations such as school principal, nurse, and minister. Low scores can be found among a few Artistic occupations, such as writer, painter, and musi-cian. Where low scores are found in other occupational samples, they are usually in jobs for which there is considerable turnover and minimal selec-tion, such as kitchen workers or untrained manual workers.

PRIMARY SCALES

The goal of the discussion of each primary scale is to help the professional answer questions such as "How do persons with high or low scores usually feel and behave?" and "What does it mean to be a person with such a score in this context?" The responses to such questions are derived from the following sources: (a) accumulated practitioner experience; (b) psychological theory, as an aid in determining the meaning of the scores; and (c) systematic research, including correlations with behavior, with other tests, and with earlier editions of the test.

The description of each of the 16 primary scales is presented in the following format:

- *Rapid Reference:* Common descriptors for high and low scores on the scale are listed.
- *About the Scale:* This section describes the global scales to which the primary scale contributes and provides significant correlations between the primary scale and the scales of other personality measures. The measures most commonly referred to are the MBTI, NEO, PRF, and CPT (see Rapid Reference 3.4). Further information regarding the correlations is given in *The 16PF Fifth Edition Administrator's Manual* (Russell & Karol, 2002).
- *High Scores:* The typical behaviors, attitudes, thoughts, and feelings of high scorers are described, and the advantages and disadvantages of extreme scores are discussed. Reference sources cited in this section are listed in Rapid Reference 3.1.
- *Low Scores:* The preceding information is reviewed relative to low scorers.
- *Occupational Implications:* Job-relevant behaviors, attitudes, and occupations of high and low scorers are discussed. The latter are generally defined according to Holland's occupational types (Holland, 1997): Realistic, Investigative, Artistic, Social, Enterprising, and Conventional. Occupational profiles are drawn from the references presented in Rapid Reference 3.4.
- *Counseling Implications:* This section describes typical behaviors, attitudes, and feelings that are relevant to the process of working with high and low scorers.

Rapid Reference 3.5

Low and High Descriptors for Warmth (A)

Low	Warmth: Scale A	High
Reserved, aloof, detached, formal, retiring, objective, impersonal, unemotional, prefers things or ideas, prefers solitary work, uncompromising		Caring, sympathetic, feeling, softhearted, generous, affectionate, expressive, emotionally responsive, attentive to others' needs, gullible

Warmth (A)

About the Scale

Warmth (A) was the first scale to emerge from Raymond B. Cattell's factor analysis of the personality domain. Thus, it is the biggest dimension of personality in terms of its variability among people and its impact on behavior. Not surprisingly, the meaning of this scale is widely known and discussed. In books, movies, and everyday conversations, careful attention is paid to whether individuals are warm, caring, and kindhearted or are of a contrary disposition.

This personality dimension plays a fundamental role in the global (Big Five) scale of Extraversion (along with Liveliness, F+; Social Boldness, H+; Privateness, N-; and Self-Reliance, Q2-), where it represents the desire to move toward others in order to seek emotional closeness and connection. Warmth also plays a small role in the global scale Tough-Mindedness, where it contributes to the low (open-minded) pole called Receptivity and represents the quality of openness to people. High scorers on Warmth tend to be interested in, attentive to, and responsive to others.

In terms of item content, high scorers endorse items saying that they enjoy people who show their emotions openly, that they like taking care of other people's needs, that they enjoy listening to people talk about their personal feelings, and that they enjoy jobs working with people. Low scorers say that friends would describe them as objective and formal, that they would prefer being a scientist or working on an invention rather than working with people, and that they are uncomfortable talking about or showing feelings of affection or caring.

Warmth (A) has substantial correlations with scales from other tests that are consistent with the nature of the scale as described in Rapid Reference 3.6. For instance, it correlates highly with Extraversion from the MBTI, with Nurturance and Affiliation from the PRF, and with Empathy and Sociability from the CPI. It also has high correlations with the Warmth and Gregariousness facets on the NEO Extraversion scale.

High Scores

Each of the 16PF primary scales that contribute to a high score on the global Extraversion can be conceptualized as a basic motivation for moving toward versus away from other people. Warmth describes the basic human desire to move toward others for emotional closeness, attachment, and connection. This quality includes the tendency to empathize, sympathize, or feel for others; to express affection, to share personal feelings, and to engage in emotional exchanges with others; to be good-natured, friendly, and adaptable around others; and to respond to others' needs in a helpful, generous, and considerate fashion. High scorers on Warmth (A) tend to have a genuine interest in people, and they find interacting with others to be intrinsically rewarding. They focus their attention on others, consider the impact of their decisions on others, and are often able to anticipate others' needs. They are motivated by a basic desire to help as well as by a need to have close emotional connections with others. Karson et al. (1997) note that for extremely high scorers, relationships are central to their identity definition and that they may rely on their friendships as a means of feeling adequate about themselves.

H. B. Cattell (1989) finds that individuals who are high on Warmth (A+) form strong personal attachments and have many of the basic traits necessary for developing an emotionally intimate relationship—one in which the partners are caring and supportive of each other, are attuned to each others' feelings and needs, are open to sharing their needs with one another, and are reliant on each other for fulfilling those needs. Cattell notes that in the long run, warm individuals tend to get along best with partners who, like themselves, are caring and attentive. She theorizes that to some degree, this scale depends on early social experiences, starting with bonding in infancy and continuing through family and peer relationships that strongly shape later social expectations and attitudes. In her sample, persons scoring high on the scale reported being raised in relaxed homes by parents who used reasoning rather than punishment to control behavior.

Although the qualities of high Warmth (A+) are often perceived as positive in our society, persons with extremely high scores may be unhappy or less effective in situations in which they have to work or function alone or have to perform impersonal tasks or functions. H. B. Cattell (1989) points out that such people may be uncomfortable in situations in which interpersonal contact is not accessible and that these people may experience strong feelings of loneliness. In fact, an extremely high score on Warmth (A+) may lead to underachievement because intellectual and creative development usually depends on spending time alone studying, concentrating, reflecting, or practicing. Cattell also notes a negative correlation between Warmth and college grades, which suggests that extremely high scorers naturally prefer the company of their peers to studying alone and so pursue social opportunities outside the classroom. Another finding of Cattell's study is that extremely high scorers reported that their dislike for being alone led them to rush into premature social relationships that were not always in their best long-term interests, such as a hasty remarriage after the loss of a spouse.

An additional potential disadvantage of extremely high scores is that such a strong desire for closeness or the approval of others may affect one's ability to disagree with others and to express independent opinions, ideas, or needs in various relationships or situations. H. B. Cattell (1989) notes that extremely high scorers may want to be on good terms with everyone, even to the extent of going out of their way to please casual acquaintances. Karson et al. (1997) observe that extremely high scorers may prioritize other people's feelings above all other concerns and thus may have trouble as a parent, supervisor, or friend in setting limits or otherwise frustrating or disappointing others. Another finding of the latter authors is that those high on Warmth may be overly trusting of others and gullible at times.

Low Scores

A low score on Warmth (A-) indicates a tendency to keep a certain emotional distance between oneself and others, thus appearing to be detached, impersonal, or formal. Low scorers are reserved, tend to enjoy being alone, and may not find interacting with others to be particularly gratifying. People with low scores are less likely to be concerned about how their actions or decisions affect others. Their thinking tends to be precise and critical, and they also may be uncompromising, inflexible, or categorical in their approach. They prefer to focus their energy on nonsocial interests such as books, hobbies, projects, or work. They often show a strong ability to work independently on tasks that involve abstract ideas, technology, or objects and that provide little social contact or reinforcement.

Low scorers have a strong capacity to be objective, even in emotional situations. They tend to pursue their own independent ideas, activities, and opinions despite strong pressures to conform. For example, leaders of unpopular political movements, pioneering scientific schools, or innovative artistic trends often show this single-mindedness in their ability to resolutely pursue their ideas and beliefs in the face of great disapproval, rejection, or even hostility from others. These qualities often make them extremely independent, original, and effective individuals.

Extremely low scorers may have a limited ability to form and maintain close relationships, and they may be uncomfortable in situations that require a great deal of closeness with other people. H. B. Cattell (1989) points out that these individuals may remain on an emotionally superficial level with most people, mistaking the sharing of common goals and activities for intimacy. They may get along best with a partner who does not require much emotional closeness, support, or attention. Cattell also notes that in order to preserve a comfortable emotional distance, reserved (A-) individuals often withdraw from their partners when the latter express a desire for intimacy. For example, Cattell finds that the spouse with the higher score on Warmth often complains about his or her partner's indifference and is usually the initiator of marital therapy. Karson et al. (1997) suggest that extremely low scorers may avoid social closeness because of a history of unrewarding, austere interpersonal relationships, which sometimes involve frustration, disappointment, or neglect (the "burnt child" syndrome). These authors caution that before drawing this type of conclusion, the professional should check the individual's scores on Emotional Stability (C) and other primary scales that make up the Anxiety global scale.

Occupational Implications

This scale tends to have a strong influence on occupational choice. Individuals who are high on Warmth (A+) usually enjoy occupations that involve personal contact with people. High scores are found among occupations in Holland's Social theme, particularly those that involve providing nurturing or emotional support such as counselor, teacher, nurse, and social worker. High scores are also found among occupations in Holland's Enterprising theme, including various business roles such as supervisor, manager, executive, and salesperson. This trait may lead to general positive effects at work in that high scorers tend to receive more promotions than do low scorers and tend to be elected leaders of small groups, where they are viewed as making socially significant contributions (Cattell, Eber, & Tatsuoka, 1992). H. B. Cattell (1989) points out that people who are high on Warmth value feeling appreciated in their work situation and that having a congenial working environment can be important to them and strongly affect their level of work satisfaction.

Individuals who are low on Warmth (A-) tend to be found in occupations that involve an objective, logical, or practical focus and little close, personal interaction with others. Often, they are comfortable working independently and are not especially concerned about having a congenial work environment. Low scores are found among occupations in Holland's Investigative theme, including a wide range of scientific and technical professions (e.g., physicist, chemist, mathematician, computer analyst, engineer); in various Artistic occupations (e.g., writer, sculptor, designer); and in a range of Realistic occupations (e.g., electrician, forest ranger, farmer).

Counseling Implications

Karson et al. (1997) note that because most forms of psychotherapy are interpersonal in nature (i.e., involve relationships with the therapist or family members or group members), high scorers are often easy to engage in therapy. They note that "joining" techniques, through which the therapist establishes a working alliance by developing emotional bonds, are likely to be effective with high scorers. In contrast, low scorers often dislike therapy's emphasis on feelings and relationships and may need a clear rationale that links such discussions with the presenting complaint.

Reasoning (B)

About the Scale

The Reasoning (B) scale does not contribute to any of the 16PF global scales. It is included in the test as a brief ability measure to provide a more complete picture of the individual. See Rapid Reference 3.6 for descriptors of the Reasoning (B) scale. Because cognitive ability affects many aspects of human functioning, Reasoning (B) scores are frequently useful in making important discriminations in the interpretations of other scales. For example, persons who are high on both Reasoning (B+) and Abstractedness (M+) are likely to find success being imaginative and creative and therefore find their "absent-minded professor" qualities to be accepted and tolerated by others.

Raymond B. Cattell provided this scale as a compromise between having no measure of ability (as is true of most personality tests) and devoting half the testing time to a full-length measure of intelligence. He believed that the Reasoning (B) scale would provide the professional with a general estimate of where a client falls on this important domain of individual differences. As such, this scale is valuable, but it cannot replace longer, more reliable tests dedicated to measuring intellectual ability. When information about this aspect of personality is of importance to a client's evaluation, the results of the Reasoning (B) scale should be augmented with additional testing.

The goal in constructing this 15-item scale was to balance items that measure the ability to solve problems using three types of reasoning: verbal, numerical, and logical. Examining these three types of items independently may prove useful to the professional when an individual's score is inconsistent with other indicators of cognitive ability. The individual may have strong abilities in one or two of the areas but may do poorly in another.

Rapid Reference 3.6

Low and High Descriptors for Reasoning (B)

Low	Reasoning: Scale B	High
Low abstract reasoning ability, less able to solve abstract reasoning problems, prefers hands-on (rather than academic) training		High abstract reasoning ability, good problem-solving skills, quick at grasping abstract relationships, performs well in academic settings

The Reasoning (B) items use simple language and concepts that were found to be familiar in most cultures. In the 16PF Fifth Edition, the items appear together at the end of the test booklet. This placement enables the assessment of reasoning ability separate from that of personality, and it also permits the scale to be omitted (if desired). When the scale is omitted, the test may need to be hand scored because Reasoning scores are necessary for a number of predicted scores in some interpretive reports.

Scale B demonstrates reliabilities that are consistent with its short length and validities that compare well with those of other measures of cognitive ability. Research has shown that Scale B has a correlation of .56 with the Full Scale score on the Wechsler Abbreviated Scale of Intelligence (Tsanadis, 2002), .68 with the Wonderlic (Wonderlic Personnel Test, 1992), .61 with ACT scores, and .37 with the Raven's Matrices (Conn & Rieke, 1994; Mead, 1999; O'Connor & Little, in press). Correlations with other measures of ability include a .61 with the Information Inventory (Altus, 1948), a short measure of general intelligence that correlates well with the Wechsler Adult Intelligence Scales–Revised (WAIS-R) and WAIS, and a .51 with the Culture Fair Intelligence Test (IPAT, 1973), a measure of nonverbal intelligence that contains four subtests (Conn & Rieke, 1994). Scale B also correlates significantly with scales of other personality measures such as the CPI's Intellectual Efficiency scale, the PRF's Need for Order scale, and the MBTI's Intuition scale. Reasoning scores show some small correlations with other 16PF scales, including Vigilance (L-) and Openness to Change (Q1+). These may reflect that people who are more curious and intellectual (Q1+) learn and process more information, and that those who are rigid and defensive in their thinking (L+) may be set in their viewpoints and not take in new information flexibly.

Using the normative sample of 10,261 individuals, mean differences for Scale B were examined between males and females, between Whites and non-Whites, and between people under 40 years of age and people 40 years of age and older. Effect sizes were computed to determine whether mean differences existed. The results indicated that there was no difference between males and females, between Asian Americans and Whites, or between people under 40 years of age and people 40 years of age and older. However, there was a meaningful difference between Blacks and Whites, and between Hispanics and non-Hispanic Whites, findings that are consistent with those for similar ability measures (Sackett, Schmitt, Ellingson, & Kabin, 2001).

High Scores

In the 16PF literature, Scale B is described as a brief measure of reasoning or intellectual ability. High scorers tend to be seen as bright, quick learners and as adept at abstract thinking and problem solving. They are able to grasp abstract relationships and relationships between part and whole quickly and are typically successful students. This scale has shown significant correlations with performance in school and in work settings. In a clinical or counseling setting, a high score may indicate that the individual was able to concentrate on the test items and therefore is not likely to be highly depressed or anxious.

Low Scores

Low scorers tend to be less adept at solving abstract reasoning problems than do high scorers. Although high scores consistently reflect strong reasoning ability (i.e., they are not easily obtained by chance), there are various possible reasons for a low score on this scale. Because of the verbal nature of many of the items, a low score can result when a test taker has a reading disability, speaks English as a second language, or is educationally disadvantaged. Some people may receive low scores if they have not read the instructions carefully or have misunderstood them. Others may score lower than expected because they are having concentration problems or may be unmotivated or disinterested for various reasons. For example, high levels of fatigue, stress, depression, anxiety, or distractibility may disrupt concentration and hamper a test taker's ability to solve the abstract problems. Another possibility is that the individual was trying to make a bad impression for some reason. Any of the preceding scenarios could result in a score that underestimates a test taker's true level of ability.

Particular attention should be paid to low scorers who on the basis of other available evidence (e.g., educational attainment) would be expected to perform reasonably well. In such a situation, an examination of each of the three types of ability items is recommended; for example, the test taker may do well on the numerical items but experience

CAUTION

Professionals should always be cautious in interpreting the results of the 15-item Reasoning (B) scale and avoid overgeneralizing from such a short intellectual measure. When information about intelligence is important to a client's evaluation, a full-length measure of intelligence should be administered.

difficulty with the verbal items, or vice versa. Discussing the specific troublesome items with the low scorer may be useful in obtaining insight into how his or her attitude or the testing situation might have affected performance. Such a discussion also could help by exploring the individual's experiences in other contexts that have required reasoning ability (e.g., school or work).

Occupational Implications

In a collection of 230 occupational samples, those with the highest scores on this scale are scientist, engineer, dentist, computer programmer, accountant, teacher, and manager (particularly upper-level manager); this finding is consistent with the nature of the trait measured by the scale. The occupational samples with the lowest average scores tend to represent jobs that do not require much training or abstract thinking, such as cook, laborer, janitor, farmer, and kitchen worker. In the author's proprietary database, the scale has a well-documented positive correlation with performance in training situations and to a lesser extent with job performance.

> # CAUTION
>
> Be careful in interpreting low scores on Reasoning (B) because they may not represent low reasoning ability for a variety of reasons:
>
> - Low reading ability or lack of fluency with English
> - Confusion, depression, anxiety, stress, fatigue, or distractibility on the part of the client
> - Lack of motivation or cooperativeness on the part of the client

Counseling Implications

High scorers on Reasoning (B+) are more likely to benefit from insight-oriented therapy than are low scorers; the latter tend to respond better to concrete suggestions on how to do it, so to speak. In an insightful comment on scale interactions, Karson et al. (1997) note that a person's score on Reasoning (B) can be helpful in understanding the implications of his or her scores on other scales. For example, a high score on Privateness (N) may suggest worldliness and shrewdness for a person who is high on Reasoning, whereas it may indicate a simple lack of communicativeness for a person who is low on Reasoning. In a counseling setting, the professional might decide to try a sophisticated approach with the former person and a more down-to-earth approach with the latter. Similarly, a practitioner might find a person low on Abstractedness (M) to be practical if Reasoning is high but plodding if Reasoning is low. The latter person not only would be unresponsive to imaginative approaches in counseling but also would be confused and perhaps inclined to be offended by the effort.

Emotional Stability (C)

About the Scale

Emotional Stability (C) plays an important role in the global Anxiety scale along with the other contributing primary scales of Vigilance (L), Apprehension (O), and Tension (Q4). As indicated by the descriptors in Rapid Reference 3.7, low scores on Emotional Stability are in the direction of high Anxiety, which represents a temperamental, emotionally reactive quality often associated with low self-esteem. High scores contribute to low Anxiety because they indicate a calm, even-tempered quality and a high tolerance for frustration. Because this scale correlates strongly with the Impression Management (IM) scale, its score may be affected by socially desirable responding.

In terms of item content, high scorers tend to agree that they usually feel able to handle life and its demands, that they recover from upsets quickly, and that they usually go to bed at night feeling satisfied with their day. Low scorers say that they would plan their life differently if they had it to live over again, that they feel as though they can't cope when small things keep going wrong, and that they have more ups and downs in mood than most people do.

Rapid Reference 3.7

Low and High Descriptors for Emotional Stability (C)

Low	Emotional Stabilty: Scale C	High
Reactive, temperamental, emotional, easily upset, reactive to stress, feels unable to cope, avoids dealing with problems, immature, volatile, dissatisfied		Calm, mature, steady, persevering, even-tempered, emotionally resilient, high tolerance for frustration, copes with stress, good problem-solving skills

Correlations with other measures are consistent with the descriptors in Rapid Reference 3.4. The contribution of low Emotional Stability (C-) to Anxiety is supported by correlations with all of the NEO Anxiety facets (particularly Anxiety, Vulnerability, and Self-Consciousness) as well as with the PRF's Defendence and Aggression scales. High Emotional Stability (C+) correlates with the CPI's Self-Acceptance, Well-Being, Independence, and Self-Realization scales, and it correlates higher than any other 16PF scale with the Coopersmith Self-Esteem Inventory. Correlations with the CPI's scales of Psychological-Mindedness, Empathy, Tolerance, Intellectual Efficiency, Capacity for Status, Social Presence, and Good Impression suggest that high scorers on Emotional Stability are resourceful in recognizing their own and others' feelings objectively, in thinking clearly, and in presenting a socially desirable self-image. Of all the 16PF primary scales, Emotional Stability is second only slightly to Tension (Q4-) in its social desirability, as indicated by its high correlation with the Impression Management (IM) scale. (Response-style indices are presented later in this chapter.)

High Scores

Above-average scores on this scale indicate a self-reported ability to remain calm, unruffled, and steady in facing life's ups and downs. High scorers tend to be even-tempered and to recover more quickly than low scorers from stress and emotional upsets. These individuals tend to cope with day-to-day challenges and disappointments in a more modulated way because of their ability to put their feelings aside and look calmly and realistically at problems. Even in emotional situations, they try to take into account different viewpoints, interests, and practical issues in solving problems. Thus, they tend to be seen as handling difficult circumstances in a mature, resourceful way rather than as being distracted or overwhelmed by them. They usually tolerate frustration well and can delay gratification when necessary. Therefore, they tend to use their energy productively and persevere toward their goals rather than procrastinating, quitting, or acting impulsively when faced with obstacles.

In earlier forms of the 16PF Questionnaire, this scale was called Ego Strength because it emphasizes the executive functions of personality. Among the adaptive ego functions identified by Freud were accurately perceiving the internal and external worlds, storing up experiences in memory, avoiding negative events, postponing or suppressing unacceptable internal impulses, and learning to bring about change in the world to satisfy other impulses. Raymond Cattell (1979) viewed the ego as fundamentally a problem-solving structure that mediates between needs and the environment. His conceptualization of ego functions included identifying needs and external reality, generating a range of potential solutions and their consequences, weighing and selecting successful alternatives, delaying satisfaction and tolerating frustration, and implementing solutions with patience and persistence.

Karson et al. (1997) view Emotional Stability (C) as central to interpreting the other scales in a 16PF profile. They find that average to above-average scores on Emotional Stability affect the meaning of many other traits, particularly in moderating the expression of extreme scores. For example, they point out that individuals with high scores on Dominance (E+) who also were above average on Emotional Stability (C+) expressed their dominance in a modulated, socially appropriate manner because of their abilities to tolerate frustration, defer needs, and manage conflicting agendas. In a similar way, these authors note that a high score on Emotional Stability (C+) when combined with a high score on Warmth (A+), often results in a generous, magnanimous, sociable quality. In contrast, a high score on Warmth (A+) combined with a low score on Emotional Stability (C-) suggests a socially attentive quality that involves being focused on the approval of others for a sense of well-being. Karson et al. also point out that for extremely Socially Bold (H+) individuals, Emotional Stability (C) scores may distinguish between those who are socially confident and spontaneous and those who compulsively seek the attention of others to compensate for feelings of insignificance.

H. B. Cattell (1989) sees Emotional Stability (C) as similar to the ego's problem-solving capacities that function "to overcome the obstacles that humans inevitably encounter as they attempt to sustain their lives and meet their needs" (p. 39). She notes that these capacities come into play most clearly when a person is actively involved in solving a problem or in a situation in which the environment offers no automatic means for satisfying a need. The ego's process of adaptation may at times include changing the environment to meet the individual's needs or, at other times, changing himself or herself in order to live harmoniously within the environment. Specific ego functions that Cattell notes are anticipation, planning, reality testing, memory, judgment, self-regulation, integration of information, and self-comforting.

H. B. Cattell (1989) also identifies characteristics that distinguished her high-scoring (C+) sample from her lower scoring (C-) sample. Individuals who were high on Emotional Stability (C+) acknowledged and confronted problems promptly rather than procrastinating, despite the effort and unpleasantness involved. High scorers also accepted and prepared themselves for inevitable negative events; for example, they would mentally rehearse such events and their possible responses or they would take other positive preparatory action, such as planning ahead to meet emergencies or eventualities. Cattell notes that high scorers tend to have a balanced sense of timing in that they allocate sufficient time for their priorities and are neither hurried nor late in their daily activities.

In addition, H. B. Cattell (1989) points out that people with high scores on Emotional Stability (C+) typically adopt a stoic philosophical attitude about life—that is, they view effort, frustration, and loss as inevitable parts of life, thereby avoiding unrealistic expectations or disappointment. The high scorers in Cattell's study also tended to reframe and simplify their problems into familiar, concrete, specific terms rather than become intimidated by abstract or judgmental meanings. Generally, Cattell's high-scoring (C+) sample maintained a positive self-image, engaged in little self-blame or criticism, and quickly discerned the limits of their own control or responsibility. Cattell notes that in an effort to preserve their self-image, high scorers (C+) sometimes adopt unrealistic viewpoints, a defense mechanism that sharply contrasts with the tendency of low scorers (C-) to hold distorted viewpoints that produce feelings of poor self-worth. According to Cattell, C+ individuals are more self-accepting than C- individuals in that the former do not place perfectionistic demands on themselves, such as setting impossible goals; rather, they are realistic about choosing among life's imperfect alternatives.

H. B. Cattell (1989) concludes that C+ individuals would serve as good companions in facing dangerous or uncomfortable circumstances because they can be relied on to solve problems, to tolerate deprivation, and to avoid making unrealistic demands. Similarly, she notes that C+ individuals are typically good marriage partners and coworkers because they deal well with frustrations, challenges, or unexpected twists of fate. She also points out that they usually are firm, reasonable, consistent parents, although they are not necessarily warm or loving ones (qualities that are determined by other scales).

Several authors note that very high scores on Emotional Stability (C+) may indicate an unwillingness to admit to having negative feelings or problems of any kind in life. Certainly, others may sometimes experience the ability of high scorers to put aside their emotions and to respond calmly in troubling situations as a lack of sympathy or compassion, especially when feelings of insecurity, self-doubt, or distress are concerned. For example, Karson et al. (1997) observe that persons with extremely high scores may not be open to acknowledging anxieties or conflicts. They point out that a large number of extremely positive self-statements need to be endorsed to attain a high score on this scale, and question "the need for such insistent declarations of positive adjustment and ego strength . . . and whether the client is protesting too much" (p. 39).

A possible explanation for extremely high scores is found in H. B. Cattell's (1989) research. The majority of her sample with extremely high scores (88%) had stressful, difficult childhoods (e.g., living with alcoholic or clearly dysfunctional parents). Cattell hypothesizes that these individuals had been challenged by their stressful environment to develop coping methods that children in more ordinary circumstances are never required to develop. Even though the effort to acquire these coping strategies probably stretched their skills to near capacity, these extremely high scorers gained considerable experience in putting aside their feelings and in solving immediate problems.

Many of the items on Emotional Stability (C) are straightforward, obvious, and hence easily faked in the socially desirable direction. For this reason, it is possible that some high scorers may be presenting themselves as more calm and resourceful than they are in reality. Karson et al. (1997) recommend that scores on the Impression Management (IM) scale should always be considered when interpreting high scores on Emotional Stability (C+). They warn that "because of the obviousness of the scale's items, high scores on Scale C indicate self-representations of ego strength more reliably than ego strength per se" (p. 38). They find that if the IM score is not significantly elevated, the likelihood that the individual was trying to make a good impression is reduced and a high score on Scale C is more likely to be accurate.

Additionally, Karson et al. (1997) point out that a high score on IM does not necessarily invalidate a high score on Emotional Stability (C+). The IM scale not only measures "faking good" but also relates to high self-esteem and the ability to create positive self-presentations—both qualities that might be expected of high scorers on Emotional Stability (C+). Thus, scores on both scales may be elevated due to desirable characteristics. Even an unrealistically positive self-presentation may represent either conscious distortion or a true self-view.

Low Scores

Persons with low scores on Emotional Stability (C-) tend to be emotional and temperamental and to react strongly to stress. In short, their lives are not dull. They frequently have a low tolerance for frustration or disappointment, and they may get bent out of shape, so to speak, when things go wrong. Their ability to bounce back from change or disruption may be low.

Extremely low scorers may seem immature, easily upset by events, or dissatisfied with people or circumstances, especially with the restrictions of life. They may feel unable to cope with the challenges of life, such as "external forces and demands as well as a variety of internal events, including competing agendas and feelings that are difficult to admit" (Karson et al., 1997, p. 37). Extremely low scorers may believe that they lack control over life events and that they react to life rather than making proactive choices. They may overreact to interpersonal stress; for example, they may "lose their cool" in arguments, thus straining interpersonal relationships. Generally, extremely low scorers tend to show a good deal of emotional fluctuation, which may affect their ability to use their capacities effectively.

H. B. Cattell (1989) investigated the subjective experience of people with extremely low scores on Emotional Stability (C-). She finds that they often feel out of touch with their feelings or are confused about what they feel or want in situations. Very low scorers (C-) who also scored low on Sensitivity (I-) or Apprehension (O-) were found to be especially unaware of important feelings or needs. Cattell notes that extremely low scorers often have a poor sense of timing in responding to situations; some tend to make decisions too quickly without due thought to consequences, whereas others vacillate and waver between alternatives so much that they "miss the boat." Extremely low scorers (C-) who are also low on Liveliness (F-) may be slow to generate potential solutions to problems. They tend to think in a narrow, constricted manner and feel stuck or unsure when confronted with unfamiliar situations that require innovative responses. Extremely low scorers (C-) who are also high on Liveliness (F+) tend to be impulsive. They often choose the first appealing idea that occurs to them, without considering the consequences or possible alternatives. In Cattell's study, low scorers (C-) who also scored very low on Perfectionism (Q3-), Social Boldness (H-), or Dominance (E-) identified good solutions but did not follow through with their plans, habitually failing to take action and to implement solutions.

Reasons for low scores on Emotional Stability (C-) should be carefully examined before it can be assumed that the preceding interpretations apply. Other sources of information about an individual's emotional stability should always be considered. For example, some test takers' low scores may result from current life events or other temporary stressors rather than a characteristic way of responding. Karson et al. (1997) discuss other possible explanations for low scores, such as a desire to "fake bad" or an attempt to communicate a "cry for help." These authors note that as with high scores, interpretation of low scores is aided by consideration of the score on the Impression Management (IM) scale; this is especially true when the circumstances for the testing provide a possible motivation to look bad. On this topic, Karson et al. state that "an IM score above the 20th or 30th percentile suggests that a low score on Scale C is valid, since any effort to look bad would typically lead to a low IM score" (p. 38). They recommend that a careful psychosocial history should be reviewed to distinguish a "cry for help" from low Emotional Stability. If the psychosocial history is consistent with higher scores on Emotional Stability, then the low score may reflect a communication to the therapist. Individuals from other cultures may also respond somewhat differently to these items.

Occupational Implications

High scorers are often found in occupations that require responding to and solving consequential problems. These include occupations in Holland's Enterprising theme (e.g., executive, business manager, sales manager) as well as some in the Realistic theme (e.g., police officer, firefighter, airline pilot) and in the Social theme (e.g., school counselor, nurse, social worker). Low scorers tend to be found in occupations that are less demanding or stressful in that they do not require responding to problems or managing responsibilities, such as cook, clerk, letter carrier, farmer, and janitor. Other low-scoring occupations are those prone to have an artistic temperament, such as writer, poet, musician, actor, and designer.

Counseling Implications

Low scores may sometimes indicate an attempt to communicate a "cry for help" and thus a willingness to respond positively to supportive counseling. On the other hand, low scorers may not respond well to the inherent challenges of the therapy process: "Low scores may indicate some difficulty in becoming objective enough to talk productively about problems and in developing a working alliance with the therapist." (Karson et al., 1997, p. 40) Average-to-above high scores generally indicate the ability to confront problems realistically and to work productively toward solutions. However, extremely high scores may indicate a reluctance to acknowledge anxiety, psychological conflicts, or problems, which could limit the process of therapy.

Dominance (E)

About the Scale

Dominance (E) is the largest contributor to the global scale Independence, which also includes the primary scales of Social Boldness (H), Vigilance (L), and Openness-to-Change (Q1). Dominance contributes the qualities of assertiveness, forcefulness, and persistence to this global scale. High scorers on Independence tend to think and act autonomously and to have a proactive effect on the world. In contrast, low scorers on Independence tend to be agreeable, accommodating, and easily influenced by others.

In terms of item content, high scorers on Dominance (E) say that they enjoy having some competition in the things they do, that they don't hesitate to criticize others when they are wrong, and that they can be tough and sharp if being polite and pleasant doesn't work. Low scorers say that they tend to be more cooperative than assertive, that they try to avoid conflict in solving problems, and that when people do something that bothers them, they usually let it go rather than mentioning it.

Correlations with other tests are consistent with the meaning of the scale as described in Rapid Reference 3.8 and thus provide evidence of construct validity. The high pole of Dominance (E+) correlates with the PRF's Dominance, Aggression, and Exhibition scales; with the CPI's Dominance, Independence, Self-Acceptance, Social Presence, and Capacity for Status scales; with the NEO's Assertiveness, Activity, Competence, and Achievement Striving facets;

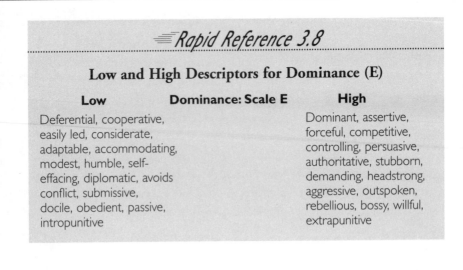

Rapid Reference 3.8

Low and High Descriptors for Dominance (E)

Low	Dominance: Scale E	High
Deferential, cooperative, easily led, considerate, adaptable, accommodating, modest, humble, self-effacing, diplomatic, avoids conflict, submissive, docile, obedient, passive, intropunitive		Dominant, assertive, forceful, competitive, controlling, persuasive, authoritative, stubborn, demanding, headstrong, aggressive, outspoken, rebellious, bossy, willful, extrapunitive

and with Coopersmith's Self-Esteem Inventory. These correlations suggest that E+ scorers are assertive, confident individuals who actively seek influence and control. The low, deferential end of Dominance (E-) correlates with the PRF's Abasement scale, with several of the NEO's Neuroticism facets (especially Self-Consciousness), and with the NEO's Agreeableness facets of Modesty, Compliance, and Straightforwardness. These correlations suggest that E- scorers tend to be agreeable and cooperative rather than confident or assertive.

High Scores

Dominance has been identified in most comprehensive studies of personality and has been studied by a number of prominent psychologists including Allport (1961), Leary (1957), Maslow (1970), McAdams (1990), and Wiggins and Broughton (1985). The meaning of this scale is consistent with the commonsense definition of the word *dominance*—that is, it refers to a broad, temperamental disposition to be assertive and forceful in approaching one's environment, whether that environment consists of people, ideas, or projects. High scorers let people know what they think, tending to be both outspoken and influential in social interactions. Karson et al. (1997) describe these individuals as powerful figures in groups, sometimes seeming confident and persuasive and at other times controlling:

> They do not hesitate to express themselves or to stand up for their rights or point of view. In groups they can be expected to play a larger

role than average, taking up more air time and setting the agenda. They are noticed by others, and their willingness to speak up implies that either they expect others to be interested in their opinions or they do not care what others think. Their self-expressiveness makes them appear confident and competent. (p. 41)

People high on Dominance (E) like to "call the shots" in social settings and may achieve leadership positions in which they can be commanding or controlling. They tend to be competitive, whether in sports or social situations or at work. They may "rock the boat" by challenging established ways or disregarding authority. H. B. Cattell (1989) points out that Dominance can be expressed in many forms and can appear in a wide variety of behaviors, including the example of the mother who claims she is "only trying to help" as she attempts to control the lives of family members.

High scorers also seek mastery over their nonsocial environment as exemplified by their assertiveness in pursuing goals and their persistence in solving problems. The latter might involve attempts to overcome forces of nature, to master a body of information, to develop expertise in some area, or to achieve lofty aspirations. High scorers also tend to be courageous and tenacious in dangerous, difficult, or discouraging situations. H. B. Cattell (1989) notes that Dominant (E+) individuals often have a reputation for getting things done because they are likely to take the initiative and to be stubborn in response to challenging events or situations. In fact, extreme high scorers may become so single-minded about how a situation should unfold that they will not consider any other outcome to be acceptable. Cattell also points out that Dominant (E+) people who are also Introverted particularly tend to express their Dominance in nonsocial areas, such as by conquering new intellectual frontiers or by "sinking their teeth into" some problem.

However, extremely high scorers may be so focused on achieving their goals that they overlook others' needs or viewpoints. H. B. Cattell (1989) notes that extremely high scorers may be intolerant of views contrary to their own, sometimes to the degree of seeing others mainly as obstacles to be overcome. They may become so focused on convincing others to accept their views and so busy thinking about what to say next to get their point across that they don't listen to what others are saying. Cattell observes that for some E+ individuals, their internal viewpoint is so strong that it affects their view of external realities even to the point of involving denial that others are independent actors outside their control.

Thus, extremely high scorers may come across as more than assertive; in fact, they may be seen as overbearing, authoritarian, aggressive, or controlling. H. B. Cattell (1989) notes that extremely high scorers frequently indicate a desire to overpower, intimidate, subjugate, or control others, often toward goals not of their own choosing. She distinguishes these behaviors from *assertiveness,* which she defines in terms of protecting one's own boundaries, time, possessions, priorities, and so forth from invasion by others, without encroaching on the rights of others. Cattell believes that extremely high scores on Dominance (E+) do not necessarily indicate her definition of assertiveness; instead, she suggests that its existence may depend on the individual's possession of other traits.

Karson et al. (1997) also distinguish between assertiveness and aggression, depending on the extent to which a person's motive is self-expression versus the control of other people: "An assertive person wants to be heard, whereas a dominant person wants to be obeyed, to impose his or her will on others." (p. 40) These authors note that very high scorers can get so caught up in their drive to get their way that they lose track of their interpersonal impact and the reactions of others. On the other hand, these authors point out that even assertiveness can be considered a form of aggression and that high scorers are generally comfortable with their own aggression as well as with other people's expressions of aggression.

H. B. Cattell (1989) observes that dominance and submissiveness are roles as well as traits and thus are interdependent: "Neither occurs in an interpersonal vacuum, since to behave dominantly generally requires that someone respond submissively, and vice versa." (p. 69) She notes that dominance in relationships is determined by a complex interaction of situational, biological, and cultural variables in addition to trait scores. Although Dominance (E) showed meaningful gender differences on previous editions, those on the 16PF Fifth Edition Dominance scale (although they were statistically significant) were not quite large enough to be of practical significance. This result likely indicates that the behaviors measured by the scale are affected by traditional male-female roles, which have evolved through changes in recent decades.

The quality of the expression of high Dominance (E+) often depends strongly on other factors. For example, dominant individuals who are also shy (H-), insecure (O+), or group-dependent (Q2-) may not show their dominance overtly, especially in new social situations in which they may be concerned about giving offense. Furthermore, those who are warm (A+), sensitive (I+), or trusting (L-) tend to express Dominance in ways that are considerate of others' needs and feelings, whereas those who score at the opposite ends of these scales may be perceived as being antagonistic or ruthless at times.

Low Scores

People who score in the low direction on Dominance (E-) show behaviors that contrast with those of high scorers—that is, low scorers tend to be agreeable and accommodating versus outspoken, cooperative and humble versus competitive, deferential and obedient versus controlling, and generally intropunitive versus extrapunitive. Low scorers usually honor others' desires, wishes, or needs rather than expressing their own; in fact, they may feel that other people are uninterested in meeting their needs. Generally, they tend to be compliant and to try to avoid conflict. Karson et al. (1997) note that in most cultures, E- traits are more consistent with gender roles of females than with those of males because women typically are socialized to facilitate the needs of others and to avoid discord at the expense of their own individual needs.

H. B. Cattell (1989) emphasizes that low Dominance (E-) can be expressed in various ways and discusses the different styles of unassertive behavior found in her sample. For example, she describes what she calls the "martyr," who follows a high standard of selflessness even though it only leads to others' taking advantage of him or her. The anxious, "walking-on-eggshells" type avoids conflict through denying his or her needs but may let off steam by displacing anger onto lower-status targets. The "passive-aggressive," agreeable individual appears to go along with others' wishes but ultimately sabotages their basic goals. The "shrewd manipulator" tends to be an astute observer of human nature and, for example, employs flattery to play on people's vulnerabilities for his or her own ends.

According to H. B. Cattell (1989), people with extremely low scores are unwilling to express their ideas, take stands, or make decisions because they feel that others will become angry, offended, or alienated by disagreement. Cattell notes that in her sample, the deferential behavior of extremely low scorers was unchanging across diverse situations, even when submissive behavior was inappropriate (e.g., with subordinates) and even when the behavior was at the submissive person's expense. Although deferential people with high self-esteem tended to view themselves as being sensitive to others' feelings, their partners were frequently frustrated: "Partners often became dissatisfied with the emotional superficiality which inevitably exists in any relationship where feelings, values, and opinions are not honestly exchanged." (1989, p. 80) H. B. Cattell points out that ironically, the extremely submissive spouses in her sample (who were paragons of accommodation) were often criticized as having "no personality of their own" by their partners and were often abandoned by their partners.

Occupational Implications

High scorers (E+) are typically employed in occupations that involve managing or influencing people or in taking initiative in managing and pursuing ideas, projects, or goals. Not surprisingly, high scorers are found in a range of occupations within Holland's Enterprising theme, including marketing manager, executive, salesperson, and lawyer. In sales occupations, Dominance is particularly related to the ability to close deals. Above-average scorers are found in various Social occupations (e.g., school principal, personnel director, psychologist), in some Investigative and Artistic occupations (e.g., scientist, engineer, airline pilot, architect, writer, dancer), and in some Realistic occupations (e.g., military officer, athlete).

Low scorers (E-) are typically found in occupations that involve minimal contact with people or contact within a prescribed or helpful role. They include some Realistic occupations, such as farmer, machine operator, and housekeeper; some Conventional occupations, such as clerical worker or bookkeeper; and an occasional Social occupation, such as nun.

Counseling Implications

In counseling situations, high scorers are more likely to show impulsive or acting-out behaviors, whereas low scorers are more likely to feel inhibited, dependent, or discouraged. H. B. Cattell (1989) notes that extremely high scorers usually seek psychological help only under strong external or internal pressure—when others convince them that they need help or when they recognize their own powerlessness in a situation. The latter is an especially difficult realization for them to accept. They are often distressed when they find themselves impotent to change a situation or to reach a goal by their usual means.

The Karson Clinical Report (KCR; Karson et al., 1995) also comments on how high Dominance (E+) may affect the therapy process:

> One obstacle to seeking help in psychotherapy in an effective manner is a tendency to view the receptive role as too submissive. [The client] may get into struggles with the therapist over the power differential and the hierarchy intrinsic to most therapies. The therapist may get further by building on the client's ideas than by offering ideas of his or her own.

H. B. Cattell (1989) confirms the sensitivity of the Dominant (E+) individual to power dynamics in relationships and recommends that professionals attempt to develop a spirit of mutual cooperation and a sense of partnership in order to sidestep power issues. At the same time, she points out that professionals must be careful to set clear limits, be prepared to have those limits tested, and be ready to discuss power issues as they arise.

People who are extremely low on Dominance (E-) may be excessively humble and accommodating and painfully submissive. Karson et al. (1997) describe such low scorers as awkward and unskilled at displaying their anger because they are out of touch with it or lack practice in integrating it. Whereas high scorers can usually externalize and discharge angry feelings, low scorers are less able to vent and typically choose to put aside angry feelings. Occasionally, their stored-up anger may be tripped by some event and pour out unexpectedly, as Karson et al. explain:

> Very low scorers basically present themselves as sheep, that is, as less aggressive than any human can be. This suggests that their anger is disowned and unacknowledged, so that when it occurs, they are unprepared to express or deal with it. (p. 42)

H. B. Cattell (1989) discusses the importance of Dominance (E) in marriages, noting that open conflict often results when both partners are Dominant and want to approach their disagreements from a competitive win-lose position. Cattell suggests that such conflicts can sometimes be resolved by having each partner channel his or her energy into independent, mutually exclusive areas of control. When spouses have differing scores on Dominance (E), the highly dominant partner usually complains about his or her spouse's unreasonableness. If the lower-scoring spouse retains an assertive position, the dominant spouse can sometimes be encouraged to modify his or her behavior over time; otherwise, the dominant spouse may leave the relationship to find someone more agreeable.

Liveliness (F)

About the Scale

High Liveliness (F+) plays an important role in the global scale Extraversion along with Warmth (A+), Social Boldness (H+), low Privateness (N-), and low Self-Reliance (Q2-). What Liveliness (F+) contributes to Extraversion is a high-energy, carefree, exuberant quality, as described in Rapid Reference 3.9. The low pole of Liveliness (F-) contributes to Introversion; F- scorers may be described as serious, quiet, and subdued. The other global scale to which Liveliness (F) contributes is Self-Control. High Liveliness (F+) contributes to the low, unrestrained end of Self-Control, which is also made up of Rule-Consciousness (G+), Perfectionism (Q3+), and low Abstractedness (M-); this reflects the uninhibited, carefree, impulsive nature of high Liveliness (F+). In contrast, low Liveliness (F-) contributes to the high end of the global Self-Control, indicating the serious, deliberate, and restrained temperament of F- scorers.

In terms of item content, high scorers say that they like to amuse people with witty stories, that they like being in the middle of a lot of excitement and activity, and that they like to relax and completely let go when at a party.

≡Rapid Reference 3.9

Low and High Descriptors for Liveliness (F)

Low	Liveliness: Scale F	High
Serious, quiet, cautious, deliberate, reflective, introspective, prudent, reliable, sober, subdued, careful, takes life seriously, restrained		Enthusiastic, animated, spontaneous, carefree, fun-loving, high-spirited, energetic, exuberant, optimistic, alert, quick, excitement seeking, impulsive

Low scorers tend to prefer working on a quiet hobby rather than attending a lively party, and they like to dress neatly and quietly rather than in an eye-catching, stylish manner.

Correlations of Liveliness (F) with other measures provide construct validity for the scale. They are consistent with the interactive, fun-loving, carefree interpretation of the scale and with its contribution to global Extraversion. Liveliness (F) correlates with the PRF's Play, Affiliation, Exhibition, Nurturance, and Succorance scales; with the CPI's Sociability, Social Presence, Empathy, and Self-Acceptance scales; and with all of the NEO's Extraversion facets, especially Gregariousness and Warmth. Other correlations support the spontaneous, uninhibited, impulsive quality of high Liveliness (F+) versus the serious, restrained quality of low Liveliness that contributes to the global scale Self-Control. They include positive correlations with the PRF's Impulsivity and Play scales, with the CPI's Flexibility and (negatively) Self-Control scales, and with the NEO's Excitement-Seeking and (negatively) Deliberation facets.

Liveliness (F) is the only 16PF scale that shows consistent age trends that are meaningful and practical in their significance. Scores on Liveliness (F) tend to be highest among adolescents and young people and to decline gradually with age. This pattern may reflect a physiological decrease of physical and mental energy levels with age, and it also may reflect the maturation process resulting from life experience. For example, the somewhat lower Liveliness (F) scores among older samples may result from people's experience that life is harder than they had anticipated or that life events have not met their expectations.

High Scores

A high score on the Liveliness (F) scale (originally called Surgency) is often seen as indicating a high overall level of energy. High scorers are inclined to be enthusiastic, carefree, high-spirited, and animated. H. B. Cattell (1989) aptly compares the qualities at the high end of the F scale to the natural vitality and exuberance of children. High scorers tend to be playful and fun loving and at social gatherings, they may be identified as "the life of the party." They are often spontaneous and uninhibited in their approach to life; they may describe themselves as "doing what comes naturally."

Generally, high scorers are cheerful and have an upbeat, optimistic view of life. In most situations, they exhibit a fast-paced style and are swift and alert in responding to stimuli. They may be attracted to exciting situations or events. Frequently, they direct their energy and exuberance toward social interactions. They are talkative, animated, and entertaining, and they can be quite stimulating to be around. They have a quick, witty sense of humor and enjoy amusing people. Thus, entertainers tend to have high scores, particularly stand-up comedians.

As discussed previously, Liveliness (F+) contributes to the global scale Extraversion along with two other primary scales that are also associated with social interactions—Warmth (A) and Social Boldness (H). It is important to distinguish the differences between these scales. People who are high on Warmth (A+) are caring and concerned about others but are not necessarily talkative, energetic, or spontaneous (F+); instead, A+ people may be quiet (F-) or shy (H-) in their expression of caring and concern. Alternatively, lively (F+) people, although talkative and entertaining, are not necessarily genuinely caring (A+). Socially bold (H+) people are gregarious and talkative like F+, but they may also be thick-skinned, attention seeking people who seek out challenging or even high-risk situations. In contrast, lively (F+) people usually have plenty of internal stimulation and energy and are not thick-skinned or attention-seeking.

H. B. Cattell (1989) describes high scorers (F+) as having a divergent (rather than a convergent) thinking style. They naturally brainstorm multiple new ideas in quick succession without using internal censorship. In conversations, they tend to generate new associations fluently, often suggesting several different ways of looking at the same thing, and moving swiftly from topic to topic. As Cattell notes, high scorers tend to think fast on their feet, generating thoughts and ideas rapidly and putting them into words with few inhibitions.

This proclivity for a fast-paced, spontaneous style may have drawbacks in addition to strengths for extremely high scorers. H. B. Cattell (H. B. Cattell, and H. E. P. Cattell, 1997) observes that high scorers' elevated exuberance and spontaneity may be inappropriate for some situations, especially those that require restraint or decorum. They also may not carefully consider all the possible consequences of their behavior. Thus, other people may come to see extremely high scorers as immature or lacking in forethought. Additionally, extremely high scorers may be unable to concentrate on tasks that are routine or tedious or require careful attention (H. B. Cattell & H. E. P. Cattell, 1997). They may become bored or restless with uninteresting or lengthy projects. Thus, they may be enthusiastic starters of new projects but not adept at finishing. This quality of distractibility may predispose them to focus on a succession of novel, high-stimulus, or obvious subjects. They may miss the subtle aspects of undertakings that require the steady, patient application of attention. As a result, they may become a "jack of all trades but master of none," and they may be perceived by others as flighty, impulsive, or unreliable.

The fast-paced, impulsive style of extremely high scorers also may adversely affect their relationships (H. B. Cattell & H. E. P. Cattell, 1997). Although extremely high scorers tend to be stimulating and entertaining company, their exuberance may eventually drain others. Their fun-loving, talkative style may lead to their knowing a wide range of people, but their relationships may not mature into friendships after the initial excitement of meeting new people wears off. They may spread themselves too thin to develop many strong, enduring personal relationships. Additionally, they may have intense romantic relationships but lose interest when the novelty fades or a more interesting person comes along. They may make commitments or promises that they later find hard to keep.

To determine the ability of extremely high scorers to constructively channel their substantial energy and spontaneity, Karson et al. (1997) recommend considering their scores on scales that measure internal behavior controls. These authors note that without emotional or behavioral controls, extremely high F+ scores may indicate not only liveliness but also impulsivity and immaturity. When Liveliness (a negative contributor to the global scale Self-Control) is high, it is important to investigate scores on other control factors, such as Perfectionism (Q3+) and Rule-Consciousness (G+), as well as on global Self-Control and Emotional Stability (C+). These 16PF scales indicate different kinds of self-restraint that might provide the discipline needed by high scorers to focus their energy and impulses in a positive manner.

Low Scores

Low scorers on Liveliness (F-) tend to be serious and cautious in their approach to life. Their slow-paced, prudent style allows them to be reflective in responding to situations. They tend to approach tasks in a deliberate manner, giving careful thought to different aspects of a situation before making decisions. Not easily distracted, they can concentrate on tedious or demanding tasks for long periods of time and bring them to completion. Thus, their abilities can be diligently applied to develop a thorough understanding of a specific area and to achieve a high level of expertise. What they may lack in range of interests, they usually compensate for in depth of focus. Generally, they tend to be steady and consistent in their behavior and interests, which makes them reliable and dependable in many situations. They are likely to be appreciated at work because they are usually accountable and take their responsibilities seriously.

The general cognitive style of low scorers has been found to be the opposite of the fast-paced, divergent-thinking style of high scorers (H. B. Cattell, 1989). Low scorers are careful not only in their behavior but also in their thinking processes. They tend to move from thought to thought methodically. They are generally cautious, checking their work in a manner that avoids mistakes but at times may seem ponderous or plodding. Their deliberateness may delay their putting their thoughts into words, and consequently, they may not always think quickly on their feet. On the other hand, because of their careful and diligent approach, they tend to anticipate difficulties and avoid risks.

People with extremely low scores are not usually stimulating conversationalists, probably because of their inclination to be quiet, subdued, and limited in their breadth of interests. In social situations, they tend to be restrained and less playful and to inhibit their spontaneity. H. B. Cattell (1989) notes that extremely low scorers may lack cheerfulness, a sense of humor, or other conversational skills, and that they may be quick to notice what could go wrong rather than right in situations. Others will appreciate their mature, responsible nature, although these low scorers are not likely to be perceived as lively or vivacious.

Extremely low scorers may be so retiring and uncommunicative that they have few friends or avoid social situations as much as possible. They may inhibit their spontaneity and narrow their interests so much that they appear constricted. At times, extremely low scorers may appear to be resigned or heavy in spirit. They may feel frustrated that others are more carefree and uninhibited and have more fun. Very low scores may indicate a lack of enjoyment and zest for life. For such low scorers, self-restraint and general inhibition may be so high that they are unable to relax or are bound by habit.

Occupational Implications

High scorers tend to enjoy jobs that require enthusiasm and energy, jobs that provide excitement and variety, or those that require attention to many tasks simultaneously. Elevated scores are found in Holland's Enterprising occupational group (e.g., bank manager, marketing manager, buyer, salesperson), in the Social occupational group (e.g., school principal, flight attendant), and in a few Artistic professions (e.g., fashion designer).

A high scorer may become bored or restless in a job that is tedious or requires careful concentration, as the Cattell Comprehensive Personality Interpretation report explains (CCPI: H. B. Cattell & H. E. P. Cattell, 1997):

> Since all kinds of stimuli—especially those that are novel or exciting—compete for his attention, he may not concentrate on any one thing long enough to develop a thorough understanding of it. . . . He may not be well-suited to jobs involving thoughtful concentration on one subject for long periods of time. He would probably find this kind of work dull and uninteresting. He tends to prefer situations that are fast-paced or stimulating rather than those that require steady, careful attention.

Low scorers tend to do well in jobs that involve steady, in-depth concentration or careful attention to ongoing or demanding tasks. They can apply their abilities diligently in a particular area. Because of their serious, deliberate style, they generally are cautious decision makers and dependable employees. Low scores are found in Investigative occupations (e.g., scientist, engineer, computer programmer) as well as in some Realistic occupations (e.g., machine operator, production worker, electrician, farmer, forest worker).

Counseling Implications

Low scorers on Liveliness (F-) tend to be quiet and taciturn in their interactions during a counseling session. Extra effort may be needed to draw them out to participate fully in the consultation. H. B. Cattell (1989) notes that low scorers often seek help because they find that they "can't loosen up and have fun" or because they take everything too seriously. Their self-restraint and general inhibition may be so high that they are unable to relax or are bound by routine or habit.

People who are very high on Liveliness (F+) tend to participate actively in therapy and to particularly enjoy group modalities. In fact, they may be so talkative and fast-paced that they seem to take over the session, especially if they also have high scores on Dominance (E). Although high scorers are expressive and animated, they may not focus on the deeper issues that affect their lives and may lack insight about their contributions to these issues. Thus, extremely high scorers may externalize and act out inner feelings, especially if they lack internal controls. Some experienced commentators see Scale F as a source of hypotheses about a person's relative standing on a continuum of impulsivity-compulsivity. Persons high on Liveliness (F+) are more likely to be at the impulsive end. They are less likely to work persistently at psychological problems and may need particular help in finding ways of making the progress that they expect in therapy.

Karson et al. (1997) emphasize the importance of interpreting extremely low scores in the context of current life events, especially those involving loss, failure, or disappointment. Low scores on Liveliness (F-) often indicate a situational reaction to a setback, in which the individual may be expressing anger about life and liveliness. Karson et al. point out that although this scale is not a measure of depression, extremely low scorers may feel hopeless and pessimistic, and they may be trying to communicate these feelings. Extremely low scores, especially in combination with other traits, may indicate a general lack of enjoyment and zest for life.

Karson et al. (1997) recommend considering extremely low scores on Liveliness (F-) in conjunction with scores on other scales that indicate further inhibitions (e.g., submissiveness, E-; or Apprehension, O+) or that indicate social withdrawal (e.g., being reserved, A-; shy, H-; or self-reliant, Q2+). They also suggest evaluating scores on other scales that indicate further impulse control (e.g., Perfectionism, Q3+; Rule-Consciousness, G+; Emotional Stability, C+). Although high scores on these behavioral control scales may be constructive for someone high on Liveliness (F+), they may indicate too much self-restraint and inhibition for a low scorer. Karson et al. note that in combination with extremely low Liveliness (F-) scores, "the C+ score may signal difficulty in allowing feelings and impulses to emerge. The high score on Q3 may indicate perfectionistic standards in the face of which the F- person has thrown in the towel." (p. 44)

Rule-Consciousness (G)

About the Scale

As shown in Rapid Reference 3.10, high scores on this scale are in the Rule-Conscious direction, whereas low scores are in the Expedient direction. Rule-Consciousness (G+) is a primary contributor to the global scale Self-Control along with the primary scales of Perfectionism (Q3+) Liveliness (F-), and Abstractedness (M-), with the latter two being in the negative direction. Within the context of Self-Control, Rule-Consciousness (G) concerns conformity with societal rules, in contrast to Perfectionism (Q3), which emphasizes personal orderliness, planning, and attention to detail. High scores on Rule-Consciousness (G+) are susceptible to motivational distortion because certain test takers may endorse the scale's items, which concern cultural ideals and virtues, to appear more responsible than they are in reality. As a result, this scale correlates strongly with the Impression Management (IM) scale.

In terms of the scale's item content, high scorers report that they always carefully consider what's right and proper when making a decision and that they believe people should insist on strict adherence to moral standards. Low scorers believe that most rules can be broken for good reasons and that being free to do what they want is more important than good manners and respect for rules. The rules referred to within the context of the scale's items are usually culturally centered. For this reason, highly religious persons with a fine moral sense may not receive a high score on this scale if their morality transcends that of the general culture.

≡ Rapid Reference 3.10

Low and High Descriptors for Rule-Consciousness (G)

Low	Rule-Consciousness: Scale G	High
Expedient, careless of rules, low acceptance of group standards, nonconforming, undependable, disregards obligations		Rule-conscious, dutiful, conforms to group standards, dominated by a sense of duty, conscientious, moralistic

The essence of the scale concerns a person's internalization of societal rules of behavior—that is, the belief that a rule is a rule and should be followed. Lord (1997) summarizes the trait's influence on behavior as the "degree to which societal standards of behaviour and externally imposed rules are valued and followed" (p. 43). Consistent with this interpretation of the scale are its correlations with other measures of socialization, conscientiousness, and conformance. For example, it correlates positively with the CPI's Responsibility, Socialization, Self-Control, and Achievement via Conformance scales and with PRF's Achievement, Order, Endurance, and Cognitive Structure scales. It also correlates positively with all of the NEO's Conscientiousness facets. Low scores correlate with the PRF's Impulsivity, Play, Autonomy, and Change scales; with the NEO's Impulsiveness, Excitement Seeking, and Openness to Values facets; and with the CPI's Flexibility scale. The latter correlations are consistent with the two possible interpretations of the low end of the scale: Low scores may be achieved by having few internalized standards or by developing independent, nonconforming values.

High Scores

Persons who are high on Rule-Consciousness (G+) have strongly internalized society's standards of right and wrong and use these standards to judge and restrain behavior. They are attentive to moral issues and are concerned that things be done properly in most situations. High scorers tend to be strict followers of rules and principles, depicting themselves as dutiful, virtuous, and persevering. They respect those in authority, follow rules conscientiously, uphold standards, and so forth. They tend to achieve good grades in school and positive performance ratings at work.

High scorers have a strong conscience that guides their behavior and judges how they ought to act or think. Some authors compare this scale with the dynamic concept of superego, in which moral ideals from the environment are internalized and used to control impulses. H. B. Cattell (1989) points out that these ideals

> achieve action when they powerfully restrain self-satisfying impulses, or put duty before personal gain. In this action, [superego] resembles an omnipresent overseer, dispensing disapproval whenever its rules are broken and approval when its rules are followed. (p. 106)

Thus, a high score on Rule-Consciousness (G+) can be a source of self-restraint and self-control. A high score on G also can modulate the effect of extreme scores on other scales, such as the impulsive quality of Liveliness (F+), and can compensate for a low score on another control scale such as Emotional Stability (C) or Perfectionism (Q3).

Instead of reflecting actual behavior, a high score may represent a desire to appear conscientious or conventionally virtuous. Test takers wishing to make a good impression may endorse many of the scale's items, which concern socially desirable behaviors, rather than admitting their actual behavior. Therefore, a high score on Rule-Consciousness (G+) should always be checked relative to the score on the Impression Management (IM) scale as well as other pertinent information about the test taker.

Although the qualities of high Rule-Consciousness (G+) are often seen as positive in our society, persons with extremely high scores may appear to be rigid, moralistic, or self-righteous in some situations. They tend to have lofty moral standards and to judge themselves and others accordingly. Extremely high scorers tend to see right and wrong in black-and-white terms, with few gray areas. They may demand adherence to the rules even if doing so is clearly not in people's best interests. Thus, they may be ineffective in a situation that requires flexibility or an adaptation of the usual rules. Extremely high scorers also may experience a strong sense of guilt or inadequacy when they believe they are breaking rules or undermining principles, particularly if they also score high on Apprehensiveness (O+).

The strong consciences of very high scorers can unwittingly provoke feelings and reactions reminiscent of childhood in others, and as a consequence, high scorers may be reacted to as parental figures. Sometimes others perceive G+ individuals as judging them, condescending to them, or trying to tell them what to do. However, control of others is a feature of Dominance (E) and has little or nothing to do with Rule-Consciousness. The combination of attention to rules (G+) along with interest in influencing others (E+) and drive for change (Q1+) would be consistent with berating others to follow the rules, but not G+ by itself.

Low Scores

The low end of Rule-Consciousness (G) indicates a casual attitude toward rules and a lack of assimilation of society's expectations. Those with scores at this Expedient pole of the scale may display behaviors consistent with a need for spontaneity, play, or excitement seeking as well as behaviors denoting a need for autonomy, unconventionality, or flexibility (as confirmed by the scale's correlations with other measures). This trait is adaptive in work that permits flexibility of approach and requires only minimal attention to fixed ways of doing things. For example, low scores are found among artists, university professors, and psychotherapists. Low scorers tend to receive only average or even mediocre grades in secondary school or college. On the other hand, low scores are associated with greater achievement in programs that feature some form of artistic expression, counseling, or therapy.

An individual may receive a low score (G-) because he or she has a poorly developed sense of right and wrong or, alternatively, because he or she ascribes to values that are not based on conventional mores. H. B. Cattell (1989) notes four variants among persons with low scores on this scale (excluding that variant of test takers deliberately skewing their responses to look bad). These variants, all of which involve some kind of rejection or at least lack of adoption of society's central values, are (a) amorality, (b) moral immaturity, (c) nonconventional moral standards, and (d) postconventional moral standards.

The amorality and moral immaturity variants suggest failure to reach some stage of normal moral development. Such individuals tend to be egocentric in their orientation, and they may have only weak emotional attachments to others. Alternatively, individuals displaying nonconventional or postconventional moral standards typically have developed strong moral standards that are well conceived but do not conform to mainstream Western thought.

Extremely low scorers usually have difficulty conforming to strict rules and regulations, and as a result, others may perceive their behavior as unpredictable. Low scorers also may be manipulative or dishonest in trying to get what they want from others. Karson et al. (1997) state that

> this may reflect a rebellious stance, typically associated with adolescent differentiation from parents. . . . rules may be viewed as mere obstacles to impulse gratification. . . . Low scorers in the central range may be more inclined to cut their own path, rely on their own experience, and self-justify their behavior. (pp. 45–46)

H. B. Cattell (1989) points out that extremely low scorers may have relationships that are short-lived: "Friends became disillusioned and drifted away when the opportunism and undependability of these individuals became apparent" (p. 126). Reactions from others may depend on how well low scorers are able to hide their true motives. Cattell notes that low scorers who are also socially shrewd or bright (high Privateness, N+, and high Reasoning, B+) often make a good initial impression. For example, these individuals are often hired for jobs based on their good self-presentation in interviews, but they are then found to be erratic in their work performance.

Occupational Implications

Generally, people who are high on Rule-Consciousness (G+) possess traits that are appreciated in employees—obedience, respectfulness, and adherence to rules and regulations. High-scoring bosses may be well liked by their reports because of their consistency and the fact that they can be counted on to do what is proper in a situation. Not surprisingly, Rule-Consciousness (G) tends to be above average in most occupational samples in the authors' database (with an average mean score of 5.98 across more than 230 samples).

When the occupational samples are compared by Holland type, the lowest group is comprised of the Artistic type such as writer, painter, and designer. High scorers are found in the Conventional type, including such occupations as office clerk, bookkeeper, and bank examiner. The relatively low score for Artistic fits the stereotype of the free-spirited, unconventional, egocentric artist. That artists score low on Rule-Consciousness is probably an adaptive characteristic because artistic productivity often flourishes by going beyond the rules or thinking outside the box. In contrast, Conventional occupations usually involve structured job situations that have clear rules and procedures and that require completing tasks, solving problems, and supervising others according to a defined set of procedures.

High and low G score contrasts occur within the other Holland types, depending on how much structure and attention to clear rules and principles is required by an occupation. For example, within the Investigative theme, the professions of airline pilot, computer systems analyst, and dentist, all show high scores on Rule-Consciousness (G). These professionals need to scrupulously follow regular procedures and principles.

In contrast, those Investigative occupations that require creativity and originality, such as scientist. university professor, or psychologist, often score below average. Psychologists, for example, must be concerned with all the vagaries of human attitude and behavior; their work requires attention to patients' individual attitudes, beliefs, and problems rather than adherence to a set of expectations. A sample of physicists was also one of the lowest of all the occupational samples.

Scales like Rule-Consciousness (G) have a well-researched history of positive correlations with actual worker performance, including two comprehensive meta-analyses of studies (Barrick & Mount, 1991; Ones, Chockalingam, & Schmidt, 1993). Both studies involve scales that are conceptually similar to G and demonstrate positive correlations between these scales and job performance in a variety of jobs and work settings. Those who show up for work, follow the rules, and pay attention to their supervisors' instructions are rated as better performing employees than are those who are less inclined to do so.

Even more notable is the scale's relationship with school achievement, another area that has been researched thoroughly. The *16PF Adolescent Personality Questionnaire Manual* (Schuerger, 2001b) summarizes the research to date and presents new evidence for this scale's relationship with school performance.

Counseling Implications

In terms of the client-counselor dyad, Rule-Consciousness has important implications for the style of counseling preferred. High scorers prefer therapists and counselors who are similar to them—orderly, conventional, and rule abiding. In short, they will get along much better with counselors who are proper, conventional, and systematic than with those who are careless or casual in their promptness, attire, method of counseling, or general attitude toward rules and regulations. High scorers are dutiful, have high moral standards, and respect authority; thus, counselors who act otherwise probably will lose the respect of high scorers.

Those with G+ scores are likely to complete homework in a timely and exact fashion according to a counselor's plan. They are likely to remain focused and to have a consistent attendance record for counseling sessions.

Social Boldness (H)

About the Scale

Social Boldness (H+) contributes to the global scale Extraversion along with the primary factors of Warmth (A+), Liveliness (F+), Privateness (N-), and Self-Reliance (Q2-). What high Social Boldness contributes to Extraversion is the motivation to move toward others to seek adventure, stimulation, and attention. In contrast, low scorers on Extraversion (those at its Introverted pole) express the qualities of low Social Boldness (H-); that is, they are shy and timid, and they prefer to avoid being the center of attention.

Social Boldness (H+) also contributes to the global scale Independence along with the primary scales Dominance (E+), Vigilance (L+), and Openness to Change (Q1+). To the Independence global, Social Boldness adds an adventurous, fearless quality in dealing with others and in pursuing independent goals. High Independence scorers are eager to take on challenging people and tasks and may even seek out high-risk situations; in contrast, low scorers tend to be agreeable and accommodating to others.

In terms of the scale's item content, high scorers say that they find it easy to talk with new people at a social gathering, they can easily speak in front of a large group, and they feel they fit in right away in a new group. Low scorers say that they find starting conversations with strangers to be difficult, they tend to become embarrassed if they suddenly become the center of attention in a group, and they are usually one of the last to express an opinion when in a group of strangers. Rapid Reference 3.11 summarizes the descriptors that generally apply to high and low scorers.

Rapid Reference 3.11

Low and High Descriptors for Social Boldness (H)

Low	Social Boldness: Scale H	High
Shy, timid, modest, diffident, threat-sensitive, alert to dangers, easily embarrassed, thin-skinned, sensitive to criticism and stress		Socially bold, talkative, gregarious, adventurous, fearless, risk-taker, not afraid of criticism, thick-skinned, resilient under stress, attention-seeking

Correlations with other measures provide construct validity for the extraverted, bold, adventurous interpretation of this scale. Social Boldness correlates with the CPI's Sociability, Social Presence, Capacity for Status, Independence, Dominance, and Self-Acceptance scales; with all of the NEO's Extraversion facets (especially Gregariousness and Assertiveness); with the PRF's need for Exhibition, Dominance, Affiliation, and Play scales; and with the Coopersmith Self-Esteem Inventory. Its highest overall correlation is with the PRF's Exhibition scale, suggesting a strong attention-seeking component. The meaning of the shy end of Social Boldness (H-) can be seen in its negative correlations with the PRF's Harm Avoidance scale and with the NEO's Modesty and Compliance facets plus several Neuroticism facets (such as Self-Consciousness).

High Scores

People with high scores tend to be bold and adventurous, both in social settings and in the world in general. They tend to be daring and uninhibited, venturing forth in a fearless manner. High scorers appear confident and unworried; challenging people and situations do not intimidate them. They generally enjoy new experiences and risk taking, and they may be attracted to situations that others would find challenging or stressful.

In social settings, high scorers tend to be gregarious, outgoing, and attention seeking. In new social situations, they are confident about introducing themselves to strangers and initiating conversations. Overall, high scorers usually participate in more clubs and social groups and spend much more time in social interactions than do low scorers. They are not inhibited about speaking in front of others, whether in a small group or to a large audience, and are unconcerned about others' reactions to them. Because high scorers do not hesitate to disagree with others or confront them, they are sometimes described as being thick-skinned. Karson et al. (1997) describe this trait:

> Social boldness can be conceptualized as the willingness to cross interpersonal boundaries. . . . The socially bold individual who shrugs off failures will have more social successes than the cautious person who evaluates a situation before taking a risk. These successes will result in a number of rewarding contacts with others and a good fit in the contacts retained. In other words, socially bold people (and especially those who are also warm and assertive) are more likely to end up with friends

and colleagues who really know them and like them than are socially restrained people. Social boldness pays off, especially if a person recovers easily from the occasional rebuff. (p. 47)

Social Boldness appears to have a substantial physical component, with high scorers showing less physiological reactivity to stimulation or threat—hence the descriptor *thick-skinned*. Studies have involved physiological correlates, such as electrocardiogram (EKG) patterns, and autonomic responses, such as heart rate and recovery of pulse rate following fearful stimuli (Aron, 1999; Cattell, 1973; Mehrabian & Steff, 1995; Henderson & Zimbardo, 2001). H. B. Cattell (1989) reports that her H+ clients did not experience typical sensations like palpitations, weak knees, and shaking when confronting danger; a sensation in the pit of the stomach before exams; or a missed heartbeat when suddenly becoming the center of attention in a group. Cattell suggests that this scale may measure reactivity of the nervous system and that high scorers may underreact to external dangers and stressors. She points out that people with high scores may be found in a range of high-stress professions such as police officer, firefighter, political leader, and astronaut, and she notes that "the history of our species is replete with examples of persons becoming bored with secure and comfortable lifestyles and venturing forth in search of the uncertain and unpredictable" (p. 133).

High scorers enjoy the adrenaline rush provoked by feeling excited or even scared. This inclination makes them strong-nerved and resilient in high-risk or stressful situations that others might find anxiety-provoking or exhausting. Krug (1981) draws an analogy between scores on this scale and the degree of psychological "insulation" possessed by an individual. High scorers, like a well-insulated building, tend to be able to withstand external pressures impassively without expending much energy. Having such a barrier allows high scorers to withstand the wear and tear of dealing with difficult people and grueling emotional situations. This attribute accounts for much of the social and material success of socially bold (H+) individuals.

As discussed previously, Social Boldness (H+) contributes to the global scale Extraversion as do Warmth (A+), Lively (F+), Privateness (N-), and Self-Reliance (Q2-). It is important to distinguish the differences between Social Boldness (H+) and some of these other primary scales. People who are high on Warmth (A+) are caring and concerned about others, but they may be outwardly shy or quiet (H-) rather than talkative or bold; similarly, socially bold (H+) individuals, although they enjoy interacting with others, may or may not genuinely care for others. Socially bold (H+) individuals tend to approach others in a fearless, laid-back manner with the intent of seeking interaction, attention, and stimulation. In contrast, high scorers on Liveliness (F+) approach others to express their internally generated, fast-paced, exuberant energy; they are not seeking stimulation and in fact may already feel overstimulated. Group-oriented (Q2-) people like to be around others for general companionship and support but are not necessarily talkative or adventurous in their social presence; they may just sit quietly and enjoy being part of the group.

Another trait that is important to distinguish from Social Boldness (H+) is Dominance (E+). However, high scorers on Dominance (E+) tend to have a driven quality toward power, control, or mastery, whereas socially bold individuals display a more adventurous, fearless interactive quality. Although socially bold individuals may take on challenging, confrontational situations, they are more interested in experiencing the attention and stimulation involved in the process than in trying to win, predominate, or reach a particular goal. High Social Boldness (H+) and high Dominance (E+) together create a powerful combination. Such socially bold, dominant individuals confidently venture forth in the world and fearlessly pursue goals—sometimes without a lot of concern about the effects on others. On the other hand, dominant individuals who are shy (H-) may be quiet but determined. They are often content to be the quiet force behind the scenes in big endeavors. In some circumstances, they may feel frustrated because they hesitate to go for what they want.

People with extremely high scores on Social Boldness may be so thick-skinned that they do not notice signs of disapproval or rejection from others. Consequently, they may come across as arrogant or insensitive. Because they like being the center of attention, others may view them as long-winded or ineffective speakers. Extremely high scorers may be seen by others as forward, brash, or intrusive unless their boldness is tempered by traits that make them sensitive to others' feelings, such as Warmth (A+), Submissiveness (E-), Sensitivity (I+), or Apprehension (O+).

H. B. Cattell (1989) notes that extremely high scorers tend to be thrill seekers who are attracted to high-risk situations. They may get restless or bored easily when life is too safe. The latter tendency may lead them to overlook danger signals and to put themselves in situations in which their health or safety is in question. In fact, teenagers with extremely high scores typically participate in dangerous sports and associate with peers who are risk takers (H. B. Cattell, 1989). High scorers may come to the attention of the professional because they have broken society's rules or are undersocialized, circumstances that are consistent with Cattell's (1989) theory that the physiological underreactivity of extremely high scorers may leave them insensitive to the social pressures or threats of punishment that are normally used to socialize individuals.

Low Scores

Low-scoring (H-) individuals report themselves to be timid and shy in social situations. They generally prefer to avoid being noticed. Speaking up and initiating social contact with strangers may be difficult for them. They especially dislike having to speak in front of groups or becoming the center of attention in a group of strangers. They tend to prefer the company of a few close friends. With their close friends, shy people may be so comfortable and familiar that they behave contrary to their public inhibited manner, becoming instead talkative, uninhibited, at ease, or even domineering. Depending on scores on other factors such as Dominance (E), shy individuals may behave quite differently in familiar, well-known situations.

Shy (H-) people are considerate and concerned about others' feelings and reactions. Because they stand back and observe others, low scorers tend to have a well-developed sense of what others are feeling, what will upset others, and how to avoid offending others. In fact, others often describe shy people as "sweet" and find such people's sensitivity, awkwardness, and transparency attractive. How shy people can protect and use these special qualities to their advantage has become an important topic of research, and a number of books have been written on the topic, such as *Shyness: What It Is and What To Do About It* (Zimbardo, 1977) and *The Highly Sensitive Person* (Aron, 1997).

Shyness generally has a strong physiological component. People with low scores tend to show a high autonomic reactivity and an overresponsive sympathetic nervous system (Aron, 1999; Cattell, 1973; Henderson & Zimbardo, 2001; Mehrabian & Steff, 1995). Thus, low scorers are sensitive and react strongly to stimuli. They are acutely aware of subtle changes in sights, sounds, or other physical sensations. Too much arousal of the nervous system can cause distress in any person, and shy people reach a level of overstimulation sooner than do most. Shy people often develop ways to insulate themselves from excess external stimulation and stress.

Because low scorers are quiet and take fewer social risks than do high scorers, they tend to have fewer social activities and friends. Some people may mistake a shy person's quietness for a lack of interest in others (A-) or a preference for doing things alone (Q2+). To the contrary, shy people often are interested in others but just hesitant about initiating contact. They also may have strong or well-developed opinions (E+), but they may hesitate to express these opinions in group situations, instead choosing to work behind the scenes to reach their goals.

People with extremely low scores may avoid social contact and risks so much that it limits their social, personal, and occupational opportunities. They may retreat from risks that are important in achieving their goals, thus making the maxim *Nothing ventured, nothing gained* into a self-fulfilling prophecy (Karson et al., 1976). Extreme low scorers may lack confidence and feel an unreasonable sense of inferiority or self-consciousness around others. Others may see them as thin-skinned or threat-sensitive. In social situations, they may hesitate to speak up and express their feelings, needs, or opinions. Thus, their ideas may be unheard and their needs unmet. Low scorers (H-) who are also low on other Extraversion traits such as Warmth (A-), Liveliness (F-), and Self-Reliance (Q2+) may be so unsociable that they avoid social contact and seem withdrawn.

Occupational Implications

Socially bold (H+) individuals are valued in occupations in which their boldness, strong nerve, and willingness to take risks are useful, including those that demand the ability to face wear and tear in dealing with people or grueling emotional situations. High scores can be found in many Enterprising occupations (e.g., salesperson, manager, executive, attorney) as well as in some Social occupations (e.g., minister, teacher, school principal). High scores also are found in some adventurous Realistic occupations (e.g., police officer, firefighter, airline pilot, race car driver) and in some Artistic occupations (musician, broadcaster, reporter).

Shy (H-) individuals tend to prefer jobs that do not involve a great deal of social interaction as well as those that do not involve stress, conflict, or physical danger. Low scores are found in occupations such as physicist, librarian, accountant, engineer, mechanic, and farmer.

Counseling Implications

Karson et al. (1997) note that some people with extremely high scores may be narcissistic in their behavior in addition to being generally bold. They may be insensitive to others' feelings, and they may ignore their own feelings about social failures or see these failures as reflecting badly on others rather than themselves. They may prefer superficial interactions or the early stages of relationships, in which interactions are based more on a social façade rather than on the whole person.

H. B. Cattell (1989) notes that high-scoring individuals sometimes come to a professional's attention because they are undersocialized or have opposed some of society's rules. She theorizes that the low physiological reactivity of high scorers to punishment or threats may make them immune to normal pressures toward socialization or conformity. Thus, they may prefer solution-oriented counseling to introspective approaches. Cattell also points out that because H+ individuals are risk-takers and thrill-seekers who desire adventure and challenge, they may resort to manufacturing these types of experiences when no constructive outlets are available. She suggests that the expression of high scorers' fearlessness usually depends on the other traits they possess. For example, those H+ individuals with high scores on Rule-Consciousness (G+) are more prone to constructive uses of their abilities because their boldness is balanced by strong internalized standards of right and wrong. Cattell also discusses the special circumstance of adolescents who have extreme scores on both Social Boldness (H+) and low Rule-Consciousness (G-), noting that survival-experience programs like Outward Bound are often more effective than hundreds of hours of counseling for these individuals.

At first, shy (H-) individuals may be hard to draw out and set at ease in a consulting relationship, particularly if they are also low on other Extraversion scales (e.g., low on Warmth, A-, or high on Privateness, N+, or Self-Reliance, Q2+). Counselors in a variety of settings rate these generally introverted people as difficult to access; however, if such people can overcome their initial shyness and become comfortable with the counselor, their awareness of their uncomfortable feelings and their sensitivity to feedback may make them responsive to counseling. As mentioned previously, a number of books (e.g., Aron, 1997; Zimbardo, 1977) provide insight and solutions for shy people.

Sensitivity (I)

About the Scale

Sensitivity (I) is key to understanding both poles of the global scale Tough-Mindedness. At the high end of this global, low Sensitivity (I-) adds tough, unemotional, logical qualities. At the low (Receptive) end of this global, high Sensitivity (I+) contributes openness to emotions, intuition, and aesthetics. As can be inferred from the descriptors listed in Rapid Reference 3.12, a high score on Sensitivity (I+) contributes to a low score on Tough-Mindedness. Other primary scales that contribute to the low (Receptive) end of Tough-Mindedness are Openness to Change (Q1+), Abstractedness (M+), and Warmth (A+).

In terms of the scale's item content, high scorers indicate that they enjoy the beauty of a poem more than football strategy, they prefer imaginative love stories to action movies, and they enjoy cultural events. Low scorers say they are interested in mechanical things and inventions, felt a preference for math over English in school, and recall spending more time building things than reading when they were children.

The very nature of the Sensitivity (I) scale implies the likelihood of gender differences in raw scores. Based on the descriptors in Rapid Reference 3.13, an extremely high score would seem to endorse the emotionally sensitive, tender-minded, aesthetic qualities perceived as stereotypically feminine, whereas an extremely low score would seem to endorse the tough, unemotional, rational

---

⟨Rapid Reference 3.12⟩

Low and High Descriptors for Sensitivity (I)

Low	Sensitivity: Scale I	High
Utilitarian, unsentimental, tough, objective, realistic, rational, hard, unemotional, has few illusions, few artistic responses, functional, acts on facts and logic, avoids sensitive feelings, cynical		Emotionally sensitive, aesthetic, sentimental, tender-minded, emotional, kindly, indulgent, empathic, intuitive, artistic, theatrical, romantic, acts on sensitive intuition, subjective, sympathetic, seeks support

qualities perceived as stereotypically male. Sensitivity (I) indeed exhibits the largest difference between genders, with women tending to have higher scores than men. Because of the significant gender distributions, separate-gender norms as well as combined-gender norms are available for this scale.

Sensitivity (I) shows correlations with scales from other tests that not only support the concept validity of the scale but also are consistent with many other research findings about the scale. The openness to both emotional sensitivity and artistic interests inherent in the scale is reflected in correlations with most of the NEO's Openness facets (Aesthetics, Feelings, Values, and Fantasy) and the Agreeableness facet Tender-Mindedness; with the MBTI's Intuitive and Feeling scales; and with the CPI's Femininity/Masculinity scale. The tough, task-focused quality of low scorers is also supported by negative correlations with the NEO's Assertiveness, Achievement Striving, and Activity facets and with the PRF's Endurance scale. A positive correlation with the PRF's Harm Avoidance scale corroborates high scorers' sensitivity to pain and suffering.

High Scores

Two characteristics primarily define high scorers on Sensitivity (I). The first is an artistic and aesthetic sensitivity: High scorers are artistic and imaginative and appreciate beauty, art, literature, music, plays, and a range of aesthetic values in their everyday lives. The second characteristic is a profound awareness of one's own feelings and those of others. High scorers experience their own feelings intensely and are strongly aware of the feelings of others, which they may express as empathy. When sensitive persons hurt, they hurt indeed, and when others hurt, sensitive people participate in the feeling. Extremely high scorers may evidence a kind of emotional fragility that can involve feeling vulnerable, trying to avoid hardship and unpleasantness, and seeming fussy, clinging, or demanding. In short, they tend to bruise easily.

Some authors (e.g., H. B. Cattell, 1989) view Sensitivity (I) as similar to Jung's concept of the judging functions. Jung (1928) described this concept as a habitual tendency to respond to events and experiences in either a thinking or a feeling mode. Individuals at the thinking pole of Sensitivity (I-) focus on objective or logical ways of evaluating experience and may be unsentimental and tough. By contrast, individuals at the feeling pole of Sensitivity (I+) evaluate the world and make decisions based on emotional reactions, subjective intuition, personal taste, and aesthetics. Thus, high scorers on Sensitivity (I+) tend to be finely attuned to their own and others' feelings as well as sympathetic, compassionate, and kind. H. B. Cattell (1989) describes one such I+ individual:

> He is fastidious, tasteful, romantic, artistic, repulsed by whatever appears crude or harsh, brimming over with sympathy and sentimentality. He is indulgent, easily hurt, and expectant that others will have the same acute sensibilities as he does, and that they will, therefore, treat him lovingly and gently. (p. 154)

Not surprisingly, those in the helping professions (e.g., teacher, social worker, school counselor) have high scores on this scale, as do those in artistic occupations. In the authors' database of more than 230 occupational samples, all the samples with above-average scores on this scale are in Holland's Helping or Artistic occupations.

Karson et al. (1997) note the similarity of this scale's poles to traditional gender-role traits as well as its correlation with the Minnesota Multiphasic Personality Inventory's (MMPI's) Masculinity/Femininity scale. Furthermore, Karson et al. note that low-scoring women and high-scoring men may be viewed as androgynous, which represents a flexible approach to the world. H. B. Cattell (1989) also suggests that midrange scores may represent a versatile ability to move between thinking and feeling responses: "Since this versatility allows for the incorporation of both subjective and objective reality, it can lead to a more complete understanding than when one is overemphasized." (p. 156)

Extremely high scorers may be so sensitive to feelings that they have trouble distancing themselves from their emotions and focusing on objective, factual aspects of situations. They may be easily upset or emotionally highstrung. In their relationships, extremely high scorers may expect sympathy, reassurance, and support so much that they are perceived as clinging or burdensome. They may avoid rough or strenuous activities and recoil from coarse or ugly circumstances. At times, their emotional sensitivity may cause them to agonize over harsh decisions, causing them to be ineffective at work.

Scores on other scales affect the behavioral expression of high Sensitivity (I+). If Extraversion scales are low, such as Warmth (A-), Social Boldness (H-), Liveliness (F-), or Self-Reliance (Q2+), sensitive (I+) people are likely to keep their strong emotional responses to themselves. They may be unable to express their needs, find comfort from others, or respond to others' needs. Additionally, for people with extremely high scores, their own empathy may lead them to expect equal treatment from others—frequently an unrealistic expectation. They may have trouble finding partners able to provide the attention and understanding for which they yearn. On the other hand, H. B. Cattell (1989) points out that high Sensitivity scorers who are also socially bold (H+) can be quite resilient and dynamic in addition to compassionate, and she notes the examples of several civil-rights activists who show this score combination.

Dr. David Watterson (personal correspondence) discusses the interaction of high Sensitivity (I+) with the Dominance (E) and Vigilance (L) scales. The coemotionality of a high score on both Sensitivity (I+) and Vigilance (L+) may be expressed as hypersensitivity and distrust when accompanied by a low score on Dominance (E-) or as a kind of angry assertiveness when accompanied by a high score on Dominance (E+). On the other hand, if Vigilance (L-) is low, the high Sensitivity (I+) usually finds expression in compassionate behavior.

Distinguishing between the sensitive, empathic qualities of I+ and the caring qualities of Warmth (A+) is helpful, particularly because both contribute to a responsiveness to people and to low global Tough-Mindedness. Although I+ people are perceptive about others' feelings, they may not use this information sympathetically unless they are also A+. Similarly, although A+ people care about others, if they have a low score on Sensitivity (I), they may be incapable of emotional understanding or accurate empathy, and their attempts to be friendly may turn out quite insensitively. Thus, the use and expression of the I+ individuals' awareness of feelings depend on other traits.

Low Scores

Persons with low scores on Sensitivity (toward the utilitarian, unsentimental pole) tend to experience the world with far less emotional content than do high scorers. Consistent with the "thinking" pole of Jung's dichotomy mentioned previously, low scorers usually focus on objective information, logic, and reason. Thus, they tend to be attuned to the physical realities and functional aspects of their environment, such as mechanical or technical matters or logical decision making.

Low scorers (I-) may be effective and resourceful in emergencies because they do not let their feelings interfere with their focus on facts. They tend to have few illusions about life, accepting harsh realities or Spartan-like circumstances without complaint. This tough, objective way of experiencing the world is often associated with male stereotypes. Persons with low scores seem to be able to put aside feelings and focus on reason and fact when evaluating a situation—a useful characteristic when problems are tangible and minimally involve people and feelings.

The price paid for the assets of lower Sensitivity seems to be a lowered ability to grasp what is going on within oneself and others at a feeling level. Consultants often comment on the challenge of helping low-sensitivity managers open up to identify or experience their feelings or those of others. Frequently, managers are a bit below average on the scale, in the utilitarian (I-) direction, but if their scores are very low, the emotional experiences of their employees are invisible to them or—even worse—deprecated by them.

Extremely low scorers tend to be so detached from their own and others' emotions that others may see them as tough, superlogical, or constricted. Thus, extremely low scorers tend to have few empathic responses to the world. They especially avoid tender, vulnerable, or needy feelings. H. B. Cattell (1989) points out that because such low scorers are inclined to devalue sensitive feelings in themselves and others, they may have negative reactions to I+ people, finding the latter's emotional approach to the world almost incomprehensible. Cattell also notes that the inability of extremely low scorers to comprehend emotional reactions can cause difficulties in their interpersonal relationships. For example, the second author recalls a married client who knew that he was missing most of what his wife was presenting of her emotional life. "I know it's real, but I just don't have a clue. It's like an entire other world that I can't see the shape of," he declared.

Occupational Implications

This scale is a valuable resource because it shows the strongest differentiation among occupations of any of the primary scales; that is, scores on Sensitivity (I) are a better predictor of occupational fit than those of any other primary scale. This probably occurs because scores on Sensitivity (I) provide important information about how people think and how they perceive the world, as well as their cognitive style, interests, and ability to deal with facts versus feelings. In the second author's database of occupational samples, those with above-average scores on Sensitivity (I+) include various Artistic occupations (e.g., writer, poet, photographer, musician, designer) as well as many of the Social or helping occupations (e.g., teacher, counselor, nurse, minister, psychologist). At the low end of the scale (I-), appear Realistic and technical occupations (e.g., mechanic, forester, firefighter, police officer, dentist, engineer, pilot), and Conventional occupations (e.g., accountant, actuary, credit manager).

Counseling Implications

High scorers, because they are usually aware of and in touch with their feelings, are generally attuned to the goals and methods of the counseling process. Unless they also have high Privateness (N+) scores, high scorers should be able to speak of their emotions readily; this is documented in the second author's personal client database, which also gives evidence that persons scoring high on the scale appear in a counselor's office with much higher frequency than do those low on the scale. Karson et al. (1997) note that extremely low scorers typically do not seek help unless they are compelled to do so by family members and that they "are likely to view the whole process as nonsense or as a threat to their self-esteem" (p. 49). Alternatively, Karson et al. caution that high scorers may be sensitive to criticism, and as a result, they may need confrontational interventions to be couched in an accepting, supportive manner.

A client's preference for the style and focus of a session can be inferred from his or her score on Sensitivity (I). Generally, low scorers prefer the session to be factual, logical, and practical, whereas high scorers prefer an approach that is sensitive, supportive, and emotion-centered. To the degree that a counselor can adjust his or her approach, the fit to the client will be better if the score on Sensitivity is taken into account.

Vigilance (L)

About the Scale

Vigilance (L) contributes to the global scale Anxiety along with Apprehension (O+), Tension (Q4+), and the low reactive end of Emotional Stability (C-). As part of the Anxiety complex, high Vigilance (L+) adds a wary, distrustful component. High scorers tend to be alert to others' motives and intentions as well as to unfairness. As Anxiety rises, scores on Vigilance tend to rise as well. Vigilance (L+) also contributes to global Independence along with Dominance (E+), Social Boldness (H+), and Openness to Change

(Q1+). High Vigilance (L+) makes the independent person attentive to others' motives and able to think strategically and competitively in developing and reaching their goals.

In terms of the scale's items, high scorers say that a difference usually exists between what people say they will do and what they actually do, that being frank and open leads others to get the better of them, that more than half the people they meet are untrustworthy, and that paying attention to others' motives is important. Low scorers tend to respond *false* to the preceding descriptions, which indicates that they believe most people are good-hearted, can be trusted, and regularly tell the truth.

The scale descriptors in Rapid Reference 3.13 are supported by correlations with other instruments. Consistent with the central meaning of Vigilance, trusting versus distrusting, are its significant negative correlations with the NEO's Trust and Straightforwardness scales. A sense of emotional rigidity and social distance is supported by negative correlations with the CPI's Empathy, Tolerance, Psychological-Mindedness, Flexibility, and Sociability scales and with three of the NEO's six Extraversion facets. The elements of psychological discomfort, insecurity, and alienation can be seen in positive correlations with five of the NEO's six Neuroticism facets, including Anxiety and Angry Hostility. Similarly, the presence of the latter psychological elements is indicated by scale L's positive correlations with the PRF's Defendence and Aggression scales and its negative correlations with the CPI's Well-Being and Self-Acceptance scales.

≡Rapid Reference 3.13

Low and High Descriptors for Vigilance (L)

Low	Vigilance: Scale L	High
Trusting, unsuspecting, accepting of one's lot in life, may be taken advantage of by others, ready to overlook affronts, tolerant, easy to get along with, ready to forgive and forget, may be exploited or fooled, gullible		Vigilant, suspicious, wary, skeptical, alert to others' motives and intentions, hard to fool, thinks strategically, dwells on affronts and frustrations, oppositional, competitive, resentful, holds grudges

High Scores

Persons with high scores on Vigilance (L+) habitually question "the motives behind what others say and do" (Lord, 1997, p. 43). They are distrustful of others and unlikely to be swayed by what others say. They may pride themselves on being skeptical, critical observers. Thus, they are not easily fooled or taken advantage of. Because of their sensitivity to others' intentions and their attentiveness to others' motives, high scorers can be effective strategic thinkers in competitive situations.

The characteristics of high scorers are adaptive in a number of circumstances and occupations. For example, a social worker with a suspicious attitude might rightly contemplate, "Hmm—what is really going on in this family?" Some bank examiners show high average scores on Vigilance, consistent with their need to be alert to errors. Some samples of salespersons also have high scores, consistent with their desire to close a deal and "get one up on" competitors. An L+ attitude also may prove useful in the occupations of lawyer, police investigator, and military officer because these positions involve being aware of others' motives and thinking strategically. In some competitive business environments, executives also find L+ traits useful. Certainly, the last thousand years of human history evidence many situations in which being suspicious of and alert to the motives of others might pay off.

To a considerable degree, distrust of others has a sound foundation in everyday life. Some people simply are not trustworthy. Yet, why are some people more sensitive to this fact of life? That every test taker does not score at the L+ pole suggests that in addition to naturally occurring events that reinforce distrust, L+ people have something special that accounts for their consistent tendency to wariness. This something special might be a learning experience involving an event or series of events in which being skeptical was useful or would have been useful, an inborn propensity to suspicion, or a combination of the two.

High scores may be seen in members of socially disadvantaged subgroups who have been treated poorly in a society. Such L+ scores should be interpreted carefully because for such groups, suspicious attitudes may be realistic and based on actual abuse and inequities experienced over a long period. Indeed, members of oppressed minority groups in the U.S. normative sample tend to score higher on Vigilance than do others. Some practitioners also note higher scores, if only for a time, for clients who have suffered greatly at the hands of others.

People with extremely high scores generally find it hard to trust others. They often expect to be misunderstood or taken advantage of by others, and they look for hidden meanings and ulterior motives to support their suspicious viewpoint. Their negative expectations may make them distrustful, oppositional, and hard to get along with; these expectations and behaviors may negatively affect their relationships. Some authors (e.g., Karson et al., 1997) see anxious insecurity as the source of the behavioral elements of extremely high scorers, a classic explanation involving the externalizing and displacement of angry feelings resulting from insecurity.

H. B. Cattell (1989) considers a secure social identity—"the degree to which one feels identified with others"—to be at the heart of extremely high scores. Cattell holds that high scorers feel alienated from most people because their personal boundaries "are so tightly drawn that they feel separate from others" (p. 170). Regardless of the cited differences in explanation for extremely high (L+) scores, most authors agree that suspicion (in part) results from a sense of insecurity about oneself.

High scores on Vigilance may be accompanied by jealousy, envy, or resentment. In this context, H. B. Cattell (1989) describes a theory of jealousy, which involves individuals' feeling deprived of something important while perceiving that others have access to the desired object or situation. These individuals may feel inadequate, ashamed, or resentful when they see the disparity, that they are unable to address. Their frustration may turn into depression, and they may exhibit hostility toward those whom they blame for the unfairness. As an illustration of such a circumstance, the second author recalls a client with a high Vigilance score who exclaimed, "I've been robbed!" on hearing of the good fortune of an acquaintance. Upon reflection, the client tracked the statement back to his expectation that "no matter what happens, I will get a bad deal" —that is, the client viewed the good fortune of the acquaintance as an instance of his own bad luck because *he* did not have the good fortune. The client's expectation of bad luck validated his envy.

Sometimes animosity and hostility become habitual in extremely high Vigilance scorers. For some, the animosity is active and brings the desired results, at least on a short-term basis; that is, people rush to placate them or to fulfill their wants. When such active animosity is consistently rewarded, the habit persists. When the animosity is passive or at least not florid, it is expressed in small ways (e.g., by remaining in the passing lane when someone honks to

CAUTION

Vigilance Is Not Paranoia

Although Vigilance has some common elements with "paranoia," it is not the same.

- High Vigilance lacks the delusional ideation found in paranoid schizophrenia.
- High Vigilance lacks the withdrawal found in paranoid personality disorder.
- High Vigilance is a normal-range trait that is useful to people such as therapists, lawyers, police detectives, and military leaders in being sensitive to motives and strategies.

pass). In such passive cases, it is difficult to determine what the aggressive person achieves, except perhaps the satisfaction of the aggressive motive. Aggression of this kind, like envy, is not conducive to happiness.

Low Scores

Persons with low scores on Vigilance (L-) express trust in others and a willingness to accept the motives of others. They tend to be tolerant and to expect fair treatment, loyalty, and good intentions from others. Thus, they are markedly lacking in suspiciousness, competitiveness, and jealousy. H. B. Cattell (1989) describes low scorers as having such a strong underlying identification with their fellow human beings that they "bordered on the mystical feeling of oneness reported by religionists of all faiths" (p. 184). Low scorers typically are not concerned about being taken advantage of by others, and they are not prone to criticizing others. One therapist, describing a client with very low scores on Vigilance, reported, "He didn't have a bit of trait hostility in him." Such an accepting attitude is consistent with the correlations provided previously, such as those with the CPI's Empathy, Tolerance, Psychological-Mindedness, Self-Acceptance, Well-Being, and Flexibility scales.

The chief advantage of a low score on Vigilance resides in the interpersonal ease that it represents. H. B. Cattell (1989) describes low scorers as "above all, easy to get along with . . . Uninterested in competition and status, they were generous and cooperative . . . People usually reported that they 'felt accepted' by them" (p. 185). Lacking jealousy and the tendency to blame others, low scorers are able to enjoy wholeheartedly the good fortune of others. Being trusting, they expect human nature to be virtuous and honorable. They can accept life on its own terms without undue concern about how others are doing. Because of their generally tolerant attitude and their lack of passive or active aggression, low scorers tend to be more popular in groups than do high scorers. Not surprisingly, they tend to be constructive team players because of their adaptability and easygoing style.

A disadvantage of very low scores is a lack of wariness, even in situations that warrant it. Extremely low scorers may be taken advantage of because they do not give enough thought to the intentions and motivations of others. In highly aggressive environments, a person with very low scores on Vigilance may get badly surprised by the hostile actions of coworkers, con artists, or others with devious intentions.

Occupational Implications

High and low scores on Vigilance (L) occur in a range of Holland's occupational types, with only small regularities describing the kind of occupational group more likely to show higher average scores. The average score on the scale for all occupational groups is 5.2, a little below the general population mean, which is consistent with the findings for the global scale Anxiety. In this context, bank examiners, therapists, lawyers, detectives, and military officers have already been mentioned as examples of occupations for which above-average Vigilance (L+) is job relevant. Among Holland's occupational types, persons in Artistic and Helping professions show slightly higher averages on Vigilance than do workers in hands-on occupations such as technician, skilled craftsperson, and farm worker.

Counseling Implications

The counselor working with a high scorer (L+) faces substantial trust issues. As Karson et al. (1997) explain, "The power differential in the therapy dyad may be difficult for high scorers to handle. They may require so much 'democratizing' of the relationship that the therapist loses the leverage needed to bring about change." (p. 51)

Persons with extremely high (L+) scores may be unaware of their suspicious, resentful feelings and how they are acting out these feelings. When their guarded perspective is an essential part of their self-esteem, they fail to recognize the less desirable aspects of high Vigilance. In dealing with a high scorer who has these tendencies, a counselor has to carefully approach the topic of high Vigilance indirectly because direct confrontation usually leads to lengthy arguments. The best plan might involve beginning with concrete issues presented by the client and then (after some rapport has been established) discussing the client's suspicious tendencies from a practical angle, such as how they impede progress toward a goal. Another tactic could involve asking the client whether suspicion and resentfulness have caused any problems in daily life. Still another possibility is to suggest that the client attempt to turn his or her wariness and suspicion into a healthy competitiveness. The latter works best with clients who are already progressing in recognizing the disadvantages of their high Vigilance. Overall, focusing on clients' underlying self-doubt and unworthiness and trying to build up their self-esteem will be more effective than confronting misperceptions.

As a preface to introducing a discussion of high Vigilance, the second author has asked clients about major losses or disappointments, either recent or in the past at critical developmental times. Typically, clients receive good insights from such an unusual beginning. However, when the counselor chooses to help a client deal with high Vigilance, the key point is to help the client recognize the distrust and quit buying into it. If the client can see that maintaining an attitude of distrust is a choice, then he or she has taken the biggest step toward amelioration of the problems caused by the distrust.

Two final aspects of this scale are notable for their counseling implications. First, high Vigilance (L+) is not paranoia as defined in psychiatric nomenclature. The items in the Vigilance scale lack the delusional and withdrawn qualities associated with paranoia. Scale L measures a normal-range personality trait. Second, as noted by H. B. Cattell (1989), two patterns involving Vigilance (L) and Apprehension (O) are helpful in score interpretation. One pattern, by far the most common, occurs when high Vigilance (L+) is accompanied by high Apprehension (O+). Clients with this pattern have the discomfort common to high anxiety and low self-esteem. As the anxiety increases, so does the tendency to blame others and see others in a poor light (high Vigilance). The other pattern, which is rare, involves high Vigilance (L+) and low Apprehension (O-). Persons with this pattern display arrogance and grandiosity rather than the low self-confidence of the previous combination. They successfully employ the defensive aspect of Vigilance; that is, they blame others, never themselves.

Although people at the low, trusting pole of Vigilance (L-) are less likely to request counseling, Karson et al. (1997) do make recommendations for working with extremely low scorers:

> To be extremely trusting, people have to be exceedingly unaware of and unprepared for hostility. This level of denial may extend to their own hostilities as well. Treatment of low scorers often involves gentle prob-ing of motives, their own and others', to develop comfort with and preparation for normal ranges of human aggression. (p. 51)

Abstractedness (M)

About the Scale

Abstractedness (M) plays a role in both the Tough-Mindedness and Self-Control global scales. The high (M+) pole of Abstractedness contributes to the low end of Tough-Mindedness (i.e., Receptivity), where it provides a quality of openness to abstract ideas, fantasy, and imagination. The other (M-) pole of Abstractedness contributes a down-to-earth focus on practical things to the high end of Tough-Mindedness. To the high end of global Self-Control, the low (M-) pole of Abstractedness also contributes an ability to focus attention on concrete, practical matters. The high (M+) pole of Abstractedness contributes to the low end of Self-Control (i.e., Unre-strained), where it adds a creative, fanciful, absentminded quality.

In terms of the scale's item content, high scorers tend to say that they pay more attention to thoughts and imagination than to practical matters, that their thoughts are often too deep and complicated for others to understand, and that they sometimes lose track of time when working hard on some-thing. Low scorers tend to say that their thoughts usually concern sensible, down-to-earth matters, that they are always doing what needs to be done rather than daydreaming, and that their ideas are realistic and practical.

Correlations of Abstractedness (M) with other measures are consistent with its descriptors shown in Rapid Reference 3.14 and thus provide con-struct validity. Those correlations that support the tendencies of high (M+) scorers to be creative and to be open to abstract ideas, fantasy, and feelings include positive correlations with four of the NEO's six Openness facets (Fantasy, Aesthetics, Feelings, Actions); positive correlations with the MBTI's Intuitive and Perceptive scales and a negative correlation with its Sensing

≡Rapid Reference 3.14

Low and High Descriptors for Abstractedness (M)

Low	Abstractedness: Scale M	High
Grounded, practical, solution-oriented, down-to-earth, realistic, pragmatic, concerned with concrete issues, literal, unimaginative		Abstracted, imaginative, idea-oriented, absorbed in ideas, creative, contemplative, interested in theory and philosophy, absentminded, impractical

scale; and, positive correlations with the PRF's Sentience and Understanding scales. Other correlations underscore the contribution of Abstractedness (M-) to global Self-Control because they support the tendencies of low scorers to show self-restraint, to accept conventional viewpoints, and to prefer order and structure. These correlations include negative correlations with the CPI's Self-Control, Socialization, Achievement via Conformance and Responsibility scales, and structural vector Norm-Favoring (v.1) and a positive correlation with its Flexibility scale; negative correlations with all of the NEO's Conscientiousness facets (Order, Deliberation, Self-Disclosure, Competence, Dutifulness, Achievement Striving); negative correlations with the MBTI's Sensing and Judging scales; negative correlations with the PRF's Order and Cognitive Structure scales and positive correlations with its Impulsivity, Change, and Autonomy scales.

High Scores

This scale tends to reveal the types of things to which people give thought and attention. High (M+) scorers frequently focus on abstract ideas, theories, and creative thinking rather than on practical things. They are contemplative and imaginative, and they have active mental fantasy lives. In fact, people with high scores may be so focused on abstract ideas that they seem as if they are sometimes attending to ideas and images playing out on an internal screen. High scorers may focus their abstract attention on either internal or external issues, depending on their other personality traits. For example, high scorers who are Extraverted may focus their abstract thinking outward, producing insightful observations about interpersonal issues or applying their ideas to constructive activities.

People with high scores attend to their abstract associations to the observable environment. That is, they try to understand the meaning of particular information by integrating it into their existing knowledge. They connect thoughts, memories, and ideas evoked by external stimuli, often making associative leaps generating unique ideas. For example, while watching a thunderstorm approach, an M+ person might think about how it is that light travels faster than sound, whereas an M- person watching that same approaching storm might think about whether his or her car's windows were closed.

High scorers tend to arrive at novel solutions to problems and to generate new ideas. They introspect and visualize possibilities that others do not. In most situations, they stand back and see the big picture—the forest instead of the trees. Thus, they are well suited for roles requiring innovation and vision. They also tend to have an intense inner life and to concentrate deeply on subjects in which they are interested. As a result, their thinking tends to be creative and unconventional, and may be out of step with ordinary everyday thinking, particularly when they develop ideas without considering the practical realities of people, processes, and situations. Their ideas may be so original and unusual that both they and their ideas are seen as unconventional or odd. For these reasons, H. B. Cattell (1989) notes that the abilities of high scorers are sometimes underestimated or undervalued. That high scorers' imagination and deep concentration can spur them to great creativity is borne out by the fact that Abstractedness (M+) is found to be a consistently good predictor of creative potential.

H. B. Cattell (1989) notes that Abstractedness (M) is related to Jung's typology of cognitive styles, a helpful association in understanding the meaning of this scale. Low (M-) scorers tend to rely on Jung's Sensing function — that is, they usually prefer depending on immediate information obtained via their five senses, and they are attentive to facts, details, and practical concerns. In contrast, high (M+) scorers tend to rely on Jung's Intuition function. They attend to overarching patterns and meanings among their perceptions by connecting ideas, thoughts, and associations; by making inferences; and by speculating about implications. Most people use both Sensing and Intuition functions, but some may come to rely so strongly on one that they neglect the other.

To a somewhat lesser degree, Abstractedness (M) also correlates with Jung's other set of cognitive dimensions, Judging versus Perceiving. High (M+) scorers tend to be at the Perceiving pole—they are flexible and spontaneous in their decision making and are inclined to take time to consider a wide range of information before reaching conclusions. They are not bothered by ambiguity. On the other hand, low (M-) scorers tend to be at the Judging pole. They want to make decisions quickly and in an organized, methodical fashion.

People with extremely high (M+) scores may be so absorbed in abstract ideas that they find it hard to shift their attention to practical matters or may even be oblivious to such concerns. In fact, the M+ pole is sometimes described as the "absentminded professor" pole. When extremely high scorers are thinking intently about something, they may lose track of time, forget appointments, or overlook other practical issues. Thus, extremely high scorers may be seen as inattentive or easily distracted from routine, monotonous, or detailed tasks, unless the task is something that particularly interests them. Moreover, their inattention to practical matters may cause them to be accident prone, especially when they are under stress. Karson et al. (1997) note that extremely high scorers are not good candidates for tasks requiring sustained attention or close monitoring of operations, such as that demanded of air traffic controllers, some factory positions, and persons monitoring children.

Karson et al. (1997) recommend considering M+ individuals' scores on other primary scales that indicate the ability to control attention and to focus on practical or uninteresting topics. An M+ score coupled with high scores on Rule-Consciousness (G+), Perfectionism (Q3+), or Emotional Stability (C+) often suggests the ability to restrain or modulate impractical tendencies and to channel creative abilities. On the other hand, an M+ score coupled with low scores on these control scales may exacerbate the impracticality of extremely high scorers, making it hard for them to apply their creativity in a fruitful manner.

Low Scores

People with low (M-) scores tend to focus on obtaining information via their five direct senses—generally, the concrete, observable realities in their immediate environment. They are inclined to stay in the "here and now," paying attention to day-to-day matters and functioning in a practical, down-to-earth way. Low scorers tend to have excellent memories and to notice and remember even small details. They are alert to practical needs in their environment, and they are good at maintaining operations, manipulating objects, and following established procedures. Their practicality and dependability are usually valued at work and at home. In emergencies, their practical focus may be especially valued. They prefer situations that are predictable and contain few ambiguities. H. B. Cattell (1989) observes that in her experience, low scorers "felt most comfortable in situations which had minimal imponderables and that required little innovation, allowing them to act in standard, reliable ways" (p. 201). This is consistent with its association with Jung's Sensing and Judging functions, mentioned above.

Low scorers may be so absorbed in concrete, factual realities that they are not interested in complicated abstractions or conceptual issues. They tend to be doers rather than thinkers and to be more concerned with the how than with the why in most situations. Thus, they are disinclined to be introspective. This avoidance of introspection means that low scorers pay more attention to the concrete than to the abstract; it does not mean that they are so focused on the external reality that they ignore the internal reality. For example, low scorers may attend just as closely to a headache or hunger (concrete, internal) as they do to a leaky pipe or spilled milk (concrete, external). Their focus is on the phenomenon itself (i.e., the concrete), whether it be internal or external—not on their ideas about the phenomenon or on its larger meaning (i.e., the abstract).

H. B. Cattell (1989) notes that extremely low (M-) scorers may be so focused on immediate physical matters that stepping back to focus on larger conceptual issues is hard for them. Just like extremely high (M+) scorers, extremely low (M-) scorers may not be able to shift back and forth flexibly between concrete observation and abstract reflection. They may be unable to transcend immediate, practical realities to see the big picture; that is, they may be so concrete and literal that they are unable to "see the forest for the trees." Generating a diverse range of possible solutions for a problem is not their strong suit. Thus, they are not candidates for occupations that demand innovation, creativity, or a sense of vision. Because of their inability to reflect on the big picture, extremely low scorers also may have difficulty organizing their fund of specific information into meaningful wholes or relating it to broader frameworks of knowledge. In fact, Cattell observes that "M- people characteristically lack imagination and so do not conjure up the kinds of images and possibilities that high-scoring . . . individuals create" (p. 201).

Karson et al. (1997) point out that the interpretation of low (M-) scores in a work setting may be complicated by the fact that this scale correlates significantly with social desirability. People who recognize that admitting their absentmindedness may be a liability attain low scores on Abstractedness just as genuinely down-to-earth people do. Thus, low (M-) scores need to be considered in conjunction with scores on the Impression Management (IM) scale.

Occupational Implications

Scores on this scale are strongly related to job performance and satisfaction. Among 16PF scales, low Abstractedness (M-) is the best single predictor of scores on Holland's Conventional theme. The temperament of low scorers is best suited to occupations that require a focus on practical issues, alertness to the immediate environment, sustained attention to detail, and the maintenance of systems and operations according to clear, orderly procedures. Thus, they typically succeed in Conventional occupations such as bookkeeper, payroll clerk, credit manager, data entry clerk, and bank manager. Low scorers are also found in some Realistic occupations that require attention to concrete matters, such as electrician, machine operator, police officer, firefighter, fitness instructor, and airline pilot. Low scorers are not suited to occupations that require abstract, innovative thinking.

High scores on Abstractedness (M+) have consistently been found to be strong predictors of creative potential (Cattell et al., 1992; Conn & Rieke, 1994; Guastello, 1993; Walter, 2000). Not surprisingly, then, high (M+) scores are strong predictors of Holland's Artistic theme and are found in creative occupations such as writer, sculptor, musician, photographer, and architect. The M+ quality of imaginative focus on abstract, theoretical ideas also contributes to high scores in scientific professions (e.g., physicist, biologist, chemist, mathematician) and in other professions that deal with abstract concerns (e.g., psychologist, teacher, priest). In addition, Karson et al. (1997) point out that when high (M+) scores are obtained in conjunction with high scores on other scales indicating self-control (e.g., Perfectionism, Q3+; Rule-Consciousness, G+; Emotional Stability, C+), creative efforts are likely to be channeled constructively. As discussed previously, high (M+) scorers are not suited to occupations that require sustained attention to concrete details or routine procedures.

Counseling Implications

A client's score on Abstractedness (M) has salient implications for choice of counseling technique. Typically, high (M+) scorers can be comfortable with and profit from creative or unusual counseling techniques, whereas low (M-) scorers prefer concrete, well-organized, and traditional counseling approaches.

In terms of client-counselor interaction, an M+ client may tempt an M+ counselor into taking imaginative byways that may not be advantageous to the client. Two imaginative people can get so interested in abstract ideas that they lose sight of the counseling goal. On the other hand, an M+ counselor can also have trouble in keeping a session on target with an M- client. The low scorer's lack of introspection and proclivity to focus on concrete facts and details instead of the big picture may challenge the professional's ability to communicate abstract or latent meanings. To the degree that the professional is able to adjust his or her style, adopting a structured, traditional counseling style that stresses procedures and "homework assignments" is likely to work best with low scorers.

Scores on Abstractedness (M) have special implications for marriage counseling. Marriages between people with opposite scores on this scale can prove challenging. Initially, high-scoring partners may find their low-scoring partners to be practical and predictable, but over time, they may come to see them as boring and dull (H. B. Cattell, 1989). Conversely, low-scoring partners may come to view their creative, abstracted high-scoring partners as absentminded, impractical, and inattentive to important details. On the positive side, this scale can be a contributor to marital stability. That is, M+ partners can find each other highly entertaining and can develop mutually satisfying routines.

Privateness (N)

About the Scale

Privateness (N) is part of the global scale Extraversion. As can be seen from Rapid Reference 3.15, high scores on N are in the Introverted, private, nondisclosing direction, whereas low scores are in the Extraverted direction, forthright and willing to talk about personal matters. The other scales that are part of Extraversion contribute Warmth (A+), group-orientation (Q2-),

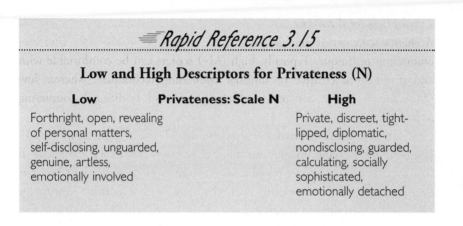

≡*Rapid Reference 3.15*

Low and High Descriptors for Privateness (N)

Low	Privateness: Scale N	High
Forthright, open, revealing of personal matters, self-disclosing, unguarded, genuine, artless, emotionally involved		Private, discreet, tight-lipped, diplomatic, nondisclosing, guarded, calculating, socially sophisticated, emotionally detached

Social Boldness (H+), and Liveliness (F+), to which low scores on Privateness (N-) add the willingness to speak openly and unguardedly about very personal matters.

In terms of the scale's item content, high scorers say that they tend to keep problems to themselves rather than discussing them with friends, that they have difficulty speaking of personal matters, and that people find getting close to them to be hard. Low scorers say that they tend to open up and talk about their feelings readily and that they give more than minimal responses to personal questions.

Correlations with other measures are consistent with the scale's pole descriptions in Rapid Reference 3.15 and with its contributions to the global scale Extraversion. For example, the low pole of Privateness (N-) correlates with several of the NEO's Extraversion facets (especially Gregariousness and Warmth) and with the CPI's overall Sociability vector (v.1). The low end of Privateness (N-) correlates most strongly with the NEO's Trust facet; with the PRF's Succorance, Affiliation, Exhibition, and Nurturance scales; and with the CPI's Social Presence, Capacity for Status, Self-Acceptance, Empathy, Tolerance, and overall Self-Realization (v.3) scales. These correlations suggest that low scorers on N are likely to be trusting and open in their social life and are as likely to feel the need of emotional help (i.e., succorance) as they are to provide it. The meaning of the high pole of Privateness (N+) can be seen in its correlations with the PRF's Autonomy scale, with the MBTI's Thinking (vs. Feeling) scale, and with several of the NEO's Neuroticism facets. These correlations suggest that high scorers may withdraw somewhat from people and feelings in order to preserve and protect their need for autonomy.

High Scores

Those with high scores on Privateness (N+) do not care to reveal their personal thoughts or feelings. In fact, H. B. Cattell (1989) refers to a high score on this scale as a representation of the "social mask, which people don in order to cover whatever about themselves they wish to hide, and to present, instead, an image designed to invoke the kind of responses they desire from others" (p. 208). This masking tendency seems to be conscious and deliberate for some people. They want to make a particular impression and refuse to reveal anything about themselves that runs counter to that impression. For others, the masking tendency is so firmly ingrained that it does not serve any conscious intent. These people simply do not talk about themselves.

Using data from earlier 16PF editions, some commentators (Cattell et al., 1992; H. B. Cattell, 1989) emphasize the shrewdness and sophistication of high scorers on Privateness (N+). They assert that high scorers are astute observers of human nature, adept prognosticators of the probable impact of their actions on others, and alert predictors and interpreters of others' motives and reactions. In short, N+ scorers are socially sophisticated individuals who use their social skills strategically to achieve their goals, whether these goals happen to be altruistic or self-serving. Consistent with the idea that N+ people are astute social observers is their attention to good manners and knowing the appropriate etiquette for an occasion, which make a good impression, avoid giving offense, and may ingratiate them to others.

Other authors (Karson et al., 1997; Lord, 1997) emphasize the lack of self-disclosure itself, without the inference about shrewdness or sophistication. Consistent with this emphasis is the observation that even in counseling settings in which truly shrewd clients would realize that self-disclosure is valued, N+ clients can go for months or years without disclosing key personal information.

For people with extremely high scores, the tendency to withhold personal information may become second nature or automatic and may severely limit their ability to develop close relationships with others. Although such discreetness may have begun as a way to avoid sharing personal information with others who are manipulative or controlling, it also makes a person hard to get to know. H. B. Cattell (1989) states

> I have observed firsthand how this occurs in marital therapy. Often the N+ partner seems unable to take off his or her social mask, seriously impeding the development of intimacy. Because these N+ people are unable to be spontaneous and share their feelings, their spouses routinely complained of "not knowing" them, or that they were "not real." (p. 213)

The presence of other traits often determines the expression of high Privateness (N+). For example, an N+ person who is also controlling (E+) and suspicious (L+) might be quite manipulative or devious and thus a powerful force with which to contend. Occasionally, one meets an N+ person who is also above average on Warmth (A+). Acquaintances or coworkers frequently describe their relationships with such a person as "friendly, but I never feel that I really know him." A two-way exchange of confidences is unlikely with this warm but private person, who typically knows much more about others than they will ever know about him. Another combination that tends to give this same impression of being "nice, but taciturn" is the interaction of high Privateness (N+) with low Vigilance (trusting, L-). Such a person, who has little or no hostility, will smile benignly while refusing to speak of personal matters.

Low Scores

Persons with low scores on Privateness (N-) are forthright and self-revealing, readily speaking of personal matters. To a fellow passenger on a bus or to another customer in line at a store, they candidly disclose problems with their children, serious medical concerns, or issues with their spouses. From a counselor's point of view, this aspect of the scale means that a low-scoring client is not likely to have difficulty speaking of private matters.

An early edition of the *Handbook for the 16PF* (Cattell et al., 1992) notes that low scorers possess "genuine emotional expressiveness and natural warmth and liking for people . . ." (p. 101). This aspect of low scorers is supported by correlations reported earlier in this section, particularly those with the PRF's Nurturance and Succorance scales, the NEO's Trust facet, and the CPI's Empathy and Tolerance scales. Low scorers on N express personal feelings and possess emotional genuineness and openness that they employ in both giving and receiving emotional nurturance.

Low scores are also viewed as indicative of artlessness and naivete in human interactions—that is, an unsophisticated willingness to talk about oneself with minimal internal censorship (Cattell et al., 1992). Sharing this viewpoint is H. B. Cattell (1989), who describes low scorers as having a childlike straightforwardness in that they are not concerned with impressing others or putting their best foot forward. Although most people find low scorers open, honest, and genuine, some people may react less positively to their direct style and see them as tactless or thoughtless.

At a higher level of interpretive inference, H. B. Cattell (1989) points out that extremely low scorers may have a naive, simplistic social orientation that pervades their social awareness and expectations of others. Being out of touch with the complex workings of human nature and motivations, they may be unaware of how they sound to others or what others might do with personal information they reveal. They may have limited insight into others' reactions or lack social sophistication and skepticism. Unfortunately, the latter may make them vulnerable to being taken advantage of or manipulated by devious people.

Because low scorers tend to be transparent about their thoughts, needs, and intentions, their other traits may be accentuated. For example, forthright (N-) people who are also controlling or domineering (E+) may come across as blunt or obviously controlling. Similarly, the indifference of aloof (A-) people and the insensitivity of I- people tend to be much more apparent if they are also (N-) forthright. H. B. Cattell (1989) distinguishes between the common, naive expression of low N and the more aggressive "I've got to be me" form that tends to be apparent when N- is accompanied by high scores on Dominance (E+) and Openness to Change (Q1+).

Occupational Implications

As noted previously, high scorers are typically found in occupations in Holland's Conventional type, such as secretary, clerk, accountant, and bookkeeper, which involve a certain level of formality and do not require close personal interaction. They also may be attracted to occupations that require diplomacy or strategic forethought, such as public relations manager, therapist, or attorney.

Counseling Implications

In terms of the quality of the counseling dyad, Privateness (N) is one of the most important 16PF scales. Counselors typically find that clients high on the scale (N+) resist revealing intimate details of their lives and attitudes. They may be friendly, even moderately outgoing and easy to speak with about casual things, but in terms of discussing private matters, they will be resistant. They are not deliberately trying to sabotage the counseling work; rather, they just tend to automatically avoid talking about personal topics. For example, such a client might—with difficulty—speak of problems at work but never mention his attraction to his wife's sister or his troubles with his mother.

Karson et al. (1997) describe problems that can arise in marital therapy when partners have widely disparate scores on Privateness (N). Each partner may find the other's behavior hard to understand, or they may interpret the behavior as having the same meaning it would have coming from themselves:

> Low scorers often think high-scoring partners are unhappy with them, since low scorers would only stop communicating to distance themselves from others. Meanwhile, high scorers may perceive their low-scoring partners as intrusive and relentless in their pursuit of information sharing, prompting the high scorers to vigorously defend their privacy. The end result can be a vicious circle. (p. 53)

These authors have found extremely high scorers to be personally guarded, often maintaining their privacy at the expense of developing close relationships with others. This behavior may reflect a fear of closeness or an expectation that others will misuse any personal information they are given.

Apprehension (O)

About the Scale

Apprehension (O) plays a central role in the global scale Anxiety along with the primary scales of Emotional Stability (C-), Vigilance (L+), and Tension (Q4+). What the Apprehension scale contributes to global Anxiety are the qualities commonly attributed to worriers—tendencies to be apprehensive, insecure, and self-doubting. This scale is one of three 16PF scales that show meaningful gender differences, with women on average scoring higher than men. The scale also shows an element of social desirability, with the self-assured low end (O-) as the socially desirable pole.

In terms of the scale's item content, high scorers say they are sensitive and worry about what they have done or should have done, that they are upset when others criticize them, and that it is hard for them to get to sleep when they are upset about something. Low scorers say that they worry less than most people, that they are not upset if others dislike them, and that they do not reconsider their decisions.

Correlations with other tests provide construct validity and support the scale descriptors listed in Rapid Reference 3.16. The scale's contribution to global Anxiety and the apprehensive quality of high (O+) scores are supported by positive correlations with all of the NEO's Neuroticism facets; positive correlations with the PRF's Nurturance and Harm Avoidance scales; and negative correlations with the CPI's Self-Acceptance and Well-Being scales. That high scorers are modest and uncertain of themselves in social situations (whereas low scorers are self-assured and self-satisfied) is supported by negative correlations with the CPI's Independence, Dominance, Capacity for Status, and Social Presence scales; negative correlations with the PRF's Dominance, Exhibition, Social Recognition, and Autonomy scales; and a negative correlation with the NEO's Assertiveness scale and a positive correlation with its Modesty scale. The tendency for high scorers to focus on feelings and low scorers to focus on thinking is supported by a positive correlation with the MBTI's Feeling scale and a negative correlation with its Thinking scale.

High Scores

People with high (O+) scores tend to be seen as worriers—somewhat similar to the style of the main character in Woody Allen films. Because they are attentive to what can go wrong in situations, they may be able to anticipate

≡ Rapid Reference 3.16

Low and High Descriptors for Apprehension (O)

Low	Apprehension: Scale O	High
Self-assured, unworried, self-satisfied, unperturbed, self-confident, placid, untroubled by guilt or remorse, complacent, little empathy for others' insecurity or worry, insensitive to criticism, assumes self-worth		Apprehensive, worried, self-doubting, nervous, insecure, lacks confidence, self-reproaching, guilt-prone, concerned for others, feels obligations, sensitive to criticism, self-depreciating

dangers or the consequences of actions and be more prepared for them. Because they are apprehensive, high scorers typically consider the consequences of their actions, especially their effects on other people. They also tend to notice others' reactions to them. They usually have a strong sense of obligation, and when things go wrong, they are more likely to consider whether they themselves are to blame. They may replay incidents in their mind and speculate as to whether they said or did the right thing at the time. In addition to worrying about the past, they may spend time worrying about what could go wrong in the future. Because they tend to be self-critical, they usually take criticism from others seriously.

H. B. Cattell (1989) points out that although the O+ personality style may involve subjective discomfort, it has inherent social value because it provides a counterforce against natural human selfishness, greed, cruelty, and irresponsibility. Cattell notes that her O+ clients were likely to make personal sacrifices, work hard, consider the impact of their actions on others, and demonstrate commitment to fairness and social justice. She comments further that her O+ clients "were justly lauded as good, humane, and virtuous by those who knew them" (p. 225). Cattell also notes that priests and nuns in her clinical study showed high scores and that high scorers generally tended to have more religious feelings and spiritual concerns than did low scorers.

Extremely high (O+) scorers may have a low sense of self-worth or self-esteem, which can induce them to feel emotionally inadequate when they are dealing with others. They may make a poor self-presentation if their insecurity, discomfort, or self-doubt become apparent to others. Extremely high scorers may doubt their own judgment, be self-blaming, or become easily discouraged. Because of their insecurity, they may not feel accepted in groups. They may be prone to feelings of guilt or loneliness. They may feel that they are to blame for negative situations over which they have no control, and their willingness to accept blame may make them susceptible to manipulation by others. High scorers who are also high on Rule-Consciousness (G+) may have rigid moral standards that lead to harsh self-censure.

Several authors note the importance of determining whether high (O+) scores represent a transitory reaction to recent life events or are characterological in nature (Karson et al., 1997; Lord, 1999). H. B. Cattell (1989) reports that the majority (72%) of high scorers in her clinical sample were the reactive type who "had recently experienced failure, illness, reduced status, bereavement, or some other loss" (p. 224). Their scores usually returned to lower levels after their lives had returned to normal or their grieving process had been completed.

Low Scores

People with low (O-) scores tend to be self-assured, confident, and unworried. They usually do not doubt themselves or question their own actions or decisions. Their judgments of themselves tend to be positive. Because they have a strong sense of self-acceptance and self-worth, they feel that they deserve respect and love and that they deserve to have their needs met. Their self-confidence makes them a strong presence around others and often leads to social success. Not surprisingly, managers, executives, and other leaders tend to have low scores on Apprehension.

The strong self-confidence of low scorers (O-) may make them insensitive to others' vulnerable feelings. Unless O- scorers are also warm (A+), submissive (E-), shy (H-), or sensitive (I+), they may have trouble empathizing with others' feelings of insecurity or worry. Extremely low scorers may be so self-assured and confident that they appear to be self-satisfied or complacent. Lord (1999) notes that low scorers are inclined to selectively attend to their own positive characteristics and to activities that showcase their talents. Extremely low scorers usually are unconcerned about others' opinions of them and are not upset by others' censure. They may ignore the effects of their behavior on others as well as feedback from others. Thus, they may miss opportunities for self-evaluation or self-improvement. Karson et al. (1997) comment on one reason for this self-complacency and insensitivity to others: "Low scores often mean that the conscience is not active or not being listened to." (p. 54)

In regard to extremely low (O-) scores, H. B. Cattell (1989) observes that although a constantly high level of self-confidence may be subjectively desirable, it is unlikely to be based on accurate self-appraisal. If self-esteem is unshakable, she points out, it does not serve its purpose of providing feedback about one's behavior through twinges of shame, guilt, or doubt. Cattell advises that because extremely low scorers seldom accept blame or experience remorse, it is wise to consider carefully what constitutes the bases of their self-esteem. For example, they may block or deny awareness of negative aspects of themselves in order to maintain their positive self-image. They also may avoid situations that would reveal their inadequacies (e.g., avoid attending college, developing intimate relationships, or having children). This approach to maintaining high self-esteem may have been developed in response to adverse circumstances and therefore may be excessively strong or rigid.

Occupational Implications

The self-assurance and resilience of low (O-) scorers are valued in a range of occupations, especially those that involve positive self-presentation, confident decision making, or dealing with stress. Among these occupations are many in Holland's Enterprising theme, such as salesperson, manager, executive, banker, marketer, and lawyer. Persons in the hands-on, no-nonsense Realistic occupations, such as electrician, mechanic, athlete, firefighter, and police officer, also tend to have low scores. Additionally, low scores are found in some Investigative occupations such as engineer, scientist, airline pilot, and dentist. In the authors' database, of 29 low scoring samples, 11 are in business occupations (e.g., manager and salesperson), seven are in scientific occupations, six are in hands-on occupations, and only five are in helping professions.

Fewer occupational samples show high average (O+) scores on this scale and the great majority of these are in helping professions, such as Roman Catholic nun, teacher, therapist, nurse, and social worker. A few are creative artists, such as ballet dancer and editorial worker. The fact that high scorers show an affinity for helping and Social occupations may suggest why women score higher than do men on Apprehension. Certainly the presence of high scores in child-care occupations (Walter, 2000) make sense since care of children requires empathy and constant attention to things that could go wrong.

Counseling Implications

Several authors note the importance of distinguishing whether high (O+) scores are reactive or characterological in nature. Thus, they recommend asking high scorers whether they have experienced recent losses or failures and whether how they currently feel is different from how they felt a year ago or even several years ago. For those who are reacting to situational problems, H. B. Cattell (1989) suggests a problem-centered approach rather than one that focuses on basic self-attitudes.

Because an extremely high (O+) score reflects a negative self-evaluation, such a score should be considered in conjunction with scores on Rule-Consciousness (G) and Perfectionism (Q3). A high score on either of these latter scales coupled with an O+ is indicative of rigid or unreasonably lofty standards. Individuals exhibiting such scores may be judging themselves harshly and feeling guilt or shame because they have not reached their high self-imposed standards. A high Apprehension (O+) score should also be checked relevant to the score on Liveliness (F). A combination of high Apprehension (O+) and low Liveliness (F-) may indicate feelings of discouragement or hopelessness. Karson et al. (1997) note concerns relative to counseling high (O+) scorers:

> Apprehension (O+) is resistant to therapeutic efforts to change it. Telling someone not to worry does not help. Often the therapist may find focusing on another problem to be more productive. . . . Arranging for satisfying compromises around impulse expression leads to a reduction in worrying more than a frontal attack on the worrying itself. (p. 55)

Low (O-) scorers usually do not experience much psychological discomfort. Thus, they typically do not seek counseling unless they are encouraged to do so by a spouse or partner. H. B. Cattell (1989) notes that the partners of O- scorers may feel a lack of emotional contact or communication. In short, they are missing the kind of empathic, vulnerable, meaningful responses that are important in the development of intimate relationships; this is because their self-assured O- partners lack understanding of or sensitivity to feelings of doubt, remorse, guilt, or shame. Cattell also points out that low scorers may not accept their fair share of responsibility and blame when things go wrong in a relationship. Conversely, high (O+) scorers tend to assume all the blame themselves when a relationship is troubled—a situation that may be exploited by a partner who tends to deny blame.

Openness to Change (Q1)

About the Scale

Openness to Change (Q1) contributes to the global scales of Tough-Mindedness and Independence. The high (Q1+) pole contributes open-mindedness to new ideas and unconventional approaches to the low

Receptive end of Tough-Mindedness, which is similar to the Big Five factor Openness. The low (Q1-) pole contributes a quality of attachment to familiar, traditional ways of doing things to the high end of Tough-Mindedness. To the high end of the Independence global, the high (Q1+) pole adds original thinking and innovative viewpoints. At the low end of Independence (Accommodating), the low (Q1-) pole provides the tendency to adhere to established ways rather than challenge the status quo.

In terms of the scale's item content, high scorers report that they prefer thinking of innovative ways to do things rather than following well-tried ways, they prefer experimenting with new ways of cooking or making things rather than following established directions, and they like to read about current social problems. Low scorers report that they feel secure and confident when they do what is familiar and routine, they do not care for people who are different or unusual, and they believe that trouble results from questioning and changing established methods.

Correlations with other measures are consistent with the descriptors listed in Rapid Reference 3.17. Scale Q1 correlates positively with all six of the NEO's Openness facets and with the MBTI's Intuitive scale. It also correlates positively with the PRF's need for Change, Understanding, Sentience, and Autonomy scales and with the CPI's Tolerance, Intellectual Efficiency, Capacity for Status, Achievement via Independence, and Flexibility scales. These correlations suggest that high scorers like to think creatively and independently about wide-ranging ideas and concepts. Negative correlations suggest that low scorers are more circumscribed, structured, and set in their viewpoints and thinking than are high scorers. These include negative correlations with the PRF's Order and Cognitive Structure scales, with the MBTI's Sensing and Judging scales, and with the NEO's Order and Self-Consciousness facets.

High Scores

The central core of the high (Q1+) pole of this scale is well captured by Lord's (1997) phrase "openness to new ideas and experiences" (p. 77). High scorers like to think freely and openly about things, without barriers or restrictions to logical thought. Thus, they tend to view things in new ways and to apply ideas from one field to another in creative ways. They enjoy experimenting with different solutions to problems rather than complacently accepting the tried-and-true solutions. Their interest in new or unusual

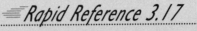

Rapid Reference 3.17

Low and High Descriptors for Openness to Change (Q1)

Low	Openness to Change: Scale Q1	High
Traditional, attached to familiar, prefers status quo, resistant to change, doesn't question how things are done		Open to change, experimenting, questions established methods, open-minded, freethinking

approaches is not based on a sense of seeking change just for the sake of change. Instead, they question established ways because they naturally notice how improvements could be made. For example, they may seek change because they find traditional ways to be illogical or ineffective or because they view the status quo as unsatisfactory or unfair.

The attitude to change expressed by high (Q1+) scorers is not essentially political; rather, it is a broader tendency toward inquiry, critical thinking, and creativity. For example, this tendency applies equally well to physical challenges (e.g., repairing a leaky roof), to conceptual challenges (e.g., understanding the makeup of DNA), to interpersonal challenges (e.g., planning an enjoyable family activity), and to personal challenges (e.g., determining how to be more assertive). Although high scorers can rock the boat, their exhortations for change generally arise out of principle. H. B. Cattell (1989) notes that high scorers are often unselfish champions of the underdog and that their criticism of established methods usually is based on real concerns that are overlooked or ignored by individuals who are more complacent.

More generally, H. B. Cattell (1989) views this scale as an indicator of an individual's basic psychological orientation to change. She notes that change requires perceptual readjustment, which is mediated by emotions as the individual lets go of old connections and forms new attachments. To differentiate the attitudes of high (Q1+) and low (Q1-) scorers to change, Cattell uses the metaphor of train passengers. High scorers are those passengers who prefer to sit facing forward, where they can constantly watch new scenes and assimilate new information. Low scorers are those passengers who prefer to sit facing backward, where they can linger on things present and past that demand few perceptual readjustments. Although most people are versatile in their preferences for forward-looking versus backward-looking views, some strongly prefer one or the other.

A real strength of high (Q1+) scorers is that they embrace the future. They anticipate the future and—depending on other aspects of personality—are eager to give the future a chance. They rejoice at change and—depending on their other traits—enjoy seeing others make positive changes in their lives. Frequently, they are found in the ranks of reformers, innovators, or entrepreneurs, where their interest in change is met with approval and encouragement. On an individual level, Q1+ scorers are prone to be proactive in solving problems in their own lives and in the lives of those around them.

A weakness of extremely high (Q1+) scorers is that they may become so focused on experimenting with improvements, they overlook the good in the way things are currently done. They may reject traditional approaches without careful consideration. Extremely high scorers also may be sensitive to issues of unfairness or injustice in established ways and thus may not function well as subordinates in a hierarchical structure. When they are in a slow-moving or restrictive environment, persons with extremely high scores may become frustrated or critical, especially if they also score high on Dominance (E+) or Vigilance (L+).

Unless they are endowed with high levels of tact (N+) or interpersonal sensitivity (e.g., Warmth, A+; Sensitivity I+), extremely high (Q1+) scorers may question and stir up situations, causing considerable discomfort. When they can claim the moral high ground because of the existence of real abuses, extremely high scorers can become intransigent to an extent that is counterproductive. If persons with extremely high (Q1+) scores also have high scores on Reasoning (B+), Dominance (E+), and Vigilance (L+), they may be forceful about their viewpoints and intellectually or verbally aggressive (Meyer, 1989).

Low Scores

Persons with low (Q1-) scores are content and comfortable with the status quo and place more value on what is than on what might be. They tend to respect traditional ways and do not question established methods. Because of their confidence in the tried-and-true approaches, they are cautious about new ideas. They seem to genuinely like the status quo and thus may have a steadying influence in situations. They prefer life to be predictable and familiar, even if it is not optimal. If they were to adopt a motto, it might be "Hold fast to what is good." They tend to maintain long-lasting friendships and to be stable, faithful marriage partners who are firmly attached to home and family (H. B. Cattell, 1989).

Because of their resistance to change, persons with extremely low (Q1-) scores may remain in less-than-optimal situations. Initiating change and dealing with the ambiguity, unfamiliarity, and confusion of transitions are difficult challenges for them, and thus they may resign themselves to remaining in unsatisfying situations, such as routine or frustrating jobs (H. B. Cattell, 1989). They also may have trouble adjusting to life's normal transitions or coping with unexpected demands. They may be so set in their ways that they overlook promising new ideas or approaches. Their limited ability to think creatively or originally may lead others to view them as unimaginative or old-fashioned. Karson et al. (1997) note that extremely low scorers may lack flexibility in adjusting to novel circumstances, causing them to have a limited array of possible responses or solutions; this is a good example of how an extreme characteristic, useful in some situations, can impede a person's long-term best interests. Just as high scorers may have a progressive pose, extremely low scorers may have a conservative pose stiffened with a sense of moral rightness.

Occupational Implications

High (Q1+) scores are consistently predictive of interests representing Holland's Artistic and Social themes. Those who need to be able to think creatively or "outside the box" typically are high scorers (e.g., writer, painter, designer, musician). Generally, the more an occupation allows room for independence of ideas and actions, the more receptive it is to persons with high (Q1+) scores. For this reason, scientists, researchers, and engineers also tend to have high scores. Additionally, high scores are found in Social occupations that require openness to innovative ideas and flexibility in dealing with all kinds of people, such as social worker, psychologist, personnel manager, and executive. Many studies indicate that high scores are predictive of creative potential in a wide range of fields (Cattell et al., 1992; Conn & Rieke, 1994; Guastello, 1993; Walter, 2000).

Managers tend to have average to above-average scores on Q1, but their scores are not extremely high unless they represent senior management. Forty-two out of nearly 50 samples of managers showed average or above-average scores, but only a few (mostly senior executives) actually had high scores. Occasionally, a consultant will encounter a company in which the majority of management is low on Openness to Change (Q1-). Such a company can function adequately in a static environment, but if the company's market becomes more competitive, management's attitudes and methods may no longer be effective. Upper-level management may recognize the problem and hire new blood to shake up the status quo and change the company culture. The resulting clash of attitudes and styles between old and new managers may be difficult to control. Typically, many of the old guard have to leave for the situation to stabilize.

Low (Q1-) scorers tend to be loyal employees and to do well in jobs that require steady adherence to set policies or procedures. Persons in many Conventional occupations—such as clerical worker, insurance agent, credit manager, and bookkeeper—show low scores, probably because they involve following set rules or systems in very structured environments. Persons in occupations that protect the status quo, such as police officer and firefighter, also show relatively low average scores on the scale. Additionally, low scores are found in some Realistic occupations that involve traditional, structured tasks (e.g., mechanic, farmer, janitor, cook).

Counseling Implications

Low-scoring (Q1-) clients are not likely to feel much motivation for change, particularly if signs of security needs (e.g., high anxiety) are present. Thus, treatment may progress slowly. Low scorers may be motivated to seek counseling around the time of a life change or transition. This is because they are typically uncomfortable about making readjustments or finding new coping strategies when their old ones are no longer adaptive. Because low scorers are traditional and prefer tried-and-true methods, professionals who use unusual or unorthodox methods may have difficulty gaining credibility and establishing rapport with them.

High-scoring (Q1+) clients are likely to be eager for rapid change and progress and to take reasonable risks to make some gains. Practitioners working with couples have noted that if one partner is high on Openness to Change, he or she will not be satisfied simply talking about problems but will want to move forward with change. In fact, high scorers are likely to take action and leave an unsatisfactory or frustrating relationship. Thus, they are less likely to be stuck in unrewarding life situations.

Karson et al. (1997) also note the significance of disparate Q1 scores in couple's therapy. Often the low (Q1-) scorer's contentment with the status quo leads to a perception of his or her high-scoring (Q1+) partner as demanding, immature or irresponsible. Conversely, the high scorer may see the low scorer as a conservative stick-in-the-mud. The high scorer does not realize that his or her desire for innovation ruins the low scorer's enjoyment of the status quo; the low scorer does not realize that his or her attachment to the familiar deadens the high scorer's imagination. Each partner has to learn to empathize with the other's mode of enjoyment and find ways to avoid imposing his or her own view on the other.

Counselors, social workers, and psychologists, who generally tend to be high (Q1+) scorers, may grow impatient with low-scoring (Q1-) clients who are unwilling to take the risks advised in counseling sessions. In such situations, professionals need to avoid interpreting the hesitation of their clients as resistance in the classic sense and instead should recognize it as the simple playing out of a personality style.

Self-Reliance (Q2)

About the Scale

Self-Reliance (Q2) contributes to both poles of the global scale Extraversion. At the Extraverted end of this global scale, low Self-Reliance (Q2-) contributes the motivation to seek companionship and social support. At the Introverted end of the global scale, high Self-Reliance (Q2+) contributes a desire to be self-reliant and autonomous in doing things and making decisions. Rapid Reference 3.18 summarizes the descriptors that apply to the high (Q2+) introverted, self-sufficient, solitary direction of the scale and to the low (Q2-) extraverted, group-oriented, affiliative direction of the scale.

In terms of the scale's item content, high scorers report that they prefer to plan alone, without suggestions or interruptions from others; that they can easily spend a whole morning alone; and that they would rather work alone in an office setting. Low scorers report that they prefer to work, plan, or solve problems with others rather than alone and that they prefer to do things with a group of people rather than on their own.

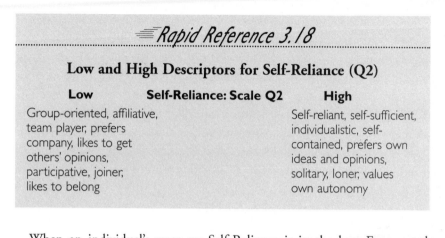

≈Rapid Reference 3.18

Low and High Descriptors for Self-Reliance (Q2)

Low	Self-Reliance: Scale Q2	High
Group-oriented, affiliative, team player, prefers company, likes to get others' opinions, participative, joiner, likes to belong		Self-reliant, self-sufficient, individualistic, self-contained, prefers own ideas and opinions, solitary, loner, values own autonomy

When an individual's score on Self-Reliance is in the low, Extraverted direction (Q2-), scores on the other primary scales that contribute to the global Extraversion are likely to be elevated. The latter scales are Warmth (A+), Liveliness (F+), Social Boldness (H+), and Privateness (N-). Moreover, Self-Reliance has a special relationship with the primary scale Warmth, and together, these two scales are sometimes called the motivational component of Extraversion; this is because both low Self-Reliance (Q2-) and high Warmth (A+) are in the affiliative direction and denote tendencies to enjoy being with others and to be concerned about others. These tendencies contrast sharply with the extraverted tendencies represented by Social Boldness (H+) and Liveliness (F+), which concern seeking attention or stimulation from social interactions.

Correlations with other tests provide evidence of construct validity and are consistent with the scale descriptors in Rapid Reference 3.4. For example, Self-Reliance (Q2) correlates negatively with all of the NEO's Extraversion facets, with the MBTI's Extraversion scale, and with the CPI's overall Sociability vector (v.1). These correlations support the nature of Q2- as an aspect of global Extraversion. Negative correlations between Self-Reliance and the PRF's Affiliative, Nurturance, and Succorance scales and with the CPI's Empathy scale and the NEO's Altruism facet, point to low scorers' having an active interest in caring connections with others and to high scorers' lacking that interest. A positive correlation between Self-Reliance (Q2+) and the PRF's Autonomy scale reflect high scorers' preference for acting alone.

In addition, Self-Reliance (Q2+) correlates positively with three of the NEO's Neuroticism facets and negatively with the CPI's Well-Being and Self-Acceptance scales and with Coopersmith's Self-Esteem Inventory. These findings suggest that high (Q2+) scorers are more prone to experience emotional discomfort than are those who have low or more moderate scores. The direction of the causality is not clear. One explanation may be that the more participative low (Q2-) scorers are buffered through difficulties by their supportive social networks. Another explanation is that perhaps persons who feel insecure prefer to withdraw from participation with others.

High Scores
High (Q2+) scorers on Self-Reliance prefer to work, relax, or solve problems alone. They are generally self-sufficient and resourceful, and they value their autonomy. They do not seek feedback from others and are able to make up their minds independently, a distinct advantage in situations that require taking individual initiative or swift action. As with low Warmth (A-) individuals, those high on Self-Reliance (Q2+) tend to adhere to their own opinions and decisions in spite of pressure from others to conform. H. B. Cattell (1989) notes that although clients in her Q2+ sample spent much time alone, they rarely felt lonely. High scorers typically value not only their privacy but also their freedom to make independent choices. To others, high scorers may often appear confident because they express so little need for reassurance or assistance.

The desire for autonomy at the high (Q2+) end of this scale is sometimes confused with Dominance (E). Whereas persons high on Dominance seek power and control and like to have influence over others, persons high on Self-Reliance are not concerned about influencing others. In fact, high (Q2+) scorers do not want much to do with others; they are concerned with their own autonomy, preferring to function independently. Thus, whereas those who are high on Dominance (E+) move toward others to seek influence and control, those who are high on Self-Reliance move away from others to avoid being controlled.

Some authors note disadvantages to extremely high (Q2+) scores (e.g., Cattell et al., 1992; Schuerger & Reigle, 1988; Sherman & Krug, 1977). Extremely high scorers may find it hard to work collaboratively and to participate in the give-and-take discussions required to achieve a common goal.

They may be uncomfortable interacting closely with others and may be seen as actively avoiding interaction. They may be especially sensitive to others' attempts to advise or control them. When they have to work in a group, they tend to focus narrowly on the problem at hand, ignoring the interpersonal aspects of the process and neglecting the interpersonal consequences of their actions (H. B. Cattell, 1989).

Another disadvantage of extremely high (Q2+) scores is that they may indicate an inclination to be too self-sufficient. Extremely high scorers seldom seek support or advice from others, and they may have difficulty relying on others even when they need help. Thus, high scorers may pay a price for their self-sufficiency. Because they prefer to rely on themselves for solving problems, they may refuse what could be invaluable assistance from others. Furthermore, because they rarely ask for advice or support from others, they may be viewed as snobbish, "above it all," or elitists (H. B. Cattell, 1989). Overall, extremely high scorers' need for autonomy may limit their capacity for close or intimate relationships.

Low Scores

Persons with low (Q2-) scores prefer doing most activities with others. They enjoy being around people and go out of their way to find companionship. In work groups they tend to be team players, sensitive to ways of maintaining group harmony. Because they don't particularly like to make decisions by themselves, they are often collaborative in their decision making. They easily turn to others for help or support when a problem arises and usually welcome even unsolicited advice or suggestions from others. They generally benefit from the ideas, resources, and support that others can provide. Generally, people like Q2- scorers, who take pleasure in helping others and contributing to the well-being of others, are more likely to find satisfaction in life than are people who, for example, are interested in controlling or competing with others. No one objects if you want to take care of the needs of others or just enjoy being around others, but many will object if you try to assume power or prominence.

People with extremely low (Q2-) scores feel a need to belong and do not enjoy being alone. They dislike being cut off from social interaction and may become uncomfortable if they are isolated from contact with others for any length of time (H. B. Cattell, 1989). Thus, extremely low scorers may carefully avoid offending or alienating others in order to maintain their social connections. Their strong need for acceptance may cause them to be unassertive or conforming in situations or unwilling to take the initiative. Extremely low scorers may depend on others for some of their ideas and opinions, and they may feel threatened when differences arise between them and others. Thus, some of their relationships may be seen as enmeshed, and they may feel anxious when important relationships are ending. Additionally, in situations in which help is not available or others are providing poor advice or direction, low scorers may be ineffective. Their strong desire for belonging also can make low scorers vulnerable to exploitation by others.

Occupational Implications

People with low (Q2-) scores tend to be found in occupations that involve teamwork and cooperation. Many of these occupations are in Holland's Social theme, such as elementary teacher, police officer, social worker, and nurse. Low scorers also are found in Enterprising occupations such as bank branch manager, over-the-counter sales, and service jobs.

Those with high (Q2+) scores tend to be found in occupations in which individual enterprise and resourcefulness are valued in preference to teamwork or conformity (H. B. Cattell, 1989). For example, high scores are found in Holland's Investigative and Artistic types, which include quite a few occupations that involve working alone much of the time. Artistic occupations such as writer, musician, and architect tend toward the high end, which is consistent with the stereotype of the artist as a loner. Similarly, high scores are found in Investigative occupations (e.g., scientist, psychologist, computer scientist) and in some Realistic occupations (e.g., forester, farmer, carpenter). People in these occupations, like artists, seem to find the autonomy adaptive in their job settings.

Although high (Q2+) scorers tend to score in the Introverted direction on the other 16PF Extraversion scales, those who instead have above-average scores on Warmth (A+) tend to be well suited to work as consultants. They not only show genuine interest in others and can enter social situations easily but also can keep their own counsel and make independent decisions.

Counseling Implications

The score on Self-Reliance is important in that it signals the degree to which the client will accept counseling suggestions or follow through on therapeutic "homework." For clients with very high (Q2+) scores, recommending that they do something contrary to their own ideas is a waste of time. Helping them to discover what works for them is the most effective course of action.

Because extremely high (Q2+) scorers dislike collaborative, help-seeking behaviors, they usually seek counseling only as a last resort or because someone has pressured them to get help. They are often reticent about personal matters because they do not like to ask for help or rely on others. They even may be passively resistant to the counseling process if they feel that they don't have any other way to protect themselves from verbal encroachment. In relationship counseling, extremely high scorers may feel threatened by impositions on their autonomy.

Extremely low (Q2-) scorers may seek counseling in regard to relationships. Their relationships may suffer from self-imposed restrictions such as avoiding assertive behavior or disagreements out of fear that they will offend others (H. B. Cattell, 1989). When an important relationship ends, they may feel lonely, uncomfortable, or anxious. Clients who score very low on the scale may form a dependent relationship with the counselor, and as a result, these persons may need assistance in planning for other support when the therapeutic relationship ends.

Perfectionism (Q3)

About the Scale

Perfectionism (Q3) plays a central role in the global scale Self-Control to which Rule-Consciousness (G+), groundedness (M-), and seriousness (F-) also contribute. Perfectionism denotes an organized and orderly approach to life and the tendency to pursue tasks and goals in a conscientious manner. These qualities are based on self-discipline, self-restraint, and control of impulses.

Correlations with other measures support the meaning of the scale description in Rapid Reference 3.19. The high pole of Perfectionism (Q3+) correlates with all of the NEO's Conscientiousness facets (particularly Order, Deliberation, and Achievement-Striving); the PRF's Order, Cognitive Structure, Endurance, and Achievement scales; the CPI's Self-Control, Socialization, Achievement via Conformance, and Norm-Favoring (v.1) vector; and the MBTI's Judging scale. These correlations suggest a tendency to be organized,

═Rapid Reference 3.19

Low and High Descriptors for Perfectionism (Q3)

Low	Perfectionism: Scale Q3	High
Tolerates disorder, unexacting, flexible, uncontrolled, casual, undisciplined, spontaneous, careless, lax, not concerned about details, follows own urges, not goal-oriented		Perfectionistic, organized, self-disciplined, conscientious, reliable, persevering, orderly approach to life, planful, thorough, exacting, detailed, has clear goals and ideals

planful, and persevering in pursuing goals. The low, unrestrained pole of Perfectionism (Q3-) correlates with the CPI's Flexibility scale; the PRF's Impulsivity, Play, and Change scales; and the NEO's Impulsiveness, Gregariousness, and Openness to Fantasy facets. These correlations suggest that whereas high (Q3+) scorers tend to be orderly, organized, and achievement-oriented, low (Q3-) scorers are more impulsive as well as more flexible and playful.

In terms of the scale's item content, high (Q3+) scorers say that they like to get started on their chores right away; that they dislike having a messy room; and that if a job is going to be done, it should be done thoroughly. Low (Q3-) scorers say that they can be quite comfortable in a disorganized setting, that they would rather leave some things to chance than make complex plans, and that they think that some jobs do not have to be done as carefully as others.

High Scores

High (Q3+) scorers tend to be organized and planful in their approach to life. They think ahead about things that need to be done. They pursue goals in an orderly and persevering fashion, and they can be counted on to achieve goals in a timely manner. While working on a project, they tend to be thorough, persistent, and attentive to details. They also are inclined to take care of the things around them and to keep them in good repair. All in all, high scorers appreciate organized environments and predictable tasks. These qualities combine to make high scorers valued employees and coworkers, who are regarded as hardworking, responsible, and reliable. They tend to have good work habits and to pull more than their share of the load. They also may be valued as good neighbors because they generally take care of their property and maintain high standards of behavior (H. B. Cattell, 1989).

High (Q3+) scorers tend to have high standards for whatever they do. When obstacles or problems arise, they usually persist in taking the steps necessary to overcome them and get things done. They tend to be goal-oriented and to have a clear idea of who they are and how they want to live. Scores on other scales indicate the kinds of goals that they have—for example, intellectual versus practical (M) or social versus nonsocial (A). Their strong self-image contributes to their concern about maintaining a respected social reputation.

In general, the behavior of high (Q3+) scorers is governed by self-restraint and self-discipline, particularly in controlling impulses. Being organized, accurate, and timely on projects involves being persistent in confronting obstacles, attentive to important details, and denying distractions no matter how pleasant they may be. High scorers tend to be able to channel their energy into constructive, goal-oriented activities. They usually have strong control over their emotions and behavior. The latter quality is what makes Perfectionism such an important contributor to the global scale Self-Control. Karson et al. (1997) describe the scale's significance in this way: "Q3 is most useful as an indicator of ability to control emotions, particularly anger and anxiety." (p. 61) These authors also describe Q3 as being "usually a good indicator of the ability to bind anxiety" (p. 60).

It is important to distinguish Perfectionism (Q3) from the other major contributor to Self-Control, Rule-Consciousness (G). Rule-conscious individuals are highly concerned with following rules and social standards and with being morally correct; they are focused on principles of right and wrong, much like the traditional content of a strong superego. In contrast, people who score high on Perfectionism (Q3+) are more concerned with attending to the process of how things are done. They have a task-oriented style, and they want things done in a thorough, conscientious manner, so that projects are completed and goals are reached.

Extremely high (Q3+) scorers may embrace standards that are too lofty to achieve. H. B. Cattell (1989) notes that truly perfectionistic individuals are rarely satisfied with their behavior and may experience uncomfortable feelings (e.g., shame or anxiety) when they do not live up to their high standards. Extremely high scorers may disown impulses that they see as unacceptable. Their self-worth may rest on whether they are able to meet their own high standards. If they impose their standards on others, they may be seen as exacting taskmasters who are inflexible in their desire to have things done right or as judgmental of others' failures (H. B. Cattell, 1989).

Extremely high (Q3+) scorers may be so tightly controlled and focused on tasks that they seem unable to relax. The same qualities that make them so effective in completing projects in a conscientious manner may leave them uncomfortable or awkward in social or playful situations. They may be seen as humorless, inflexible, or somewhat compulsive. Karson et al. (1997) elaborate:

> Productive and creative people may score high on Q3, but very high sten scores (8 or above) are unusual in these people. Our experience indicates that when anxiety is too tightly bound, creativity and flexibility may suffer. Certainly the Q3+ person is not going to tolerate much ambiguity or disorder in life, and disorder is often essential at some stage of the creative process. (p. 60)

A Q3+ person who is overcontrolled typically scores high on the other Self-Control subscales (G+, rule-conscious; F-, serious; M-, grounded) as well as on Emotional Stability (C+).

Low Scores

People with low (Q3-) scores tend to be more casual and uncontrolled than high scorers. In short, they're inclined to "let it all hang out." Generally, they prefer to be flexible, avoiding advanced planning that would make life too structured or organized. They would rather leave more things to chance. They tend to tolerate disorder and to avoid worry about details. Their approach to life tends to be spontaneous. For example, they may change direction in the middle of a project if something more interesting comes along. In contrast to high scorers, low scorers are more playful; that is, they may impulsively follow their own urges and express their needs or feelings in an immediate manner. They may not have high personal standards or be concerned about realizing ambitions. Generally they are less task oriented and goal oriented than are high scorers. H. B. Cattell (1989) likens the qualities of low scorers to the unworried, nonstriving, here-and-now style that Buddhists call "without face."

Extremely low (Q3-) scorers may be so unconcerned about organization and task completion that they are seen as lackadaisical or unreliable. They may not be motivated to behave in planful or organized ways, especially in areas that are unimportant to them. Setting and achieving goals may require more focus and perseverance than they are prepared to expend. Thus, extremely low scorers are often underachievers. Given their ability level, they may not apply their skills effectively. As a result, their abilities may not be valued at work, and they may be passed over for promotions. They may seem to drift through life without career goals or a clear work identity.

Extremely low (Q3-) scorers may be undersocialized in the sense that they show little concern about social protocol or how others regard them. They may seem more concerned about gratifying their own immediate impulses than about meeting other people's expectations. Their lifestyle and identity may be perceived as lacking in focus, especially if other Self-Control factors are low. Certain Q3- scorers may be aware of their tendency to desire immediate gratification. Some of these low scorers are comfortable with this disposition, whereas others are acutely uncomfortable because they realize that their tendency toward carelessness may cause them trouble in the long run.

Occupational Implications

Many occupations benefit from high Q3 traits like being organized, planful, and conscientious. This scale best predicts an interest in occupations in Holland's Conventional theme, such as clerical worker, bookkeeper, and accountant. Some Enterprising occupations tend to be above average on this "get-things-done-right" trait; these include positions such as supervisor, manager, and administrator. Other jobs that attract high (Q3+) scorers are those within the Realistic theme, such as mechanic, carpenter, and machine operator. High scores also are found in some Investigative occupations such as dentist, computer programmer, pilot, and scientist. Those who score high on this scale tend to be more successful in pursuing formal academic training, which is consistent with their goal-oriented approach to life.

Low (Q3-) scores appear infrequently in most occupational samples. They are more likely to appear in artistic or creative occupations where flexibility and spontaneity are encouraged. Some helping occupations show lower average scores on the scale. For example, some samples of counselors and English teachers show averages below 5 on the scale. Understandably, a counselor who is a high (Q3+) scorer on Perfectionism might have trouble being patient and supportive trying to work with the complicated lives of clients who continue to make poor decisions.

Counseling Implications

High-scoring (Q3+) individuals prefer orderly presentations and well-established procedures. They like sessions to be well organized and focused and to proceed systematically from one aspect to another. They may become dissatisfied with a counselor who has a casual demeanor; they want a thoroughly professional atmosphere. Typically, they consider sessions to be teaching events rather than opportunities for personal expression or transformation. They tend not to focus on the relationship between client and counselor.

Clients with very low (Q3-) scores, by contrast, welcome ambiguity and spontaneity in the counseling sessions, particularly if their score on Abstractedness (M+) is also high. They may not respond well to structure or formality, and they are unlikely to follow through on "homework assignments."

A client with high Anxiety usually experiences it as aversive; however, if Perfectionism (Q3+) is also high, the client probably will be functional and able to take appropriate problem-solving steps. Although the anxiety is painful, it is said to be "bound" by the active, focused competence indicated by the high score on Perfectionism. Persons with this pattern may respond well to reassurance and encouragement.

Tension (Q4)

About the Scale

Tension (Q4) contributes to the global scale Anxiety along with Emotional Stability (C-), Apprehension (O+), and Vigilance (L+). What Tension adds to Anxiety is the quality of being full of nervous energy and drive. As the descriptors in Rapid Reference 3.20 indicate, high (Q4+) scores on the scale are in the tense direction, whereas low (Q4-) scores are in the Relaxed direction.

In terms of the scale's item content, high scorers report that they become frustrated easily, get annoyed when others cause changes in plans, and become restless and fidgety when forced to wait for something. Low scorers say that they do not mind being interrupted when they're doing something, find it easy to be patient, and can stay relaxed during an argument.

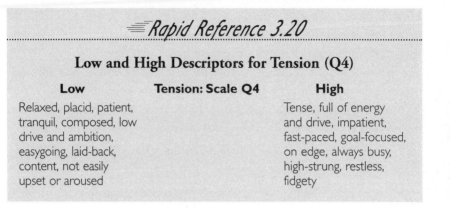

===Rapid Reference 3.20

Low and High Descriptors for Tension (Q4)

Low	Tension: Scale Q4	High
Relaxed, placid, patient, tranquil, composed, low drive and ambition, easygoing, laid-back, content, not easily upset or aroused		Tense, full of energy and drive, impatient, fast-paced, goal-focused, on edge, always busy, high-strung, restless, fidgety

Social desirability can influence scores on Tension because the scale's items are fairly transparent. A low (Q4-) score can signal a desire to present oneself favorably, whereas a high (Q4+) score can indicate a tendency to present oneself unfavorably. Therefore, an extreme score in either direction on the scale should always be checked relative to the score on the Impression Management (IM) scale.

The central concept of Tension (Q4) is driven energy in contrast to the self-blaming insecurity (O+), suspiciousness (L+), and emotional lability (C-) that define the other Anxiety scales. Correlations with other measures are consistent with this conception of the scale as well as with the descriptions in Rapid Reference 3.4. For example, Tension correlates positively with all of the NEO's Anxiety facets, especially Angry Hostility, and with the PRF's Defendence and Aggression scales. Supporting the restless, driven, temperamental qualities seen in the Q4+ person are a positive correlation with the NEO's Impulsiveness scale and negative correlations with the CPI's Self-Control, Responsibility, and Flexibility scales. That the impatience included in high Tension can limit empathic understanding and helpful cooperation is supported by negative correlations with the CPI's Empathy, Tolerance, Psychological-Mindedness, and Sociability scales; with four of the NEO's Agreeableness facets (Compliance, Trust, Straightforwardness, and Altruism); and with the PRF's Nurturance scale. Some practitioners note that Tension can be an important component of drive in a work setting, a conception supported by a positive correlation between Q4 and the need for Achievement scale of the EPPS.

High Scores

Persons with high (Q4+) scores display a lot of drive and energy. They tend to be fast paced and may express a sense of urgency in many situations. If this urgency is channeled to serve useful goals, it can be a positive force in developing and maintaining effective work habits and in motivating action. Not surprisingly, high (Q4+) scorers share the qualities of urgency, energy, and restlessness with Type A persons. These qualities can be most desirable in a climate that puts a high priority on getting things done, as Karson et al. (1997) corroborate:

> In many jobs, this may be an adaptive stance of acknowledging stress levels. Indeed, some businesses go so far as to actively construe impatience as a virtue since it implies that the individual has important things to do. Tension also is seen as a sign of importance and commitment to many jobs. (p. 62)

Less positive consequences of high (Q4+) scores are the tendencies to feel pressured and on edge and to be easily frustrated by obstacles or setbacks. Such tendencies may undermine the performance of extremely high scorers in demanding or stressful environments. Because they are driven and have a low frustration tolerance, they may be impatient with people or situations that slow them down. The quality of extremely high scorers on this scale is well described by Lord (1997) as "the level of physical tension expressed by irritability and impatience with others" (p. 43). Extremely high scorers can be temperamental and may impulsively say or do things that they later regret, such as criticizing others or losing their temper. They may make spur-of-the-moment decisions, become upset over minor annoyances, or blame others unreasonably. Thus, extremely high scorers may run roughshod over people in service of their urgencies, and understandably, others may react negatively to their behavior.

This possibility of abrasive interactions with others is increased if a Q4+ person also scores high on other extrapunitive scales such as Dominance (E+) or Vigilance (L+), or if the person scores low on scales reflecting self-control, such as Rule-Consciousness (G-), Emotional Stability (C-), or Perfectionism (Q3-). The possibility of abusive interactions with others is diminished if the high (Q4+) scorer's profile indicates the presence of softer qualities, such as above-average scores on Sensitivity (I+) or Warmth (A+).

H. B. Cattell (1989) notes the "decidedly unpleasant" subjective feelings that tend to accompany high scores, such as feeling jittery, nervous, on edge, or pressured. She points out that these feelings are often experienced physically, such as in stiffness of the shoulder or neck muscles. Extremely high scorers may have trouble relaxing or sitting still for very long. Their attempts to release tension may include fidgeting, tapping their feet, or pacing the floor. The restless, excitable, or overwrought feelings of extremely high scorers may also disturb their attempts to get a good night's sleep.

Low Scores

Persons with low (Q4-) scores tend to be relaxed, tranquil, and content. They are easygoing and "laid-back," and they are not easily upset by frustrations or disappointments. Even those with particularly low scores seem satisfied with their placid lifestyle. H. B. Cattell (1989) compares this languorous state to that experienced by many people after strenuous exercise, meditation, or deep, restful sleep, and she further notes that many types of drug use are aimed at achieving a similar tranquil condition. She describes her low Q4 clients as "slow to take offense, easy to get along with, and undemanding, and they are rated as comfortable companions by relatives, coworkers, friends, and other acquaintances" (p. 302). If they experience any subjective tension, they typically do not take it out on others.

Less positively, H. B. Cattell (1989) notes that extremely low (Q4-) scorers typically lack vigor and drive. Because they are content with life and tend to live in the present, they often are without ambition. Disinclined to change or to push themselves, they may be underachievers. Not surprisingly, teachers and employers may complain about the difficulty of motivating extremely low scorers. According to Cattell, the nonchalance of Q4- people may also frustrate their partners or spouses, especially if the latter are worldly or ambitious: "Among my clinical sample were several women who were annoyed by their husbands' complacency and unwillingness to exert effort to achieve social or economic success." (p. 302)

Occupational Implications

Generally, a high (Q4+) score is not a strong predictor of occupational choice. High scores on the scale are found sometimes among occupations within the Artistic theme. Creative occupations (e.g., painter, sculptor, writer) seem to tend toward showing high scores, consistent with the stereotype of the tense, driven, temperamental artist.

Occasionally, low (Q4-) scores on Tension are found in occupations for which people must function well in stressful situations, such as firefighter, police officer, and airline pilot. Perhaps for the same reason, moderately low scores on Tension are found among some occupational samples in the Social theme, such as nurse, counselor, teacher, and social worker. Moreover, impatience is not a desirable trait in the helping professions.

Some indirect evidence relates lower scores on measures of anxiety, including scales like Tension (Q4), with job performance. Barrick and Mount (1991) suggest that the relationship is complex, that high scores hinder performance, and that scores below a certain level have little effect. Other researchers point to a further complexity in the relationship between anxiety and performance. They hold that both high and low scores can hinder performance. This finding is supported by reports that suggest that moderate scores on Tension can signify a drive to achieve.

Counseling Implications

A high (Q4+) score often confirms the focus of self-referral by a client; this can be a positive sign for counseling because the client is already aware of current stresses and usually is motivated to work hard to relieve his or her subjective distress. A less positive reality is that a high score can be accompanied by restless demands for relief that are sometimes difficult to manage, particularly if the client is low on Emotional Stability (C-). Because the experience of tension can be so demoralizing for a high-scoring client, H. B. Cattell (1989) recommends counseling interventions that directly address the symptom. These suggestions include antianxiety medication, biofeedback, physical exercise, and meditation.

An extreme score in either direction on Tension (Q4) may reflect an enduring characterological trait or a transitory state that is a reaction to some current situation. Because of these possibilities, H. B. Cattell (1989) emphasizes the importance of determining the origin of the extreme score (i.e., trait or state), and if the stress is situational, investigating scores on other scales to determine contributing factors. Karson et al. (1997) note that the items tapping Tension are transparent; that is, they are easily influenced by the testing situation and by the test taker's preferred self-presentation. Therefore, the score on Tension may reflect the person's conscious self-concept or how he or she wants to appear. The score also may represent a communication to the professional that the person is in distress (high score) or not ready to acknowledge the stress (low score). As recommended previously, an extreme score in either direction on the scale should be checked relative to the score on the Impression Management (IM) scale.

SCALE INTERACTIONS

Beyond the one-at-a-time interpretation of scores presented previously, many users of the 16PF Questionnaire look at combinations of scores, also called scale interactions or score patterns. These combinations concern the way a score on one scale may interact with a score on another scale to modify the meaning of both. For example, a common combination consists of high Warmth (A+) and high Dominance (E+). Here the aggressive, overbearing qualities that can be present in E+ individuals are softened by the tendency to be concerned about others and their feelings (A+). High scorers are likely to be persuasive and socially facilitative rather than stubborn or domineering (Karson et al., 1997).

Many patterns have been noted by experienced practitioners and are reported in standard references on the 16PF Questionnaire (H. B. Cattell, 1989; Cattell et al., 1992; Karson et al., 1997; Karson & O'Dell, 1976). Most of them were subsequently tested in a small cross-validation study, and with few exceptions, the patterns were substantiated, increasing confidence in the findings of the source authors. Even so, the pattern descriptions are best thought of as hypotheses that can be explored in counseling, not as certainties.

The patterns occur with varying frequencies in the general population. The patterns were tested for frequency of occurrence in both the adult and adolescent norm groups. Patterns consisting of extreme scores on more than two scales naturally tend to be less common. The same is true of patterns consisting of two scales that are from the same global scale but in opposite directions. An example is the pattern (A-, F+), in which both elements are from Extraversion, but one is in the extraverted direction (F+), whereas the other is in the introverted direction.

Of identified patterns, only a limited selection is presented here, organized alphabetically by scale. Patterns including low Warmth (A-) are presented first and followed by those including high Warmth (A+). Within those for low Warmth, the patterns are arranged alphabetically according to the second scale in the pattern. So, for example, the first few patterns presented are

A-, E-

A-, E+

A-, F-, L+

A-, F-, H+

A-, F+

A-, Q2+

A+, E-, L+

A+, H-, I+.

As presented in Rapid Reference 3.21, the scale interactions can be used to enhance understanding of a client's profile. The authors suggest that the interactions be consulted third in the process of interpreting a profile, after a consideration of first the global scales and then the single primary scales.

Patterns Including Warmth (A)

- A-, E-: Submissive and finds others aversive; has negative expectations about relationships. This pattern is fairly common and is

≡Rapid Reference 3.21

How to Use the Patterns

For the practitioner faced with the task of interpreting a 16PF profile, the authors suggest the following guide to use of this section:

- First look at the descriptions for the client's high and low global scale scores.
- Next, look at the descriptions for the client's high and low primary scale scores.
- Finally, look at the pattern descriptions that fit the client's score combinations.

characterized by aloofness and avoidance of others plus extreme submissiveness and humility. It was first recorded by Karson and O'Dell (1976), who attribute it to aversive or punishing early relationships. There may be resentment associated with this blocked aggression.

- A-, E+: Stubborn, domineering, and indifferent to others. In contrast with the A+ E+ pattern, in which the person is likely to be friendly and persuasive, this combination indicates a mode of assertion that is unmitigated by friendliness and may seem harsh, stubborn, or aggressive (Karson et al., 1997).

- A-, F-, L+: Hostile, suspicious, and withdrawn. To the detached, indifferent introversion of A- F-, L+ adds distrust, resentment, and jealousy (Meyer, 1989).

- A-, F-, H-, Q2-: Introverted but dependent. This pattern is rare because it combines the aloof, silent, restrained qualities of Introversion (A-, F-, H-) with the extraverted trait of desiring affiliation, belonging, and togetherness (Q2-). The inference is that they are deeply dependent on others but possess few skills to satisfy their needs (H. B. Cattell, 1989).

- A-, F+: Mercurial, changeable, and unreliable in relationships. The mercurial quality of the F+ person, combined with the detached, indifferent quality of A-, has been found among persons who rush into relationships and then just as quickly depart when the novelty fades (H. B. Cattell, 1989).

- A-, Q2+: Aloof, withdrawn, little connection or attachment to others. This common pattern consists of what Sweney (n.d., p. 2) calls the "motivational component of Extraversion." These two scales denote the tendency to seek connection with and feel compassion for others. Being low on both, these individuals tend to be indifferent and aloof, perhaps because of negative experiences in childhood that have led to avoidance of others (Karson & O'Dell, 1976).

- A+, E-: Low assertiveness, compensated for by friendliness, adaptability, and approval seeking. The interaction of Warmth (A) and Dominance (E) is often revealing about a person's basic social persona. In this pattern, the person tends to seek to meet their social needs by being agreeable, attentive, and responsive, unlike the aggressive pursuit of personal objectives by persons high on Dominance (Karson et al., 1997).

- A+, F-, H-: Quiet and timid but warm. Although introverted in a shy, restrained way (F-, H-), these people express their basic warmth and caring in small, quiet ways that may not be immediately apparent. Someone with the opposite scores (A-, F+, H+) will be talkative and outgoing, but, in the long run, others will perceive that their interest is not genuine and enduring (H. E. Cattell, 1989). Although people with F+, H+ scores tend to perceive themselves as people-oriented and therefore interested in people, those who are A- may be more interested in attention and stimulation (Lord, 1999).

- A+, H-, I+: Warm, sweet, emotional feminine ego ideal (adolescent). This pattern, with the soft-hearted, generous qualities of Warmth, the emotional sensitivity and romantic sentimentality of high Sensitivity, and the modest diffidence of low Social Boldness, is presented by Farber (1990) as the popular feminine stereotype among adolescent women. It can be compared to the masculine stereotype pattern (E+, H+, I-, O-).

- A+, M-: Warmly attends to concrete. These people will be concerned and responsive to other's practical, down-to-earth needs in situations, but may have trouble seeing the deeper needs behind surface behavior (Lord, 1999).

- A+, N+: Private yet friendly person. In a seeming anomaly, persons with this pattern show genuine liking for others, yet remain guarded and unrevealing about themselves. They are seen by others as friendly, yet hard to know (Schuerger, n. d.). Lord (1999) notes that others are often drawn to A+, N+ people because they are caring and easy to confide in, but that there is not likely to be a two-way exchange of confidences.

- A+, Q2-: Caring and friendly, high need for social feedback and support. Often referred to as the "motivational component" of extraversion (Sweeny, n. d., p.2), these two scales together indicate a high need for social connection, interaction, and approval. High scorers tend to be compliant, easily influenced, and unhappy when left alone. Compare this pattern with its counterpart (A-, Q2+).

Patterns Including Reasoning (B)

- B-, F+, H+: Accident prone, inattentive to danger signals. The impulsiveness and fearless risk-taking and sensation seeking that comes with F+ and H+, when unmitigated by intelligence (low B), tends to come out in poor judgment and rash behavior (H. B. Cattell, 1989).
- B+, E+, L+, Q1+: Intellectualized hostility. This pattern is characterized as argumentative, oppositional, and distrusting (E+, L+), which in a bright (B+), critical (Q1+) person can result in verbal aggression (Meyer, 1989).
- B+, E+, M+, Q1+, Q3+: Creative potential. The combination of cognitive ability, independence, imagination, openness to new ideas, and self-discipline have been widely found to be related to creative functioning.
- B+, I+, Q3+: In an adolescent, creative potential, with good control on fantasy activity. By contrast, if Q3 is low, the fantasy is likely to be dissipated and rarely comes to fruition (P. Farber, workshop notes).

Patterns Including Emotional Sensitivity (C)

- C-, E-, Q4+: Passive but high strung. Tense, emotional, and submissive, these persons allow others to make their decisions. Once in a while they blow up at others, often deflecting their anger toward inappropriate others (H. B. Cattell, 1989).
- C-, F-: Ineffective decision-making skills. Persons with this pattern are subdued and emotional; they find it hard to generate a wide range of potential solutions. Their thinking may be narrow or constricted, and they may feel unsure about what to do when confronted by novel situations (H. B. Cattell, 1989).
- C-, F+: Ineffective decision-making skills, impulsivity. These individuals tend to respond too quickly and emotionally to problems without considering all the potential consequences or possible alternatives (H. B. Cattell, 1989).
- C-, E-, H-, Q3-: Ineffective problem-solving skills, unable to act. The lack of emotional stability (C-) accompanied by undisciplined

spontaneity (Q3-) or passivity (E-, H-) shows itself as failure to take appropriate action (H. B. Cattell, 1989).

- C+, L+, O-: Calm and confident but defensive. Although these people describe themselves as calm in facing stress, they tend to selectively attend to their own positive traits and to blame others for problems that arise. Their ability to externalize problems is self-protective and successful, at least temporarily (Karson et al., 1997).

Patterns Including Dominance (E)

- E-, C-, Q4+: Obedient, tense, displaces aggression. Because these people strongly fear and avoid conflict, they have the experience of "walking on eggshells." They follow others' instruction and deny their own needs and beliefs, often resulting in angry, unpredictable outbursts displaced onto "lower-status" people such as children (H. B. Cattell, 1989).
- E-, G-: Kohlberg's good boy/nice girl. Test takers showed immature moral notions, expecting obedience, sacrifice, and goodness to be appreciated and socially rewarded. Many show a "martyr" complex (H. B. Cattell, 1989).
- E-, F-, H-: Extreme passivity. Shy and submissive, such persons acquiesce to the wishes, whims, and wants of others in order to avoid offending or angering them. They can easily feel overburdened by external forces (H. B. Cattell, 1989). They may be sullen, resentful, and passive-aggressive in addition to immobilized (Karson et al., 1997).
- E-, I+, L-: Accepting and accomodating person with much concern and compassion for others. This pattern, noted by Dr. David Watterson (personal communication, Dec. 26, 1981), includes submissive (E-), compassion (I+), and trust (L-). With L+, the pattern may show passive-aggressive behavior rather than sensitivity.
- E-, N+: Devious expression of aggression. Sometimes the resentment of E- is expressed indirectly by shrewd, strategic people (N+), especially if they are also without self-doubt (O-).

- E+, A-, O-, Q1+, Q4+: Aggressive dominance not tempered by concern for others. The expression of Dominance is likely to be more harsh and aggressive if accompanied by any of these scales: Cold detachment (A-), thick-skinned boldness (H+), complacent self-assurance (O-), a critical and oppositional temperament (Q1+), or irritability and impatience (Q4+).

- E+, C-, F+, G-, Q3-: Impulsive, aggressive, and possibly violent when threatened. This pattern (high Dominance with any of the four indicators of low impulse control) is found in about 13% of general population adults and almost twice as frequently in adolescents. When these dominant people are frustrated or powerless, they may resort to desperate last-ditch efforts (H. B. Cattell, 1989).

- E+, F+; also E+, H+: In adolescents, impulsivity and aggressiveness. Adolescents with this pattern may tend to act out under stress (P. Farber, 1990, p. 4).

- E+, H-: Assertiveness expressed by stubbornness and behind-the-scenes activity. Standing up for oneself (E+) is difficult because of timidity and threat-sensitivity (H-). This pattern may result in inner conflict. Persons with this pattern find it hard to engage in argument, and they may not be exposed to alternate points of view (Karson et al., 1997).

- E+, I+: Stress-related problems; dominance may block nurturance. This combination can represent conflict between dominance needs and nurturance or succorance needs. The dominance need may block the other (Meyer, 1989).

- E+, I-, L+: Aggressive and hostile in efforts to be dominant. Little regard for others' feelings in the context of being aggressive and distrustful. With L- instead, may comfortably assert self with acceptance of others rather than hostility (D. G. Watterson, personal communication, Dec. 26, 1981).

- E+, I+, L-: Dominance with compassion. Dominance coupled with sensitivity and trust is expressed with respect and acceptance of others (without hostility of L+) (D. G. Watterson, personal communication, Dec. 26, 1981).

- E+, L+, Q1+: Intellectualize aggression. High scorers are critical, argumentative, oppositional, and distrusting of others (Karson et al., 1997). See also B+, E+, L+, Q1+.
- E+, Q2-: Tension between dependency and dominance. This pattern, when it occurs, often signals vacillating between dependency needs and needs for control. Persons able to balance the conflicting needs can become popular leaders (H. B. Cattell, 1989).

Scale E also appears in the following patterns already presented:

- A-, E-: Submissive and finds others aversive; has negative expectations in relationships
- A-, E+: Stubborn, domineering, and indifferent to others
- A+, E-: Low assertiveness, compensated for by friendliness, adaptability, and approval seeking
- B+, E+, L+, Q1+: Intellectualized hostility
- C-, E-, Q4+: Passive but high-strung

Patterns Including Liveliness (F)

- F-, H-, I+: Painfully sensitive. Shy, inhibited introversion plus tender emotional sensitivity creates intensity of feeling, which are bottled up rather than shared (H. B. Cattell, 1989, p. 158).
- F-, M-: Practical, serious, detail oriented person. The combination of cautiousness and restraint (F-) with a concrete detail-orientation denotes a constricted, unimaginative person who may be stoical and have a narrow range of interests. This pattern is also found generally among technical occupations (H. B. Cattell, 1989).
- F-, O+: Discouragement, pessimistic mood, lack of energy. The subdued, cautious, stoical quality of F-, when it is accompanied by the anxious, self-blaming, insecurity of O+, often indicates discouragement (H. B. Cattell, 1989).
- F+, C+, G+, Q3+: Energy and enthusiasm moderated by self-control. The exuberance, optimism, and high spirits indicated by F+ scores can lead to impulsivity and unreliability if not tempered by some form of self-control, such as Emotional Stability (C+), strong internalized standards (G+), or self-disciplined perseverance (Q3+). These help to channel and focus the energy of high

scorers (H. B. Cattell, 1989). Alternatively, when these self-control elements are combined with the subdued, cautiousness of F-, the individual may feel constricted or overcontrolled (Karson et al., 1997).

- F+, G+: Vacillation. Extreme scores on these two scales indicate a pairing of the moralistic rule-bound orientation of G+ with the carefree impulsivity and exuberance of high F. The implication is that the person has not integrated these disparate elements (H. B. Cattell, 1989).

- F+, H+: The "ascendent component" of Extraversion. Scales A+ and Q2- represent the caring, affiliative, "motivational component" in Extraversion—F+ and H+ are the "ascendent component," indicative of a need for excitement, stimulation, and attention in social interactions (Schuerger, n. d.). Very high scores signal high energy levels, thrill-seeking, and intolerance for boredom (Karson et al., 1997).

- F+, H+, I+: Dynamic personality. Depth of feeling (I+) coupled with fearless boldness (H+) and energetic optimism (F+) are often found among persons with ardent and dynamic natures—for example, among several civil-rights activists (H. B. Cattell, 1989).

Scale F also appears in the following patterns already presented:

- A-, F-, L+: Hostile, suspicious, and withdrawn
- A-, F-, H-, Q2-: Introverted but dependent
- A-, F+: Mercurial, changeable, and unreliable in relationships
- C-, F-: Ineffective decision-making skills
- C-, F+: Ineffective decision-making skills, impulsivity
- E+, C-, F+, G-, Q3-: Impulsive, aggressive, and possibly violent when threatened
- E+, F+; also E+, H+: In adolescents, impulsivity and aggressiveness

Patterns Including Rule-Consciousness (G)

- G-, O+: Identity problems and low self-concept. Common among adolescents, this pattern shows guilt feelings about breaking societal moral standards. It may also be seen as moral immaturity (H. B. Cattell, 1989).

- G-, N+: Makes good initial impression. The social shrewdness and poise of N+ (especially when combined with B+) make it easier for these people to hide their true motivations and make a good first impression. Employers often hire them based on their good self-presentation, but they are later tardy and erratic in their work; friends become disillusioned with their opportunism and undependability (H. B. Cattell, 1989).
- G-, Q3+: Self-disciplined but expedient. Although these people impose their own structure and are organized and focused on their goals, they may not respect externally imposed rules. They tend to see these as guidelines or externally imposed strictures, which they may consciously resist (Lord, 1999).
- G+, O+: Negative self-censure. This pattern indicates classic guilt in a person who reports guilt proneness along with high standards of conventional morality (H. B. Cattell, 1989).
- G+, M-, Q1-, Q3+: Holland's Conventional type. One sees the general detail orientation in high G and Q3, the conservatism in low Q1, and the properness in low M (Schuerger, n. d.).

Scale G also appears in the following patterns already presented:

- E-, G-: Kohlberg's good boy/nice girl
- E+, C-, F+, G-, Q3-: Impulsive, aggressive, and possibly violent when threatened
- F+, C+, G+, Q3+: Energy and enthusiasm moderated by self-control

Patterns Including Social Boldness (H)

Scale H appears in the following patterns already presented:

- A-, F-, H-, Q2-: Introverted but dependent
- A+, F-, H-: Quiet and timid but warm
- A+, H-, I+: Warm, sweet, emotional feminine ego ideal (adolescent)
- B-, F+, H+: Accident prone, inattentive to danger signals
- C-, E-, H-, Q3-: Ineffective problem-solving skills, unable to act
- E-, F-, H-: Extreme passivity
- E+, F+; also E+, H+: In adolescents, impulsivity and aggressiveness

- E+, H-: Assertiveness expressed by stubborn or behind-the-scenes activity
- F-, H-, I+: Painfully sensitive, shy
- F+, H+: The "ascendent component" of Extraversion
- F+, H+, I+: Dynamic personality

Patterns Including Sensitivity (I)

- I-, M-, O-: Holland's Realistic type. This tough, confident, practical combination is seen in a good many occupations in Holland's Realistic type (J. M. Schuerger, n. d.).
- I-, M+: Innovative, objective. The strong imagination of M+ coupled with the objectivity of I- seems to allow the person to see possibilities from an unemotional point of view (H. B. Cattell, 1989).
- I+, M-: Kind, sensitive, not much self-insight. Sensitive (I+) and unimaginative (M-), these persons tend toward practical good works (H. B. Cattell, 1989).
- I+, M+, Q1+: Artistic, creative. This pattern is consistent with Holland's Artistic occupational type and emphasizes aesthetic sensitivity, imagination, intuition, and interest in abstractions and new ideas. These traits are consistently found to be related to creative potential, but control traits (C+, G+, Q3+) may determine whether this potential is actualized. Without internal controls, high scorers may be overly emotional and subjective, impractical, unreliable, absentminded, or accident prone (Karson et al., 1997).

Scale I also appears in the following patterns already presented:

- A+, H-, I+: Warm, sweet, emotional feminine ego ideal (adolescent)
- B+, I+, Q3+: In an adolescent, creative potential, with good control on fantasy activity
- E-, I+, L-: Accepting and accomodating person with much concern and compassion for others
- E+, I-, L+: Aggressive in efforts to be dominant
- E+, I+, L-: Dominance with compassion

- E+, I+: Stress-related disorders; dominance may block nurturance
- F-, H-, I+: Painfully sensitive
- F+, H+, I+: Dynamic personality

Patterns Including Vigilance (L)

- L+, O-: Arrogant, grandiose. Persons with this pattern tend to be arrogant and grandiose, projecting their tensions on others (L+) successfully and showing low tendencies to guilt or self-doubt (H. B. Cattell, 1989).
- L+, Q2-: Tension between dependency and hypervigilance. Internal conflict of the approach-avoidance kind. The high suspicion indicated by L+ opposes the social neediness indicated by the low Q2 (H. B. Cattell, 1989).
- L+, Q2+: Distrust and rejection of advice. A common pattern, especially in adolescents. Distrust and rejection of others because of insecurity projected outward (H. B. Cattell, 1989).

Scale L also appears in the following patterns already presented:

- A-, F-, L+: Hostile, suspicious, and withdrawn
- B+, E+, L+, Q1+: Intellectualized hostility
- C+, L+, O-: Calm and confident but defensive
- E-, I+, L-: Accepting and accomodating person with much concern and compassion for others
- E+, I-, L-: Comfortably asserts self with acceptance and regard for others
- E+, I-, L+: Aggressive and hostile in efforts to be dominant
- E+, I+, L-: Dominance with compassion
- E+, L+, Q1+: Intellectualized aggression

Patterns Including Abstractedness (M)

- M+, Anxiety+: Accident prone. A person high on Anxiety, along with the absent-minded, internalized imagination of Abstractedness (M+), is prone to escape into thoughts and imaginations as tension increases, and lose awareness of practical, immediate things (Cattell et al., 1992).

Scale M appears in the following patterns already presented:

- A+, M-: Warmly attends to concrete
- B+, E+, M+, Q1+, Q3+: Creative potential
- F-, M-: Practical, serious, detail oriented person
- G+, M-, Q1-, Q3-: Holland's Conventional type
- I-, M-, O-: Holland's Realistic type
- I-, M+: Innovative, objective
- I+, M-: Kind, sensitive, not much self-insight
- I+, M+, Q1+: Artistic, creative potential

Patterns Including Privateness (N)

Scale N appears in the following patterns already presented:

- A+, N+: Private yet friendly person
- E-, N+: Devious expression of aggression
- G-, N+: Makes good initial impression

Patterns Including Apprehension (O)

- O-, Q3-, Q4-: Self-centered, sloppy in appearance. Persons with this pattern tend to be relaxed and self-satisfied, overindulgent to selves, and untidy (H. B. Cattell, 1989).
- O+, Q2+: Withdrawal out of a sense of unworthiness. The sense of unworthiness (O+) leads these persons to withdraw (Q2+), partly for fear of rejection (H. B. Cattell, 1989).
- O+, Q3-: Inner tension between guilt and impulsivity. This combination indicates that the client is presenting both guilt proneness and feelings of lack of control (Schuerger, n. d.).
- O+, Q3+: Bound anxiety; shame. High scores on O or other anxiety indicators, combined with a high score on Q3, denote a person who is able to bind the anxiety and probably make it work as a motivator. Cattell adds the possibility that such persons have shame from failing their own expectations (H. B. Cattell, 1989; Karson & O'Dell, 1976).

Scale O also appears in the following patterns already presented:

- C+, L+, O-: Calm and confident but defensive
- E-, A-, O-, Q1+, Q4+: Aggressive dominance not tempered by concern for others
- F-, O+: Discouragement, pessimistic mood, lack of energy
- G-, O+: Identity problems and low self-concept
- G+, O+: Negative self-censure
- I-, O-, M-: Holland's Realistic type
- L+, O-: Arrogant, grandiose

Patterns Including Openness to Change (Q1)

Scale Q1 appears in the following patterns already presented:

- B+, E+, L+, Q1+: Intellectualized hostility
- B+, E+, M+, Q1+, Q3+: Creative potential
- E+, A-, O-, Q1+, Q4+: Aggressive dominance not tempered by concern for others
- G+, M-, Q1-, Q3+: Holland's Conventional type
- I+, M+, Q1+: Artistic, creative

Patterns Including Self-Reliance (Q2)

Scale Q2 appears in the following patterns already presented:

- A-, F-, H-, Q2-: Introverted but dependent
- A-, Q2+: Aloof, withdrawn, little connection or attachment to others
- A+, Q2-: Caring and friendly, high need for social support and feedback
- E+, Q2-: Tension between dependency and dominance
- L+, Q2-: Tension between dependency and hypervigilance
- L+, Q2+: Distrust and rejection of advice
- O+, Q2+: Withdrawal out of a sense of unworthiness

Patterns Including Perfectionism (Q3)

Scale Q3 appears in the following patterns already presented:

- B+, E+, M+, Q1+, Q3+: Creative potential
- B+, I+, Q3+: In an adolescent, creative potential, with good control on fantasy activity
- C-, E-, H-, Q3-: Ineffective problem-solving skills, unable to act
- E+, C-, F+, G-, Q3-: Impulsive, aggressive, and possibly violent when threatened
- F+, C+, G+, Q3+: Energy and enthusiasm moderated by self-control
- G+, M-, Q1-, Q3+: Holland's Conventional type
- O-, Q3-, Q4-: Self-centered, sloppy in appearance
- O+, Q3-: Inner tension between guilt and impulsivity
- O+, Q3+: Bound anxiety, shame

Patterns Including Tension (Q4)

Scale Q4 appears in the following patterns already presented:

- C-, E-, Q4+: Passive but high strung
- E-, C-, Q4+: Obedient, tense, displaces aggression
- E+, A-, O-, Q1+, Q4+: Aggressive dominance not tempered by concern for others
- O-, Q3-, Q4-: Self-centered, sloppy in appearance

RESPONSE STYLE: IMPRESSION MANAGEMENT, ACQUIESCENCE, AND INFREQUENCY

It is almost axiomatic that people change the way they present according to the circumstances. A person in a classroom presents one way; on a playing field, the same person presents another way. A person develops a slant on his or her self-presentation depending on what is at stake. Thus, a person will dress neatly and professionally, sit on the edge of the chair, and adopt an attitude of conscientiousness and competence in a preemployment situation. On a personality questionnaire, the person may very well answer the questions in a way that is compatible with looking for a job. Consciously or unconsciously, a person trying for a job may be expected to feature desirable interpersonal skills and conscientiousness, or the person may otherwise try to match his or her self-presentation to the job description. Alternatively, an individual seeking disability compensation or admission to a treatment program will be influenced to give a negative self-presentation. In other words, most persons will have some "test-taking attitude" that varies with circumstances, and psychologists have concerns about whether these attitudes will interfere with accurate interpretation of responses.

When the accuracy of questionnaire results is at issue, the question may be asked, "Is the person's self-presentation so unrealistic that the usual rules for inferential interpretation are inappropriate?" This issue, under a number of headings—test-taking attitude, test-taking validity, motivational distortion, faking, impression management or response style—has occupied the attention of many test constructors. The authors of the 16PF Fifth Edition decided to address this issue, under the heading of Response Style Indices, by construction of three indicators to tap common response styles: Impression Management (IM), Acquiescence (ACQ), and Infrequency (INF). The test manual for the 16PF Questionnaire advises that the first step in interpreting any profile is to examine these scales in order to evaluate whether use of the ordinary interpretive guidelines is appropriate (Russell & Karol, 2002). The same manual suggests that extreme scores on these scales provide reason for the practitioner to look further into the accuracy of the respondent's self-presentation. In every instance, the practitioner must make the decision about whether the client's scores can be interpreted, because there are no hard and fast rules.

The 16PF Response Style Indices

Impression Management

The IM scale is a bipolar scale consisting of 12 items that are independent of the items on other scales. This scale was developed to address the issue of socially desirable response styles; its items were designed to tap both conscious and unconscious components of social desirability. The items were developed by correlating them with other measures of social desirability. The best 12 items were retained for the final IM scale. Typical items involve behaviors or attitudes that are widely accepted as good or bad according to central values of Western culture. Items were written to reflect both desirable and undesirable behaviors and attitudes. Examples (not actual IM items) are: *I am never angry at my parents, I don't tell lies, I don't try to get even with people who hurt me, I am hardly ever moody*, or *I always stop and help people who are in trouble*. The general sense of the items, if answered in the keyed direction, is of a favorable, somewhat unrealistic, idealistic presentation of oneself—a picture of someone who is always friendly, confident, and helpful around others rather than vindictive, manipulative, or easily upset.

Rapid Reference 3.22 presents correlations between the IM scale and a number of 16PF primary scales. The table is arranged according to the global factors that are most related to social desirability, in order of relationship: Anxiety first, Self-Control second, and Extraversion third. The other global scales, Independence and Tough-Mindedness, have relatively little relationship to IM. In brief, as shown by the table, high social desirability is characterized by low Anxiety, high Self-Control, and to a lesser extent by high Extraversion.

These results have been cross-validated by Kaushik (1995), part of programmatic research at Florida Institute of Technology. They are also reflected in a meta-analysis reported by Ones and her collaborators (1993) over a variety of instruments that measure constructs similar to the global scales. The two broad scales correlating most highly with social desirability are Emotional Stability (the inverse of Anxiety) and Conscientiousness (similar to global Self-Control).

A high score on the IM scale does not necessarily mean that the individual deliberately "faked" the test or that the profile is invalid (i.e., that the scores cannot be interpreted by the usual rules). A high score means that the person tended to respond to items in a particularly socially desirable manner. There are several possible hypotheses that should be explored. One is the possibility that the score represents deliberate attempts to fake the test. This possibility is rare in a business context, according to a study by Christiansen, Goffin, Johnston, and Rothstein (1994). At the other extreme, a very high score may indicate a realistic self-appraisal of a person who actually has very low anxiety and behaves in an unusually virtuous manner (e.g., religious people). Most likely explanations are in the middle—that high scores reflect

≡Rapid Reference 3.22

Correlations of Primary Scales With IM Score

Global Scale	Primary Scale	Correlation	Direction of Good Impression
Anxiety			Low Anxiety
	Q4	-.53	Relaxed, placid
	C	.50	Emotionally stable
	O	-.39	Self-assured, complacent
	L	-.39	Trusting, unsuspecting
Self-Control			High Self-Control
	M	-.36	Grounded, practical
	G	.34	Rule-conscious, dutiful
	Q3	.17	Perfectionistic, organized
	F	-.09	Serious, reflective
Extraversion			High Extraversion
	Q2	-.21	Group-oriented, affiliative
	H	.20	Socially bold, thick-skinned
	A	.16	Warm, outgoing
	N	-.12	Forthright, genuine
	F	-.09	Serious, reflective

Note. Adapted with permission from Conn, S. R. & Rieke, M. L. (2002). *The 16PF Fifth Edition Technical Manual.* Champaign, IL: Institute for Personality and Ability Testing, Inc.

either a somewhat naive or semi-conscious favorable self-image, or that it actually involves a positive quality of putting one's best foot forward. As Lord (1999) comments, "It is a sign of adjustment to try and present ourselves in ways which are appropriate to whatever situation we are in." (p. 33)

Low scores on the IM scale indicate a willingness to admit undesirable attributes. H. B. Cattell (1989) points out several reasons for low scores, in addition to the possibility that such scores might signal a deliberate attempt to look bad. She suggests that this willingness to be self-critical may be an attempt to communicate a state of subjective distress or a plea for help. It also may indicate a generally negative self-evaluation, low self-esteem, or a tendency to be overly self-critical.

Using the IM Scale

No male-female differences were found on the IM measure, so percentile norms have been developed from a combined male-female sample. The authors of the *16PF Fifth Edition Administrator's Manual* (Russell & Karol, 2002) suggest using cut-off points at percentile scores of 95 and 5, respectively, as points at which the professional should consider the client's tendency to give socially favorable or unfavorable answers.

For example, in one case, a young man named "Charles" was tested in a therapy context and then during an application for a sales job. In the counseling situation, he presented himself as low average on Extraversion (4.3) and Self-Control (3.5), high average on Anxiety (7.5), Tough-Mindedness (6.7), and Independence (7.8), and near the 25th percentile on Impression Management. However, his scores were noticeably different in the job application context: IM was near the 95th percentile (very high); Extraversion was somewhat higher, in the average range (5.5); Self-Control was much higher (7.0); Anxiety was much lower (2.8); and Tough-Mindedness and Independence were slightly lower (5.7 and 6.8, respectively). Thus, he presented himself as somewhat more out-going and easy-going, and much more calm, confident, and conscientious in the job situation.

In a situation like this, where the individual was applying for a job and wanted to make a good impression, one may well ask the questions, "Was he faking to get the job? Is it reasonable to use the ordinary rules of inference to predict performance as a salesperson?" The safest practice—barring a very high IM and most extreme scores on primary or global factors—is to use the standard rules of inference, but with caution. Charles turned out to be quite successful as a salesperson, even though the scores were unique to the job situation. When asked about it, he said, "When I was applying for that job I became that person!"

There are no firm rules by which to decide whether to use the ordinary rules for interpreting the 16PF Questionnaire. The authors hold that it would be very rare to write a report on a person like this and suggest that because of "faking good" the person should not be hired. A more proper approach is to address the favorable impression that is being created and make the assessment with some caution based on what is there: "This candidate shows significant efforts to make a favorable impression, and certain 16PF scores may be somewhat exaggerated. Nevertheless . . ." Dr. David Watterson, whose consulting practice includes daily use of the test as part of personnel evaluations, concurs. He notes that an unfavorable evaluation is appropriate in perhaps one case in a thousand, based on a combination of high IM, extreme scores on the Anxiety and Self-Control primary scales, and some additional indications from interview and correlative information.

The test manual suggests that scores at or below the 5th percentile warrant investigation. If the low IM score is combined with high Anxiety and low Self-Control, and if the situation is one in which the client may profit from appearing to have symptoms and difficulties, the possibility of an effort to "look bad" is increased. As in the case of high IM, the likelihood of exaggeration should be reported, and then the ordinary rules for inferences cautiously used.

A final consideration in evaluating Impression Management is to look at the kind of person being assessed. Dr. Watterson notes that persons with a technical bent (engineer, technician, skilled crafts) tend to have relatively low scores on IM, whereas persons in sales and management occupations tend to have above-average scores; this suggests that technical people are more concerned with technical problems and are not so oriented to "putting their best foot forward." People in professions that involve influencing, persuading, or leading others tend to have a more well-developed self-presentation, and higher scores on IM are adaptive for them. Thus, the kind of person and situation makes a difference in the evaluation of IM, and it is believed that this finding is quite general. The implication is that high scores on IM for managers and sales persons are not to be taken as seriously as high scores for persons in technical or manual jobs.

Acquiescence

Another commonly accepted response style is called Acquiescence, indicating a tendency to be agreeable and endorse personality questions regardless of their content. The Acquiescence index for the 16PF Questionnaire is scored simply by counting each *true* response among the 103 true-false items in the inventory (the *true* alternative always appears first on 16PF items and thus is the *a* choice on the answer sheet). Most respondents seem to have a balanced pattern of responses, as indicated by the 2002 norm sample. About 95% of the norm group chose the *true* response between 35 and 75 times out of the 103 items possible. About 2% of persons in the norm sample chose fewer than 35 *true* responses, and at the high end, fewer than 2% chose more than 75 such responses out of the 103 possible.

Interpreting correlations between ACQ and the 16PF personality scales is made difficult by the fact that some of the scales have an uneven split between true-keyed responses and false-keyed responses. For example, factors Dominance and Liveliness both have seven true-keyed responses versus three false-keyed responses. Nonetheless, it is still possible to conclude that high scores on ACQ correlate positively with global factor Anxiety to a moderate degree and with submissive (E-), shyness (H-), and trusting (L-). These findings are all in the expected direction for an acquiescent or agreeable personality. Karson et al. (1997) also note that when the ACQ score is very high or very low and these 16PF scales are *not* elevated, the ACQ score may represent random responding or poor comprehension.

This score, like IM, is presented as percentile rank, so the practitioner can tell easily whether the client is extreme in either direction. If the Acquiescence index is at or above the 95th percentile, inspection of the responses may help to determine whether random or patterned responding is involved. If not, the practitioner may evaluate the profile scores and interview data for evidence of self-abasement and need for approval.

Infrequency

The third response index on the 16PF Questionnaire is the Infrequency (INF) scale. It was created by identifying statistically rare item responses on the test for a large representative sample (N = 4,346). People who choose a relatively large number of these infrequent responses may be responding randomly or may be having reading or comprehension difficulties. The interpretation of a high INF score as random responding has some empirical support. A Monte Carlo study was conducted in which random responses were created for the 32 items on the INF scale. Scores on these random test responses were compared with regularly answered tests, and the results indicated that the INF scale can be useful in identifying protocols that were answered randomly.

However, the infrequent responses all happen to be *b* responses, middle responses from the 16PF a-b-c answer format. This middle response is labeled with a question mark (?), an option that implies "uncertain or cannot decide," which the test taker is instructed to avoid whenever possible. For this reason, the INF scale can be interpreted not only as an indicator of infrequent choices on the part of the person responding, but also as an indication of uncertainty about one's personal characteristics or an unwillingness to choose definitive answers.

Scores on INF are also presented as percentiles, and the authors suggest that around the 95th percentile the professional should consider random responding. At that point, the professional is advised to check for reading problems, confusion, deliberate random answering, significant uncertainty on the client's part about his or her self-concept, or other emotional problems like depression or anxiety. If the answer sheet shows any sign of patterned answering, random answering becomes most probable, which might indicate lack of interest on the part of the client, deliberate fooling around, or perhaps frustration with some aspect of the assessment. If the person is of limited intellectual background or has undergone serious trauma recently, confusion or uncertainty about self-concept becomes more likely. Finally, as Lord (1999) points out, "some people may opt frequently for the [neutral] middle ground response out of anxiety about what more extreme responses might reveal about themselves" (p. 25), displaying a mindset that can also result in a high INF score.

Karson et al. (1997) suggest one source of help in deciding between these various interpretations of a high INF score:

> Typically the other 16PF scales support these hypotheses. The oppositional client often is assertive (E+) or suspicious (L+); the ambivalent client, worried (O+) or disorganized (Q3-); the nondisclosing client, private (N+); and the uncomprehending client, verbally limited (B-). (p. 67)

If the client has a high INF score and none of the personality-based explanations seem adequate, the technical manual (Conn & Rieke, 1994) provides information that may help a professional evaluate the odds of a truly random set of responses. Such responses would not be interpretable by the usual rules.

✍ TEST YOURSELF ✍

1. **The central focus of primary scale Sensitivity (I), as seen in the item content, is**

   (a) a preference for artistic activities and enjoyments

   (b) a tendency toward affiliative relations with others

   (c) comfort in meeting new people

   (d) steady feeling of competence in handling life's demands

2. **The central focus of primary scale Apprehension (O), as seen in the item content, is**

   (a) an orientation to rules and standards

   (b) a tendency to worry and self-doubt

   (c) a comfort in meeting new people

   (d) a steady feeling of competence in handling life's demands

3. **Primary scales A (Warmth) and I (Sensitivity) show significant important male-female differences.** True or False?

4. **Which of these primary scales does NOT contribute to any of the global scales?**

   (a) Warmth (A)

   (b) Reasoning (B)

   (c) Emotional Stability (C)

   (d) Dominance (E)

5. **Vigilance (L+) does not measure paranoia.** True or False?

6. **Name two primary scales that are prominent in the Self-Control global scale.**

   (a) Emotional Stability (C) and Perfectionism (Q3).

   (b) Vigilance (L) and Rule-Consciousness (G).

   (c) Rule-Consciousness (G) and Perfectionism (Q3).

   (d) Self-Reliance (Q2) and Tension (Q4)

7. **Of the three Response Style Indices (IM, INF, ACQ), which one is most related to measures of social desirability?**

(continued)

8. **In interpreting INF it is important to remember that all of the infrequently chosen responses are**

   (a) "A" responses

   (b) "B" responses

   (c) "C" responses

9. **Most of the scale interaction patterns have been cross-validated in a separate sample from that in which they were identified.** True or False?

10. **Which would be a more common pattern, A+ with Q2-, or A+ with Q2+?**

   (a) A+ with Q2-

   (b) A+ with Q2+

Answers: 1. a; 2. b; 3. True; 4. b; 5. True; 6. c; 7. IM; 8. b; 9. True; 10. a

Four

HOW TO INTERPRET THE
16PF QUESTIONNAIRE

STRATEGIES FOR INTERPRETATION OF THE 16PF

Because of the comprehensive nature of the 16PF Questionnaire, the test can be used in a wide range of settings to help the professional gain a deep, integrated understanding of an individual's enduring personality makeup, including strengths and weaknesses. Although the 16PF results provide extensive information for the professional, no personality test by itself can furnish a complete picture of an individual; other sources of information should always be included in the evaluation process.

Generally, the test is administered after the client has met with the professional and has developed rapport and gained an understanding of the purpose of the testing. This interaction is essential because both the mutual understanding developed and the information gathered during this process are important to the interpretation of the test. Subsequent meetings may include a discussion of the test results and their meaning and implications for the purpose of the assessment. Unlike the scales of tests measuring psychopathology, the 16PF scales represent relatively common areas of everyday experience that can be easily discussed with a client. In addition to increasing self-awareness, the sharing of 16PF results can facilitate the client's sense of being fully understood and of being part of the assessment process. Even if the results are not shared, the professional's enhanced understanding of the client contributes to the development of empathy, rapport, and the client's respect for the professional.

A thorough comprehension of the meanings of the scales facilitates interpretation of the 16PF Questionnaire. Because of the long history of the test's use in applied settings, many authors and researchers have contributed several thousand articles, chapters, and books to the 16PF knowledge base. The books cover a wide range of topics that can aid interpretation, and their authors provide expertise in clinical and counseling, in career development, in employee selection and development, and in educational and research settings. Rapid Reference 4.1 provides a few basic references for the new user. Many other books (e.g., Lowman, 1991; Meyer, 1989) provide insights about 16PF interpretation, but because they are numerous and provide information about a range of tests, they are not included in this list.

Another effective source of information and insight for test users is the wide variety of computer-generated interpretive reports that summarize relationships between 16PF scores and individual behavior. Quotations from some of these reports are included in the case interpretation presented in this chapter and in subsequent chapters. Reports available from IPAT, the 16PF publisher, are listed in Rapid Reference 4.2 and are described in the appendix. Both books and reports contain a variety of expert insights plus additional scores based on prediction equations. These equations were developed in various studies that used regression analyses between the 16PF dimensions and a wide range of criteria, including leadership, creativity, achievement, self-esteem, and a range of social skills.

≡Rapid Reference 4.1

Resource Books

- *Handbook for the 16PF* (Cattell et al., 1992)
- *The 16PF: Personality in Depth* (H. B. Cattell, 1989)
- *The 16PF Fifth Edition Administrator's Manual* (Russell & Karol, 2002)
- *The 16PF Fifth Edition Technical Manual* (Conn & Reike, 1994)
- *16PF Interpretation in Clinical Practice: A Guide to the Fifth Edition* (Karson et al., 1997)
- *Personality in Practice* (Lord, 1997)
- *Occupational Interpretation of the 16 Personality Factor Questionnaire* (Schuerger & Watterson, 1998)
- *Overcoming Obstacles to Interpretation* (Lord, 1999)

16PF Computer-Based Interpretive Reports

- 16PFworld.com Report
- BIR—16PF Basic Interpretive Report (see Russell & Karol, 2002)
- CCPI—16PF Cattell Comprehensive Personality Interpretation (see H. B. Cattell & H. E. P. Cattell, 1997)
- CCR—16PF Couple's Counseling Report (see Russell, 1995)
- HRDR—16PF Human Resource Development Report (see Dee-Burnett, Johns, Russell, & Mead, 1997)
- KCR—16PF Karson Clinical Report (see Karson & Karson, 1998)
- LCR—16PF Leadership Coaching Report (see Watterson, 2002)
- PCDP—16PF Personal Career Development Profile (see Walter, 2000)
- PSR—16PF Protective Services Report (see Russell & Bedwell, 2003)
- Select—16PF Select Report (see Kelly, 1999)
- TDR—16PF Teamwork Development Report (see Russell, 1998)

Note. Please refer to the appendix for a full description of the reports.

GETTING STARTED

About the Scales

It is essential for interpreters to become familiar with the meanings of the 16PF primary and global scales that are presented in chapter 3 of this book (as well as in the resource books listed in Rapid Reference 4.1). In particular, understanding of the meaning of each primary scale and how the primary scales combine to make up the global scales is critical knowledge for interpreting the test. Rapid Reference 4.3 lists the primary scales that contribute to each global scale.

As described in chapter 2, the 16PF personality scales use a sten (standardized ten) distribution. These scores range from 1 to 10 and have a mean of 5.5 and a standard deviation of 2. (Refer to Figure 2.1 in chapter 2, which shows the normal distribution of these sten scores, including percentiles.) The farther scores are from the mean of 5.5, the more extreme they are and the more likely they are to affect behavior. A rule of thumb is that scores of 8–10 (top

16%) are high and scores of 1–3 (bottom 16%) are low. Sten 4 (16th–31st percentile) is generally considered low average, and sten 7 (69th–84th percentile) is considered high average. Scores of 5 or 6 are considered average and range from the 31st percentile to the 69th percentile.

≡ Rapid Reference 4.3

The Global Factors and Their Contributing Primary Scales

Extraversion (EX)

Introversion	Contributing Primaries	Extraversion
Reserved, impersonal, distant	Warmth (A+)	Warm, outgoing, attentive to others
Serious, restrained, careful	Liveliness (F+)	Lively, animated, spontaneous
Shy, threat-sensitive, timid	Social Boldness (H+)	Bold, venturesome, thick-skinned
Private, discreet, nondisclosing	Privateness (N-)	Forthright, genuine, artless
Self-reliant, solitary, individualistic	Self-Reliance (Q2-)	Group-oriented, affiliative

Anxiety (AX)

Low Anxiety	Contributing Primaries	High Anxiety
Emotionally stable, adaptive, mature	Emotional Stability (C-)	Reactive, emotionally changeable
Trusting, unsuspecting, accepting	Vigilance (L+)	Vigilant, suspicious, skeptical, wary
Selfassured, unworried, complacent	Apprehension (O+)	Apprehensive, self-doubting, worried
Relaxed, placid, patient	Tension (Q4+)	Tense, High Energy, impatient, driven

Tough-Mindedness (TM)

Receptivity (Openness)	Contributing Primaries	Tough-Mindedness
Warm, outgoing, attentive to others	Warmth (A-)	Reserved, impersonal, distant
Sensitive, aesthetic, sentimental	Sensitivity (I-)	Utilitarian, objective, unsentimental
Abstracted, imaginative, idea-oriented	Abstractedness (M-)	Grounded, practical, solution-oriented
Open to change, experimenting	Openness to Change (Q1-)	Traditional, attached to familiar

Independence (IN)

Accommodation (Agreeableness)	Contributing Primaries	Independence
Deferential, cooperative, avoids conflict	Dominance (E+)	Dominant, forceful, assertive
Shy, threat sensitive, timid	Social Boldness (H+)	Bold, venturesome, thick-skinned
Trusting, unsuspecting, accepting	Vigilance (L+)	Vigilant, suspicious, skeptical, wary
Traditional, attached to familiar	Openness to Change (Q1+)	Open to change, experimenting

Self-Control (SC)

Lack of Restraint	Contributing Primaries	Self-Control (Conscientiousness)
Lively, animated, spontaneous	Liveliness (F-)	Serious, restrained, careful
Expedient, nonconforming	Rule-Consciousness (G+)	Rule-conscious, dutiful

(continued)

Abstracted, imaginative, idea-oriented	**Abstractedness (M-)**	Grounded, practical, solution-oriented
Tolerates disorder, unexacting, flexible	**Perfectionism (Q3+)**	Perfectionist, organized, self-disciplined

Note. A plus (+) sign beside the letter indicates that a high score on the primary scale contributes to a high score on the global scale. Conversely, a minus (-) sign beside the letter indicates that a low score on the primary scale contributes to a high score on the global scale. The descriptions for scales that contribute in the negative direction are reversed from the usual profile direction.

All 16PF primary and global scales are bipolar; that is, both high and low poles of the scales have a well-defined meaning rather than just greater or lesser degrees of one end of the scale. High scores (right pole) are usually indicated by a plus sign (e.g., high Warmth, A+) and low scores (left pole) are indicated by a minus sign (e.g., low Warmth, A-). Generally, both the scale name and its letter indicator are given when a scale is mentioned (e.g., Rule-Consciousness, G).

High scores are not considered good, and low scores are not considered bad. Traits at both poles have some positive and some negative consequences for behavior. For example, although some may see high Warmth (A+) as good and low Warmth as not so good, being detached and objective can be important or essential in situations that require solitude (e.g., security guard, astronaut) or that require a focus on objective problems or functions (e.g., surgeon, airplane pilot, nuclear plant operator). In this way, scores at either pole of each scale usually have strengths and weaknesses for different situations.

Additionally, unlike an ability scale, on the 16PF Questionnaire "more" is not necessarily "better." Extremely high scores may result in somewhat different behaviors than do above-average scores. For example, above-average Anxiety often increases motivation and achievement in a positive way, however, high Anxiety is frequently debilitating or disruptive of achievement. Thus, the interpretation of extreme scores is often different from those that are just above- or below-average scores. To further illustrate, although low scores on many of the Anxiety scales may seem socially desirable, extreme low scores may have undesirable effects. For example, whereas low Apprehensiveness (O-) scores may indicate a desirable confident, unworried demeanor, however, extreme low scores suggest that the individual may be defended against self-doubt or self-scrutiny, making his or her confidence unshakable even in situations in which realistic self-evaluation and self-improvement may be desirable.

The relationship between personality scores and behavior is often nonlinear in this way, requiring somewhat different interpretations as scores become more extreme either in the high or the low direction. Additionally, very high or very low scores are particularly important within a profile because they signal aspects of the personality that are central to the individual's identity. Furthermore, extreme scores generally have a substantial effect on the expression of many other scores.

Accuracy of Scores

All test scores are estimates of a person's true scores on traits. Because the standard error of measurement for 16PF scales is close to 1 sten point (*SEMs* range from .71 to 1.06 for primary factor scales), a person's true score usually is in a range of plus-or-minus 1 sten point around his or her obtained score. For example, with a sten score of 7, the true score would be expected to fall at least 68% of the time within a sten score range of 6–8. Thus, the interpreter should recognize that scores could be anywhere in this range and interpret scores judiciously, based on all sources of information about the individual. Although research indicates that personality is a valid predictor of behavior (e.g., Barrick & Mount, 1991; Goldberg, in press), the correlations between personality and various behavioral criteria tend to be modest. Thus, inferences from test scores should always be considered hypotheses to be confirmed against other sources of information.

INTERPRETIVE STRATEGIES

Although a 16PF profile can seem daunting to a beginner, a strategy for interpretation can reduce the complexity of the profile into small, manageable

Rapid Reference 4.4

Steps to 16PF Interpretation

1. Consider context of assessment.
2. Evaluate the response style (validity) indices.
3. Evaluate the global scale scores.
4. Evaluate the primary scales in the context of the globals.
5. Consider scale interactions, prediction equations, interpretive report content, and comparison profiles.
6. Integrate all information in relation to the assessment question.

components. A common interpretive strategy consisting of six steps is discussed here and summarized in Rapid Reference 4.4. Each step is explained within the context of a case study to illustrate the processes performed and the information gleaned. The 16PF scores for the case study's profile are presented in Figure 4.1. This profile is interesting even though it has few extreme scores; the interactions among the particular traits make this person quite distinctive and answer many of the assessment questions.

Step 1: Consider Context of Assessment

Test interpretation does not take place in a vacuum; rather, it must consider the total circumstances surrounding the testing including the purpose for the testing. Why is the individual being referred for assessment? Are the test scores to be shared with others? Is the examinee a candidate for a job? Is testing occurring in a forensic setting for child custody or disability decision making? Is an individual's spouse insisting that they get help to improve their marriage? Is the person in some kind of a life crisis or life transition that might bring forth uncharacteristic stress reactions or coping strategies? What is the nature and duration of the client's relationship with the professional? Has the necessary time been taken to develop adequate rapport? All of these context issues affect how an individual approaches and responds to the testing process.

Any special characteristics of the individual that might affect his or her scores should be considered in evaluating the profile. Is the individual unfamiliar with tests or anxious about the testing process? What is his or her attitude about testing in general? Is the person particularly young or old? Is he or she likely to express strong gender biases in responding to test items? Does the person come from a culture in which certain questions or the whole testing process may be viewed differently? The professional needs to consider the preceding kinds of characteristics before interpreting a profile. In addition, the professional should be aware of his or her own characteristic preferences and biases in evaluating other people.

As with any test, 16PF results should be combined with other sources of information to more fully understand the individual and the context in which the testing is taking place. Whenever possible, the additional information should be sought and examined to confirm or disconfirm the results found in the testing process. Such information might include results from a previous 16PF administration, results from other types of tests, life history accounts, interview data, and communications from others involved in the referral process.

Sample Profile: Mr. Stark is a 39-year-old Caucasian engineer who has repeatedly failed to gain promotion to higher levels of management at an engineering firm. At the suggestion of his boss, he is seeking consultation in the circumscribed area of achieving his career goals. Mr. Stark has been successful technically, contributing innovative and original solutions to significant technical problems, and in this regard, he has been viewed as a rising star in the firm. During his introductory interview, Mr. Stark came across as an intelligent, ambitious, confident person who was frustrated and genuinely confused by his failure to gain promotion.

Although the assessment was performed outside the workplace and scores were not reported to his boss, Mr. Stark felt external pressure to do a self-evaluation. Because Mr. Stark did not seem to be the kind of person who would normally seek consultation or feedback, the consultant hypothesized that Mr. Stark might not have much confidence or trust in the assessment process and perhaps would feel anxious or defensive about results that reflected perceived professional inadequacies. Thus, the consultant gave special attention in the initial interviews to discussing Mr. Stark's perception of

RESPONSE STYLE (VALIDITY) INDICES

	Raw Score	Percentiles	
Impression Management	17	84%	within expected range
Infrequency	2	71%	within expected range
Acquiescence	53	32%	within expected range

PRIMARY FACTOR SCALES

Factor	Sten	Left Meaning	Standard Ten Score (STEN) 1 2 3 4 5 6 7 8 9 10	Right Meaning
A: Warmth	4	Reserved, Impersonal, Distant		Warm, Outgoing, Attentive to Others
B: Reasoning	9	Concrete		Abstract
C: Emotional Stability	6	Reactive, Emotionally Changeable		Emotionally Stable, Adaptive, Mature
E: Dominance	8	Deferential, Cooperative, Avoids Conflict		Dominant, Forceful, Assertive
F: Liveliness	5	Serious, Restrained, Careful		Lively, Animated, Spontaneous
G: Rule-Consciousness	7	Expedient, Nonconforming		Rule-Conscious, Dutiful
H: Social Boldness	7	Shy, Threat-Sensitive, Timid		Socially Bold, Venturesome, Thick-Skinned
I: Sensitivity	4	Utilitarian, Objective, Unsentimental		Sensitive, Aesthetic, Sentimental
L: Vigilance	6	Trusting, Unsuspecting, Accepting		Vigilant, Suspicious, Skeptical, Wary
M: Abstractedness	7	Grounded, Practical, Solution-Oriented		Abstracted, Imaginative, Idea-Oriented
N: Privateness	4	Forthright, Genuine, Artless		Private, Discreet, Non-Disclosing
O: Apprehension	3	Self-Assured, Unworried, Complacent		Apprehensive, Self-Doubting, Worried
Q₁: Openness to Change	8	Traditional, Attached to Familiar		Open to Change, Experimenting
Q₂: Self-Reliance	8	Group-Oriented, Affiliative		Self-Reliant, Solitary, Individualistic
Q₃: Perfectionism	7	Tolerates Disorder, Unexacting, Flexible		Perfectionistic, Organized, Self-Disciplined
Q₄: Tension	6	Relaxed, Placid, Patient		Tense, High Energy, Impatient, Driven

GLOBAL FACTOR SCALES

Factor	Sten	Left Meaning	Standard Ten Score (STEN) 1 2 3 4 5 6 7 8 9 10	Right Meaning
EX: Extraversion	4.9	Introverted, Socially Inhibited		Extraverted, Socially Participating
AX: Anxiety	4.6	Low Anxiety, Unperturbed		High Anxiety, Perturbable
TM: Tough-Mindedness	4.9	Receptive, Open-Minded, Intuitive		Tough-Minded, Resolute, Unempathic
IN: Independence	8.3	Accommodating, Agreeable, Selfless		Independent, Persuasive, Willful
SC: Self-Control	6.3	Unrestrained, Follows Urges		Self-Controlled, Inhibits Urges

Figure 4.1. 16PF profile for Mr. Stark, engineer.

Adapted with permission from Institute for Personality and Ability Testing. (1993). *16PF Fifth Edition Individual Record Form: Profile Sheet.* Champaign, IL: Author.

the reasons for the assessment and for his lack of promotion. This discussion enabled the consultant to learn about specific problems at work and Mr. Stark's view of them. It also allowed the consultant to develop rapport with Mr. Stark and to explore his anticipated gains from the assessment process and how he thought it might be useful to him. The consultant was able to develop an adequate sense of cooperation and collaboration from Mr. Stark in trying to find solutions to help him reach his career goals.

Step 2: Evaluate the Response Style (Validity) Indexes

The usefulness of test results in predicting behavior depends strongly on the individual's willingness and ability to cooperate with the testing process, particularly by responding to test items in a way that is consistent with his or her true self-perceptions. The accuracy of test results can be negatively affected by a variety of factors ranging from low reading comprehension to inability to think clearly because of anxiety or depression to crude or sophisticated attempts at intentional deception. Such factors affect whether the professional can use the ordinary rules of interpretation for an individual's scores.

Therefore, an initial and crucial step in evaluating 16PF scores is to consider the response set of the individual. First, check the answer sheet (or the item response page for computerized administration) to ensure that all items were completed with a single response and that none were left blank. (Blank items should be checked to see whether there is more than one unanswered item from any one scale.) Next, determine whether the items were responded to in a meaningful way versus randomly selected or inadequately answered because of fatigue or reading problems. The 16PF Infrequency (INF) scale is useful in addressing this consideration. An above-average score on the Reasoning ability scale (B) is another indicator that the individual was able to read and understand items and respond appropriately. Finally, determine whether the individual was motivated to present an accurate self-portrayal. This involves examination of the Impression Management (IM) and Acquiescence (ACQ) scales.

The three 16PF response style or validity indices—Impression Management (IM), Infrequency (INF), and Acquiescence (ACQ)—are presented as a raw score or percentile rather than as a sten score. Extreme percentiles are used to flag the possibility of a response set. If any of the indices is extreme, the interpreter should evaluate whether the individual's response set might be affecting the validity of the profile. Generally, the 16PF manuals suggest using the 95th percentile as the point at which to flag extreme scores, but less extreme scores also may provide useful clues. Further information about the use of these scales can be found in chapter 3.

Infrequency

This scale is comprised of the most statistically infrequent responses on the test, which are all middle (*b*) responses and appear in the test booklet with a question mark. A score at or above the 95th percentile (i.e., a raw score of 7 or higher out of a possible 32) typically serves as a flag for this index, and may indicate that the individual either (a) had trouble reading or comprehending the questions, (b) responded randomly, (c) experienced consistent indecisiveness about the *a* or *c* response choices (perhaps because of an ambiguous self-picture), or (d) tried to avoid making the wrong impression by choosing the *?* middle answer rather than one of the more definitive or extreme answers.

Acquiescence

This scale serves to raise a flag about the possibility that the individual agreed with items regardless of what was being asked. A high score results when the agreeable (*a. true*) response to true-false items is repeatedly selected; doing so 70 times or more exceeds the 95th percentile for this index. A high score might indicate that the individual (a) misunderstood the item content, (b) responded randomly, (c) has an unclear self-image, or (d) had a "yea-saying" response style. The latter two motives also might indicate that the individual will tend to agree with or defer to the professional or be highly sensitive to cues of approval or self-definition from others.

Impression Management

This scale is bipolar, with high scores reflecting socially desirable responses and low scores reflecting socially undesirable responses. The *16PF Fifth*

Edition Administrator's Manual (Russell & Karol, 2002) suggests using the 95th percentile (a raw score of 21 or greater, out of a possible 24) as a point at which to flag socially desirable responding. A raw score of 4 or lower (at or below the 5th percentile) serves to flag socially undesirable responses.

High Impression Management Scores

Three possible explanations exist for an extremely high Impression Management (IM) score: (a) the individual may actually behave in highly socially desirable ways, in which case no distortion is at work; (b) the responses may reflect a kind of unconscious distortion in that they are consistent with the individual's self-image but not with his or her behavior; (c) the individual may have deliberately presented him- or herself as behaving in a highly socially desirable manner. Although it is more common in employee selection situations than in clinical settings, such distortion may occur in any setting where the purpose of the testing gives the person a reason to respond in a socially desirable manner (e.g., in child custody evaluations). When elevated scores occur, the professional should investigate whether the profile contains at least some less desirable qualities; these particularly include high scores on the Anxiety scales (C-, L+, O+, or Q4+) as well as low scores on several Self-Control scales (G-, M+, and Q3-) and on most Extraversion scales (A-, H-, N+ or Q2+). Such scores indicate that the individual was willing to endorse some undesirable characteristics, and therefore, the profile likely reflects honest self-reflection.

Low Impression Management Scores

A low Impression Management (IM) score suggests an unusual willingness to admit undesirable attributes or behaviors. Such a score can occur when a person is unusually self-critical, discouraged, or under stress. In fact, an extremely low score may be a "plea for help" (see Karson et al., 1997). The possibility of deliberate manipulation should be considered, especially when the purpose of testing gives the individual a reason to do so (e.g., in claiming mental disability in a litigation).

Sample Profile. Mr. Stark is an educated person who has had a good deal of experience with computerized testing and assessment. His average scores on the Infrequency (INF) and Acquiescence (ACQ) indices and his high score on the Reasoning scale (B+) suggest that he had no problem in reading and understanding the test items and answering them in a meaningful way.

Mr. Stark's Impression Management (IM) score is around the 84th percentile. Although this is above average and indicates that his responses are in the socially acceptable direction, the profile probably can be interpreted using the usual rules. In job-related settings, IM scores are generally above average and often indicate positive characteristics—that the individual has a good understanding of others' social expectations and has the ability to put his or her best foot forward in an appropriate manner.

One way to investigate this hypothesis is to check the other personality scales that are typically elevated when people are trying to "look good." That Mr. Stark did not try to present a uniformly positive picture of himself is supported by the following results: (a) most of his Extraversion scores are not in the socially desirable, above-average range (i.e., he is not A+, F+, or Q2-), (b) some of his Anxiety scores are not in the socially desirable below-average range (not L- or Q4-), and (c) his Abstractedness score is not low (M-). However, the professional also should confirm these findings with data from other sources.

Step 3: Evaluate the Global Scale Scores

The global scales are generally examined next because they give a broad overview of the individual's personality. (See descriptions of the global scale meanings at the beginning of chapter 3.) The 16PF global factor scales represent the original Big Five scales (H. E. Cattell, 1996), which are so popular in the current personality literature. H. B. Cattell (1989) notes that the information provided by the global factor scales

> is analogous to the first broad outline created by an artist's brush before the canvas is filled in with the details, contrasts, and highlights that give the picture its final form. This outline, though rough, foreshadows the particulars to come. The outline also provides a general framework for organizing pieces of information as they are gleaned from each primary factor interpretation. (p. 308)

After the interpreter has developed a sense of the big picture outlined by the global scales, the scores on the primary scales can be used to fill in the fine-grain specifics of the individual's personality.

As is typical of scores on most personality scales, global scores that fall outside the average range are most noteworthy and thus become the focus of interpretation. Usually, global scores that are low (sten 1–3) and high (sten 8–10) are identified first, and then those that are below average or above average (sten 4 or sten 7) are noted. The individual's overall number of extreme global scores (those between sten 1–3 or 8–10) can be compared to the average number of extreme scores in the 16PF normative sample (N = 10,261), using Rapid Reference 4.5. Because 86% percent of the general population achieved a total of zero, one, or two extreme global scores in their profiles, 0–2 extreme scores are considered to be within the average range. The rest of the general population achieved these extreme scores in their profiles: (a) 10% had three extreme global scores, (b) 3% had four extreme globals, and (c) less than 1% were extreme on all five global factors. Thus, people with three extreme global scale scores have an above-average number of distinctive traits, and those with four or five total extreme global scores are rather unique in the distinctiveness of their personality.

Sample Profile. Because Mr. Stark's profile shows only one extreme global score, he is well within the average range for overall number of elevated

≡Rapid Reference 4.5

Number of Extreme Global Factor Scores on 16PF Profiles

Number of Extreme Scores	Percent of Sample	Cumulative Percent
0	26.4	26.4
1	35.5	61.9
2	24.4	86.3
3	10.3	96.6
4	3.1	99.6
5	0.4	100.0

Note. N = 10, 261. Based on updated norm sample released in 2002. Adapted with permission from Russell, M., and Karol, D. (2002). *16PF Fifth Edition Administrator's Manual with Updated Norms.* Champaign, IL: Institute for Personality and Ability Testing.

scores. His high score on Independence suggests that he is a self-directed individual who tends to act independently and to have a significant impact on his environment (rather than accommodating to it). People with such high Independence scores tend to be assertive and individualistic, and they are often seen as "a force unto themselves." In the next step, Mr. Stark's Independence primary scales are examined to discover the particular style of his impact on his environment.

All of Mr. Stark's other global scale scores are within the average range. His slightly below-average Anxiety score indicates that, at present, his overall adjustment potential is at least average and he is not experiencing much distress or acknowledging any problems. Mr. Stark's Extraversion is slightly below average, indicating that people and social activities do not play quite as big a role in his life as in that of the average person. His slightly above-average Self-Control score suggests that he is a reasonably conscientious individual, and his slightly below-average score on Tough-Mindedness indicates that he tends to balance emotional toughness with an openness to new ideas.

Although only one of Mr. Stark's global scores is elevated (Independence), it is important to note that his average-range global scores were attained by averaging elevated but opposite scores on the contributing primary scales. Thus, his particular combination of primary scores gives distinction to his personality.

Step 4. Evaluate the Primary Scales in the Context of the Globals

Identify the Number of Extreme Primary Scores
First, compare the individual's total number of extreme primary scores to the average number of extreme scores achieved by people in the normative sample (N = 10, 261). Rapid Reference 4.6 gives the percentage of the norm sample attaining different numbers of extreme primary scores on the 15 personality scales (excluding the Reasoning ability scale, B). The table indicates that attaining between two and seven extreme primary scores is within the normal range. The greater the number of extreme scores found within a profile, the more likely the person is to have a well-defined, individualistic personality style. An extreme score on any scale is attained when the person consistently endorses items that describe one distinct kind of behavior. Thus, extreme scale scores suggest strong, behavioral tendencies, and that shifting behavior from the preferred style may be difficult for the person, even in situations in which this style may not be ideal or appropriate.

≡Rapid Reference 4.6

Number of Extreme Primary Factor Scores on 16PF Profiles

Number of Extreme Scores	Percent of Sample	Cumulative Percent
0	1.8	1.8
1	6.6	8.3
2	12.1	20.5
3–6	61.6	82.1
7	8.6	90.7
8	4.4	95.1
9–15	4.9	100.0

Note. $N = 10,261$. Based on updated norm sample released in 2002. Adapted with permission from Russell, M., & Karol, D. (2002). *16PF Fifth Edition Administrator's Manual with Updated Norms.* Champaign, IL: Institute for Personality and Ability Testing.

When a profile contains few extreme scores, the person's behavior may not be extreme in either direction (i.e., is average), or the person may have a rather unclear self-picture on certain traits. In some cases, people who wish to avoid making a poor impression can achieve a fairly flat profile either by answering similar items in inconsistent directions or by choosing a relatively high number of *b* responses.

Sample Profile. Mr. Stark shows four extreme primary scores (excluding the B scale), which is well within the average number. He does have seven above- or below-average scores, which also influence his behavior. Thus, although Mr. Stark appears to have distinctive features in his personality, he is not extreme.

Review the Primary Scales in the Context of the Global Factor Scales

Primary scale scores that fall outside the average range represent those traits that are most definitive and descriptive and most likely to affect the individual's behavior. The interpreter should note each primary scale that is extreme as well as those that are above average or below average. The primary scales that make up each global scale are usually considered together in order to gain a thorough picture of the individual's functioning in each domain. Rapid Reference 4.3 summarizes which primary scales contribute to each of the five global scales and in which direction. The primary scores within each global scale contribute not only to the level of the global trait but also to the nature and quality of its expression. For example, if someone's above-average Anxiety score were based mainly on high Apprehensiveness (O+), he or she would be insecure and self-doubting, whereas if it were based on high Tension (Q4+) and Vigilance (L+), he or she would tend to be easily irritated and to blame others for problems that arise.

Because each primary scale may contribute in a positive or a negative direction to a global scale, the interpreter should first identify the individual primary scales that are *raising* each global factor score as well as the primaries that are *lowering* the global score. For example, a high score on the global Extraversion can come from high scores on Warmth (A+), Liveliness (F+), or Social Boldness (H+) or from low scores on Privateness (N-) and Self Reliance (Q2-). Sometimes a primary score is inconsistent with the rest of the primary scores within a global (e.g., a high score on Extraversion but a low score on Warmth, A-). Additionally, an average global scale score may be the result of a combination of extreme but opposite primary scale scores. The latter is particularly noteworthy because it indicates complex trends within an individual's personality and greatly affects the way the global scale is expressed.

This kind of disparate mix of qualities is especially useful in building a picture of an individual's unique needs and style. For example, disparate primary scores within Extraversion may help to identify what particular needs or motivations lead a client to seek social contact or to avoid social contact. In a similar way, the scales within Self-Control may elucidate some sources of internal controls but reveal other sources of impulsivity. Disparate patterns among primary scales may be explored with a client to enable an understanding of their impact or meaning. For example, the counselor might say, "On the one hand, you tend to be X, but in certain situations you also describe yourself as Y. How do these disparate qualities make a fit for you? Do you find that it is sometimes hard to express (or accommodate) both styles?"

The interpreter can build an integrated picture of an individual's functioning, including strengths and weaknesses, by putting together the scales in the following order:

1. Start with the primary scales within global Extraversion and Independence scales, beginning with whichever is most extreme. Because both of these domains tend to focus on interpersonal behavior, they can be used to build a picture of the individual's interpersonal style, both in interacting with others (Extraversion) and in influencing others (Independence).

2. Next, put together the primary scales within Tough-Mindedness and Self-Control. These scales can elucidate areas of internal functioning, particularly ways of controlling impulses and experiencing emotions, fantasy, and new viewpoints.

3. Finally, put together the scales within Anxiety. These scales indicate the individual's style of dealing with difficult feelings and situations, whether they originate in the interpersonal domain or the internal one.

Sample Profile.

Independence: Mr. Stark's high Independence score is his most outstanding global trait; all of the primary scales within this global are in the above-average direction. His high score on Dominance (E+) indicates a forceful, competitive, and opinionated person. He is also high on Openness-to-Change (Q1+) and so is likely to be an innovative individual who questions established ways of doing things. Together, these two traits suggest someone who is confident and forceful in pursuing his ideas and viewpoints and in pushing for change. His above-average score on Social Boldness (H+) further contributes to his tendency to be fearless and thick-skinned in pursuing his goals and in confronting others. He is unlikely to be inhibited by criticism or discouraged by obstacles. His high-average score on Vigilance (L+) suggests that he is more likely to be critical of others than of himself and to be vigilant about others' motives. In all, Mr. Stark's Independence primaries consistently describe someone who is very confident and forceful; that is, he is not afraid to rock the boat in advancing his ideas and goals.

Extraversion: Mr. Stark's Extraversion scores are quite mixed; two are below average and two are above average. The two primary scales in the Introverted direction—Warmth (A-) and Self-Reliance (Q2+)—make a powerful combination. Because Mr. Stark tends to be reserved (A-), he is not particularly interested in people or their feelings, and his attention is more likely focused on facts, ideas, or other objective matters. More extreme is his high score on Self-Reliance (Q2+), which indicates a solitary, individualistic style. Thus, Mr. Stark prefers to rely on his own thinking and judgment and tends to work by himself on most projects. He does not welcome advice or opinions from others and may view them as intrusions or attempts to control him.

Mr. Stark's two above-average scores on the Extraversion primaries of Social Boldness (H+) and Forthrightness (N-) may actually intensify his individualistic style. His bold, adventurous manner probably helps him to initiate contacts, take risks, and withstand stress, but sometimes it may lead him to come across as brash or thick-skinned. His boldness (H+) and his straightforwardness (N-) may lead him to speak or act before he thinks carefully about others' perspectives or the effects his behavior may have on others. At times, he may seem tactless in his interactions and unaware of or unconcerned about others' feelings. His boldness and straightforwardness also tend to make his other traits more apparent because they are expressed straightforwardly rather than cautiously or tactfully. Without considering the possible impact, he may forcefully criticize others' ideas or established ways of doing things (E+, Q1+) or indicate his disinterest in others (A-, Q2-) in a direct or indirect manner.

All of these Extraversion traits suggest someone who is detached, individualistic, and blunt. Mr. Stark is unlikely to be concerned about others' opinions or feelings or to be inhibited or tactful in expressing his own. These traits coupled with his Independence scores make a powerful combination. They describe someone who is forceful and confident in pursuing his ideas and goals but individualistic and detached in his feelings for others.

Tough-Mindedness: The traits that make up global Tough-Mindedness are often seen as descriptive of cognitive style. Thus, the score on the Reasoning ability scale (B) is usually considered at this point in the profile interpretation. Mr. Stark's high Reasoning (B+) score indicates a superior ability to understand and use abstract concepts and to solve intellectual problems.

His overall Tough-Mindedness score is slightly below average, but it results from averaging primary scores that go in opposite directions. The low, Receptive end of this scale indicates openness, and so Mr. Stark's overall scores may be seen as a description of someone who is "open to ideas, theory, and innovation but closed to people, needs, and feelings." His two below-average Tough-Mindedness traits suggest a strong potential for creative functioning. Mr. Stark shows an interest in abstract ideas and theoretical thinking, and he tends to focus on the "big picture," seeking the underlying meaning behind things (M+). This imaginative quality is complemented by his open-mindedness and tendency to seek new and original solutions to problems (Q1+). These creative qualities plus his superior intellectual ability probably have contributed greatly to Mr. Stark's success in scientific and technical innovation.

The focus of Mr. Stark's creative thinking is indicated by his other two Tough-Mindedness traits, which contribute in the opposite, positive to Tough-Mindedness. His below-average scores on Sensitivity (I-) and Warmth (A-) denote an aloof individual who tends to focus on logical, objective aspects of situations rather than on people, aesthetics, or feelings. This trait combination indicates that his creative abilities are likely to be applied to technical or scientific matters rather than to interpersonal or artistic matters. It also suggests that the forceful, individualistic qualities revealed in his other global scales are likely to come across in ways that are insensitive to people's feelings and needs. In seeking control and change (E+, H+, Q1+), he is unlikely to give a great deal of attention to the perspectives of other people.

Self-Control: Mr. Stark's high-average score on global Self-Control indicates someone who is reasonably conscientious. Mr. Stark's above-average score on Perfectionism (Q3+) suggests that he is a self-disciplined individual who tends to be organized and planful in achieving his goals. He also is likely to be respectful of rules, regulations, and standards because he has a strong, internalized set of values (G+). In fact, his overall Self-Control score would be significantly higher were it not for a score in the opposite direction—his tendency to be abstracted, imaginative, and distractible (M+).

Anxiety: There is a considerable spread among Mr. Stark's Anxiety scores, and this configuration makes a substantial difference in its expression. His low score on Apprehensiveness (O-) indicates that he is self-assured, unworried, and untroubled by self-doubt. Such characteristics likely enhance his self-confidence and resilience under stress, but such a low score also suggests that he may come across as self-satisfied and complacent. This style probably reinforces his quality of bold, critical superiority (E+, Q1+, H+) and his tendencies to be detached, thick-skinned, and insensitive to others (A-, I-, Q2+).

Mr. Stark's high-average score on Emotional Stability (C) indicates that he tends to be a little calmer than most in coping with life's ups and downs. On the other hand, this score combined with his untroubled self-assurance (O-) may indicate that his coping skills are based on a tendency to ignore things he doesn't want to hear. His low-average score on Vigilance (L+) also suggests that he may see most problems as originating outside himself.

Step 5: Consider Scale Interactions, Prediction Equations, Interpretive Report Content, and Comparison Profiles

Experienced interpreters of 16PF scores learn to identify significant combinations of primary scale scores rather than evaluating only one score at a time. Some of these combinations are presented in chapter 3. Other valuable resources for expert insight on these combinations are the books and the computer-generated interpretive reports listed in Rapid References 4.1 and 4.2, respectively. In addition, the books and reports provide scores on research-based prediction equations developed from regression analyses predicting a variety of criteria from the 16PF scales (Conn & Rieke, 1994). Prediction equation scores presented in this case study include, for example, those for leadership style, potential for creativity, self-esteem, and Holland's occupational themes. By consulting these sources, the professional can benefit from the experience of experts and from a range of research findings. The manuals for the interpretive reports often summarize relevant research conducted by the report authors and include a bibliography of related studies. Group profiles for comparison purposes are also found in the books and reports listed in Rapid References 4.1 and 4.2.

The text that follows features excerpts from various interpretive reports that were generated on the basis of Mr. Stark's scores. The reports are referred to by their acronyms, which are given in Rapid Reference 4.2. The interpretive comments are organized around the global scales, similar to the order used in Step 4.

Sample Profile: Mr. Stark's strongest scores are in the area of Independence, including average to high scores on Dominance (E+), Openness to Change (Q1+), Social Boldness (H+), and Vigilance (L+). Various reports describe these score combinations:

Mr. Stark's preferred lifestyle is highly independent and self-directed, leading to active attempts to achieve control of others and the environment. He tends to exert a strong social influence or persuasiveness. He prefers to form his own opinions and is willing to challenge the status quo. In interpersonal relationships, he leads or dominates. He likes to be in charge and may be persistent in getting his way. He is experimenting and has an inquiring, critical mind. He tends to question traditional methods and to press for new approaches. (BIR)

Mr. Stark is apt to be vehement or even forceful in his manner of saying and doing things. He is prone to be individualistic and opinionated. People with similar characteristics are often not particularly interested in beliefs contrary to their own. Mr. Stark presents himself as a highly self-determined individual who frequently says what he thinks. (HRDR)

Some reports include hand-back sections that provide feedback to consider for self-development:

Mr. Stark would most likely function with greater personal effectiveness, both on-the-job and in other personal-career situations, if he would try to be aware of and work consciously to guard against the impact of: being so overly confident about trying new approaches to some problems and situations that the benefits of first exploring what others may have to contribute to the solutions sought may be overlooked; a tendency to expect others to accept his ideas about how best to solve problems needing to be resolved; relating to others in ways that may make people feel that their ideas are unimportant, especially if they think differently than he does about the issues at hand. (PCDP)

The PCDP report provides scores from a range of leadership prediction equations (Walter, 2000). Mr. Stark's predicted score for Leadership Preference is high (7.8), indicating that he enjoys taking charge and leading others. However, most of his leadership prediction equations, such as Elected Leadership (6.6) and Effective Leadership (6.0), are in the average range. Mr. Stark's most extreme leadership score on the PCDP is a very low score on the Supportive Leadership-Subordinate role pattern, which indicates that being understanding, accommodating, supportive, or encouraging is not his typical style.

Mr. Stark's Extraversion scores present a complex picture. Although his tendency to be bold (H+) and forthright (N-) makes him more interactive with others, it also makes his other extreme scores more apparent: "He tends to be very blunt when he does speak up, and others may come to resent his outspokenness" (KCR). Mr. Stark's other two Extraversion scores, low-average Warmth (A-) and high Self-Reliance (Q2+), are in the Introverted direction, and they represent an important score combination. These two scales make up the part of Extraversion that concerns caring for others and enjoying being around people without seeking attention, prominence, stimulation, or control. Because he is both detached (A-) and self-reliant (Q2+), Mr. Stark is low on this relationship quality; this means that he probably is not inherently interested in people and generally would prefer to work alone rather than with others. In addition, he probably has not formed many strong relationships with others. Report information elaborates on some of the strengths and weaknesses of this score combination:

He is also self-reliant and thus has the potential to be a self-starter. He may be able to use these qualities to demonstrate initiative and enterprise in the workplace or to branch out on his own. . . . Mr. Stark tends to rely on his own judgment and thinking rather than on other people's. While this may make him autonomous in his decision-making, he may at times be seen as close-minded. He also may have opinions that are strongly held and not easily changed by listening to outside input. (CCPI)

He seldom gets overly concerned about what others may think is the practical thing to do. Even though he may see that others are not listening to his ideas, he is not usually bothered by this rejection because he is inclined to be mostly wrapped up in his own thoughts. (PCDP)

He prefers working alone to working in groups, which may cause stress when he is required to collaborate with others. He is not a person who can easily defer his personal agenda to the group's. (KCR)

Some reports note that Mr. Stark's high scores on Dominance (E+) and Self-Reliance (Q2+) may present potential problems for working with him on self-improvement issues:

> Obstacles to seeking help in psychotherapy in an effective manner include a tendency to view the receptive role as too submissive and his investment in being seen as self-sufficient. The therapist may get further by building on Mr. Stark's ideas than by offering ideas of his or her own. Any therapeutic orientation that depends on establishing an atmosphere of mutuality may run afoul of his aversion to collaboration. (KCR)

Mr. Stark's scores on Tough-Mindedness scales present some strengths and weaknesses for a managerial role. His combination of below-average Sensitivity (I-) and Warmth (A-) indicates a tendency to be tough and objective in decision making as well as a lack of awareness of others' feelings. Especially when it is combined with his level of drive and outspokenness (E+, Q1+), boldness (H+), and bluntness (N-), his lack of concern for others and their feelings may at times seem harsh. All of these scores contribute to Mr. Stark's extremely low score (2) on the Social Sensitivity prediction equation on the BIR, which suggests that he has a limited ability to interpret social and emotional cues. Various reports describe the effects of below-average scores on Sensitivity (I-) and Warmth (A-):

> He probably has a somewhat limited empathic understanding of others' vulnerable feelings since he tends to be out of touch with his own. His assessments of people tend to be based on what he regards as objective facts. (CCPI)

> He is a rather tough-minded, no-nonsense individual as compared to most people. His efficiency is rarely affected by emotional concerns in the sense that he does not spend a lot of time wondering how his actions and decisions will feel to himself or to others. . . . He is the kind of person who tends to keep his poise under duress, and he generally copes well when the going gets tough, partly because it is a source of pride to him to stand up to adversity. (KCR)

He may be unaware of the effect or appropriateness of his own social actions. Effectively, Mr. Stark is not overly self-conscious, but a lack of awareness may hinder his ability to understand other people. (BIR)

Mr. Stark's scores on the other Tough-Mindedness scales, Openness to Change (Q1+) and Abstractedness (M+), plus his high Reasoning ability (B+) indicate a strong potential for creative functioning. His score on the prediction equation for Creative Potential, found on the PCDP and the BIR, is high (9.1). Other reports describe these qualities:

His level of creative initiative is predicted to be high. He is likely to have the sense of venture, determination, and orientation toward ideas that are instrumental for pursuing creative interests. (HRDR)

He has a talent for innovative work that requires thinking outside the usual cultural paradigms. In addition to being open-minded and original, he is also imaginative. Stepping back to see the 'big picture' and envisioning the possibilities therein are among his strongest attributes, and so his intelligence would be best used in work that involves putting ideas together creatively. . . . His innovative temperament is unlikely to be a good match with a large, authoritarian institution or one that is set in its ways. He would fit better in a newly emerging industry or an organization where the lines of authority are not highly structured and policies and procedures are flexible. He also is well suited to an environment where individual enterprise and resourcefulness are valued rather than teamwork or conformity. (CCPI)

The PCDP report discusses the effect of Mr. Stark's Tough-Mindedness scores (Q1+, M+) and his Reasoning score (B+) on his learning style. These primary scale scores contribute to his high score (8.8) on a prediction equation for interest in formal academic learning environments:

He is very alert mentally. He can see quickly how ideas fit together and is likely to be a fast learner. Being probing intellectually and having interest in learning from lectures and books, he usually likes to learn about many things. He also strives to seek knowledge for its own sake. Mr. Stark appears to be quite able to learn well from his experiences. Within the areas of Mr. Stark's interests, and if he feels like doing it, he should be quite able to learn much from formal academic training. (PCDP)

Mr. Stark's Self-Control score is on the high side of average and contains above-average scores on both Rule-Consciousness (G+) and Perfectionism (Q3+):

He shows signs of self-control, group conformity, and conscientiousness. He is well aware of conventional standards of behavior and tries to live up to them. On the whole, then, social reinforcers like praise and the avoidance of disapproval are likely to be effective motivators for him. (KCR)

Mr. Stark's global Anxiety score is on the low side of average. Prediction equations on the BIR also indicate that Mr. Stark is high average (7) on both Emotional Adjustment and on Social Adjustment. These scores plus his low Apprehensiveness (O-) score indicate qualities of self-assurance and resilience that can be useful in leadership roles but may also have some drawbacks:

He has a firm sense of self, which structures and directs his responses to events; he is not overly susceptible to variations in self-concept, and his focus is not easily swayed by changes in mood. (KCR)

He seems to experience a rather strong sense of adequacy about his ability to handle most situations. He appears, too, to have little need to explain his actions to himself or to other people. (PCDP)

However, his self-esteem at present is above the optimal level for fairly appraising both his strengths and weaknesses. He may be defended against recognizing his own shortcomings. . . . Mr. Stark does not take his fair share of responsibility and blame when things go wrong. Any problems between him and his partner may be exacerbated by his tendency to deny his role in them. (CCPI)

In combination with his forcefulness (E+, Q1+, H+) and his insensitivity to feelings (I-, A-), his self-assurance may sometimes come across as complacence, arrogance, or a lack of concern for others' vulnerable feelings.

Further perspective on Mr. Stark's configuration of scores can be obtained from his predicted Holland occupational scores found on the BIR and his predicted career orientations (Campbell, Hyne, & Nilsen, 1992) found on the PCDP. An individual's relative standing on these six broad areas of career interest is often quite revealing. Mr. Stark's highest score within both systems of occupational interest is on the scientific Investigative (10) or Analyzing (9.7) theme, which includes jobs such as computer scientist, medical researcher, and geologist. His second highest score is in the pragmatic Realistic (9) or Producing (9) theme, which includes occupations such as electrician, airline mechanic, and engineer. He shows only midrange scores in the Enterprising (6) or Influencing (7.5) theme area—an area that relates to his aspiration for promotion to higher management. However, his highest scores within this area involve jobs that do not involve close, cooperative relationships with others, such as attorney, investment manager, and elected public official. The Social (6) or Helping (5) theme is his lowest score.

Another way to learn more about an individual profile is to compare it to group profiles. Mr. Stark's profile reveals both strong similarities and differences to group profiles of managers presented in the *16PF Fifth Edition Technical Manual* (Conn & Rieke, 1994), the *Occupational Interpretation of the 16PF Questionnaire* (Schuerger & Watterson, 1998), and the *Leadership Coaching Report Manual* (Watterson, 2002). Mr. Stark scores in the same general direction as technical managers on most of his 16 traits; that is, he is bright (B+); calm and self-assured (O-, C+); conscientious and tough-minded (G+, Q3+, I-); and assertive, bold, forthright, and innovative (E+, H+, N-, Q1+). The comparison also indicates some important differences between Mr. Stark's traits and those of the manager groups. In the area of Extraversion, Mr. Stark is so self-reliant (Q2+), aloof (A-), and unemotional (I-) that he may have trouble developing strong relationships with others or showing empathy and responsiveness. His strong scores on Dominance (E+), self-assurance (O-), Openness to Change (Q1+), and toughness (I-) also may lead to friction in his relationships.

Step 6: Integrate All Information in Relation to the Assessment Question

After considering a wide range of information about Mr. Stark's profile in the previous two steps, the interpreter's final task is to integrate and summarize the highlights of these findings in relation to the purpose of the assessment. The interpreter can build a comprehensive picture of the individual's functioning in areas relevant to the referral question by combining information from each of the global areas.

Sample Profile. Overall, Mr. Stark has many qualities that would be assets in an upper-level management position. He is very bright and can tackle even the most challenging intellectual problems (B+). He is assertive and confident in his social presence, and he is unlikely to be intimidated by problems or people (E+, H+, O-, Independence+). These traits also make him forceful and decisive in pursuing his goals; obstacles and criticism do not discourage him. He tends to be independent and self-sufficient in his activities and viewpoints and to keep his own counsel about solutions to problems (A-, Q1+, Q2+). He is particularly open to change, and his technical ideas are probably original and innovative (Q1+). He is likely to be adept at seeing the big picture and having a vision for the future (M+). Furthermore, he tends to be a reasonably organized and conscientious individual who is thorough and persevering in completing projects (G+, Q3+, Self-Control+). Overall, he is emotionally stable and he is likely to be mature and resilient in most situations (O-, Anxiety-, I-).

These strengths make him a possible candidate for upper-level management; however, important areas of his personality diverge from that of an effective executive and must be substantially developed if he is to become a solid candidate. His dominance, boldness, and confidence (E+, H+, Q1+, Independence+, O-) are at such high levels that he is likely to have problems with being overbearing, self-satisfied, and inattentive to others' viewpoints. He also is likely to have trouble building relationships and leading collaborative efforts because of his detached, individualistic style (A-, Q2+). His tendency to focus on objective aspects of situations rather than on emotional or social aspects (A-, Q2+) suggests that he may be unaware of his impact on others, inattentive to others' feelings and needs, and unable to provide emotional support and encouragement. Overall, these combined scores indicate that Mr. Stark is probably not very socially aware and undoubtedly tunes out all kinds of feedback. In all likelihood, these qualities have negatively affected his opportunities to gain promotion.

Dr. Dave Watterson, author of the Leadership Coaching Report (LCR), was asked to summarize Mr. Stark's strengths and weaknesses for functioning in an upper-level management position as well as the leadership development issues that relate to such a position. The remaining five paragraphs are a summary of his ideas. Dr. Watterson points out that Mr. Stark's profile is similar to those of many people who become interested in management positions because of their strong individual technical contributions rather than because of their people skills. He notes that Mr. Stark is likely to push for increased control over large decisions and for recognition but to have little interest in working with others from a personal standpoint. Thus, a central focus of any coaching with Mr. Stark should involve developing his social skills; however, Mr. Stark's profile indicates that he may not see this area as important for development. Therefore, the first step would be to ask Mr. Stark about his goals for being in management—why he thinks management is for him. It is not clear from his scores how receptive he is to personal growth or receiving coaching because of his dominance, self-satisfaction, avoidance of emotions, and resistance to accepting guidance or ideas from others (E+, O-, I-, Q2+). Therefore, an essential goal is to develop and encourage his active participation in the process.

Mr. Stark has high "command and control scores" (E+, G+, Q3+), which suggest that he is strongly interested in using authority and power to direct activities. He has few skills for leading from a supportive standpoint (A-, I-, Q2+, O-). In fact, the latter scores indicate that he is not skilled at working with others in ways that allow for team success or in nurturing or supporting others toward their own growth. Overall, he needs to develop the ability to assert himself in a manner that does not depend so heavily on command and control. These scores also indicate that he needs to develop the important skill of delegation because he currently tends toward micromanagement. He would be quite misplaced in a corporate culture that emphasizes relationships, collaboration, teamwork, and development of staff; he would be more likely to realize possibilities for success in a more authoritarian, structured environment.

His listening skills are probably poor for a range of reasons. He is likely to consider that his own opinions are correct (E+, O-, Q1+, Q2+), and he possibly has received support for this superior attitude because he is intelligent and creative (B+, M+, Q1+). He also may have a strong sense of how things should be done according to his own structured approach (G+, Q3+), and he may not be accepting of different approaches. Much of his communication comes across as being judgmental or critical of others (A-, E+, Q1+, O-, N-, Q4+). Overall, he generally credits his own opinions more than those of others. He is unlikely to acknowledge others or to support their ideas unless they align with his own. He will present his view first, speak with a great deal of confidence and authority, and argue to have his solution acknowledged over those proposed by others.

These scores suggest that Mr. Stark will push to achieve his own goals rather than work cooperatively with others. He will lean heavily on his power and authority in motivating others. In turn, others will see him as seeking self-recognition rather than acknowledgment for the group. Therefore, developmental goals for Mr. Stark should focus on a range of social skills including the abilities to listen, communicate, work collaboratively, share information, delegate, and support the growth of others. Because Mr. Stark is not by nature responsive to people, he may have difficulty understanding the importance of developing these skills or grasping why anyone would want to spending so much time working with people in preference to solving technical problems.

Mr. Stark is likely to resist personal development because he is overconfident, insensitive to others' input, and brandishes an authoritarian style. He is likely to see his lack of promotion as the fault of others in the firm. Perhaps the most likely way to penetrate his wall of self-confidence will be for him to hear direct feedback from his boss. The boss would need to communicate that although Mr. Stark is a great technical contributor, his ability to lead others is low, particularly in the areas of building strong mutual relationships with others and attracting the willing cooperation of others to work with him toward achieving goals. Furthermore, the boss would need to precisely state that Mr. Stark would not be considered for a promotion unless he chose to improve his relationships skills. Depending on his reaction, the firm could decide to give him incentives for changing or to continue to reward him for his strong technical expertise.

Thus, Mr. Stark's 16PF profile reveals a great deal about his strengths and limitations for a management role as well as specific approaches for feedback and development. A consulting professional in a leadership development role could profitably explore these areas.

TEST YOURSELF

1. 16PF results are best at revealing

    (a) the individual's strengths.

    (b) the individual's weaknesses.

    (c) personality disorders.

    (d) an integrated picture of the whole personality.

(continued)

2. **Many professionals discuss 16PF results directly with their clients because**

    (a) the scales represent normal everyday behavior and experience.

    (b) they increase the client's self-awareness.

    (c) they facilitate discussion of important topics.

    (d) they increase the client's feeling of involvement in the assessment process.

    (e) all of the above

3. **16PF scores are presented in sten scores ranging from 1-10, and high scores are considered good and low scores are considered bad.** True or False?

4. **The first step in interpreting a 16PF profile is to**

    (a) interpret the global scales.

    (b) consider the response style (validity) indices.

    (c) interpret the primary scales.

    (d) consider all other sources of information about the person.

5. **Scores that are low (sten 1–3) or high (sten 8–10)**

    (a) are the only scores that are important.

    (b) are central to the person's identity.

    (c) indicate pathology.

    (d) indicate that the person was anxious when taking the test.

6. **The standard error of measurement for 16PF primary scales is about 1 sten point, and thus a person's "true score" is usually in a range of plus-or-minus 1 sten point around his or her obtained scores.** True or False?

7. **A high score on the Impression Management (IM) scale**

    (a) indicates that the individual behaves in a highly socially desirable way.

    (b) may be consistent with the person's self-image but not his/her behavior.

    (c) indicates a deliberate attempt to present a highly socially desirable self.

    (d) any of the above.

8. **An essential part of 16PF interpretation is understanding which primary scales fit together to form each of the global scales.** True or False?

Answers: 1.d; 2.e; 3. False; 4.d; 5.b; 6.True; 7.d; 8.True.

Five

STRENGTHS AND WEAKNESSES OF THE 16PF QUESTIONNAIRE

T he 16PF Questionnaire was first published in 1949, after years of research trying to identify the basic dimensions of personality. Since that time, the test has gone through four major revisions, culminating in the publication of the Fifth Edition in 1993, which is the subject of the present evaluation. Although it is not by itself a complete assessment, the 16PF Questionnaire is one of very few tests available that is derived from a basic effort to sample the whole domain of normal personality.

OVERVIEW OF ADVANTAGES AND DISADVANTAGES

The 16PF Fifth Edition has many strengths as an assessment tool. These include the test's strong scientific background, its comprehensive assessment of normal personality, its multilevel structure that includes primary and global traits, its fast and easy administration and scoring, its nonthreatening item content and scales, its large recently updated standardization sample, and its long history of research and validation in a range of applied settings.

The latest revision made the test stronger. Items were updated and simplified, psychometric characteristics were improved, and delivery modes were increased to include not only paper-and-pencil and computer software, but also a fax-based system and multilingual Internet administration, scoring, and interpretive reports.

Rapid References 5.1 through 5.4 focus on the strengths and weakness of four aspects of the test: the development of the test, administration and scoring, reliability and validity, and interpretation of the test.

Rapid Reference 5.1

Strengths and Weaknesses of the 16PF Fifth Edition Questionnaire: Development

Strengths	Weaknesses
Result of scientific research into the basic elements of human personality; embedded within a comprehensive theory of personality, abilities, and motivation.	Cognitive ability scale (Reasoning B) is very brief.
Continuity with concepts and theoretical model of earlier versions (original author, Raymond B. Cattell, participated in creation of latest edition).	Due to careful refinement on the latest edition, a few of the scales (L, M, N, Q1) do not correlate well with the old scales, which had much lower internal consistency.
Multilevel model provides in-depth assessment of the entire range of normal personality, including 16 primary traits and five global (Big Five) traits, and three response style indices (a brief ability scale is also included).	Scales are not orthogonal (uncorrelated). Self-report measures can be "faked."
Test items are short, simple (fifth-grade reading level), and nonthreatening, with updated language and standardized response format.	Removal of extreme items may have limited the range of some scales.
Psychometric characteristics of the test, such as scale homogeneity, were improved.	As a result of increased homogeneity, scale meanings may be narrower than in earlier forms.
Comprehensive, nonthreatening instrument is appropriate for a range of settings, including clinical and counseling, industrial and organizational, educational, and research.	Further validation studies using larger samples are needed on latest edition.
An extension of the test to lower age ranges has been recently published the 16PF Adolescent Personality Questionnaire (Schuerger, 2001a).	

Strengths	Weaknesses
Items were reviewed for gender, race or cultural bias as well as potential ADA violations. Special attention was also given to cross-cultural translatability.	

≡Rapid Reference 5.2

Strengths and Weaknesses of the 16PF Fifth Edition Questionnaire: Administration and Scoring

Strengths	Weaknesses
Items are shorter and simpler than previous form (fifth-grade reading level). Answer format has been simplified, and Reasoning ability items (B) are separate from the personality items.	Meaning of middle answer (b.) is ambiguous.
Administration time is short: 30–50 minutes for paper and pencil; 25-35 for computer administration. Easy administration and scoring can be completed by a trained nonprofessional.	
Administration and scoring are available in paper-and-pencil, computer software, Internet format, and multilanguage Internet format; scoring and reports also available by mail-in or OnFax.	Several scoring keys required for hand scoring.
The same answer sheet is used for both hand scoring and computer scoring.	
Discounted materials and scoring available for classroom or research purposes.	
Recently updated standardization sample ($N = 10,261$) approximates demographics of the 2000 U.S. census data.	College-educated persons are somewhat overrepresented in the sample compared to the 2000 census but are representative of typical test users.

Rapid Reference 5.3

Strengths and Weaknesses of the 16PF Fifth Edition Questionnaire: Reliability and Validity

Strengths	Weaknesses
Psychometric characteristics of the test, such as scale homogeneity, are comparable to those of other tests.	
Test-retest reliability compares favorably for both short (2-week) and long (2-month) intervals.	
Joint factor analyses indicate good alignment of concepts with earlier editions. Confirmatory factor analyses support the construct validity of the scales.	
Construct validity is supported by correlations with other measures.	
IRT analyses indicate that scales generally function the same across subgroups.	Mean differences were found between some subgroups (e.g. sex, age, race) on expected primary scales, e.g. females were higher Sensitivity (I), older age groups were lower on Liveliness (F).
Mounting evidence of criterion validities for the revised test is similar to those of earlier editions in career counseling, employee selection and development, clinical and counseling.	More validity studies need to be completed on the latest edition, for example, in predicting specific job performance.

≡ *Rapid Reference 5.4*

Strengths and Weaknesses of the 16PF Fifth Edition Questionnaire: Interpretation

Strengths	Weaknesses
Comprehensively measures the whole range of normal personality.	
Multilevel structure provides in-depth picture of individual including primary traits and global (Big Five) traits.	Large number of scales makes training and experience necessary for in-depth interpretation.
Continuity of concepts with previous editions.	A few scales have narrower definitions with the refinement of the latest edition.
Nonthreatening item content, scale names, and report contents make the test useful in many settings; allows for direct client feedback which promotes self-awareness and rapport.	
Strong evidence for conceptual and applied validity of scales from research and practitioner experience over many years. Resource books provide a wealth of information for a variety of settings.	Many studies and books are based on the fourth edition.
Interpretive reports available that focus on many different settings and purposes.	

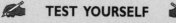

TEST YOURSELF

1. **A particular strength of the 16PF Fifth Edition Questionnaire is that**

    (a) it measures the same concepts and model as earlier forms.

    (b) it is based on scientific research into the basic elements of personality.

    (c) its non-threatening and comprehensive nature make it useful in a wide range of settings.

    (d) all of the above

2. **The 16PF Questionnaire measures the entire range of normal human personality. A correlative weakness is that it does not measure _____.**

3. **Although the test items are short, simple, and written at a fifth-grade level, the multi-level structure of the numerous scales makes training and experience necessary for in-depth interpretation.** True or False?

4. **Computer administration of the 16PF Questionnaire is about how many minutes shorter than paper and pencil administration?**

5. **The 16PF Questionnaire has no response style (validity) scales.** True or False?

6. **One significant weakness of the test is that the majority of the validity information available was collected on the previous edition.** True or False?

Answers: 1.d; 2. abnormal traits; 3. True; 4. 10–15 minutes; 5. False; 6. True

Six

CLINICAL, COUNSELING, AND CONSULTING APPLICATIONS

The 16PF Questionnaire is not meant for psychodiagnosis. However, it can be very useful in a variety of ways in counseling, clinical, and consulting settings. For example, it can be useful in quickly and objectively understanding the client's whole personality, including both strengths and weaknesses; in facilitating conversation and interaction with clients; in anticipating aspects of the client that might hinder self-awareness, progress, and communication with the professional; and in suggesting areas for further exploration. Rapid Reference 6.1 lists several of these areas that are discussed in this chapter. Moreover, a range of books and computer-generated interpretive reports (such as those in Rapid References 4.1 and 4.2) provide insights about the relationships between the 16PF scales and behavior in applied counseling, clinical, and consulting settings.

Even though some of the examples in this chapter focus on the challenges that are inherent in extreme scores, in general, emphasizing client strengths more than weaknesses is most constructive. Furthermore, adopting a cautious approach in regard to interpreting very high or very low scores is recommended. Although some clinicians believe that high (8–10) or low (1–3) scores on a scale usually signal some disadvantages (along with advantages), such scores may also indicate characteristics that are central to the client's personality and thus ones that the client will strongly resist changing. Some experienced 16PF users note that a very high or very low score is not just a number; rather, the score represents a strong self-description that proclaims, "This is who I am!" To encourage changing such a characteristic can be like trying to swim upstream and risks losing the client's good will.

=Rapid Reference 6. /

16PF Questionnaire Usefulness With Clients Who Have Adjustment Problems

Cattell's purpose in developing the 16PF Questionnaire was to provide a measure of general personality. Although the test is not meant for psychodiagnosis, many counselors, clinicians, and consultants who work with people find the test's results useful in the following four ways in a counseling context:

1. To understand the client and facilitate interaction
2. To anticipate aspects of the client's personality that could hinder self-awareness, progress, and free communication
3. To point out strengths and weaknesses in the client's makeup
4. To suggest specific areas for further exploration

USING THE 16PF QUESTIONNAIRE TO UNDERSTAND THE CLIENT AND FACILITATE INTERACTION

In this capacity, the use of the 16PF Questionnaire has five steps:

- **Step 1**: Evaluate the client's motivation for therapy and ability to grasp abstract interpretations and move beyond the concrete. For example, check the level of the global scale Anxiety to assess the client's motivation for therapy and the levels of primary scales Reasoning (B), Sensitivity (I), and Abstractedness (M) to assess the individual's likely capacity for abstract or emotional insight.

- **Step 2**: Evaluate the client's likely emotional accessibility and capacity for interrelatedness in the consulting relationship by assessing the levels of the primary scales such as Warmth (A), Social Boldness (H), Privateness (N), and Self-Reliance (Q2).

- **Step 3**: Estimate the client's primary motivation pattern(s) to enable selection of interventions that would be most compatible with the client's preferences and motives.

- **Step 4**: Evaluate the client's preferred style of social interaction by assessing patterns of the primary scale scores within the global Extraversion and Independence scales.

- **Step 5**: Evaluate the client's emotional resources, resilience, and durability by assessing the patterns of the primary scores within Anxiety and other scales affecting self-confidence.

Suggestions relevant to each of these steps are presented in the sections that follow.

Step 1

The following are general considerations in understanding the client's motivation for therapy and ability to benefit from insight therapy:

- Check the level of global Anxiety to estimate the client's overall level of motivation for self-development. Sound experience and theory assert that a person who is experiencing psychological discomfort has a stronger motive for therapy or counseling than does one who has no discomfort. Within Anxiety, low Emotional Stability (C-), high Apprehension (O+), and high Tension (Q4+) scales are the most likely to indicate subjective distress or discomfort, whereas high Vigilance scores (L+) often indicate that the client may be blaming others for their distress. Motivation for change and self-improvement also may be indicated by high scores on the Openness to Change (Q1) scale; low Q1 scorers usually prefer to keep things the way they are.
- Clients with higher scores on Reasoning (B) and Abstractedness (M+) are more able to profit from abstract explanations, patterns, and principles rather than from concrete procedures and suggestions. In fact, clients who are high on scale B may become bored if the pace of a session is too slow or the focus too simple. Those with high scores on Abstractedness (M+) tend to show an interest in and understanding of abstract ideas (such as interpretations) and imagination; high scorers on Sensitivity (I+) tend to be much more aware of emotions and their importance. On the other hand, clients who are low on these scales generally do not react well to abstractions, preferring concrete suggestions.

Step 2

This step concerns evaluating a client's emotional or interpersonal accessibility, or how ready the client is to speak openly to the professional.

- Estimate the client's accessibility for general interaction by examining the levels of the primary scales Warmth (A), Liveliness (F), Social Boldness (H), Privateness (N+), and Self-Reliance (Q2)—the scales from global Extraversion. Typically, clients who score average or higher on these scales are easily engaged in conversation and discussion—the higher the scores, the greater the readiness to engage socially. Low scorers tend to be more silent, withdrawn, and detached, and they may require extra encouragement. Clients who are average to above on Warmth (A+) and average to below on Self-Reliance (Q2-) are more able to develop a close, trusting relationship with the therapist. Persons who score extremely high on these scales may also turn out to be more in need of support and approval (A+, Q2-), more self-centered and attention-seeking (H+), or more flighty and impulsive (F+).
- Based on the level of the primary scale Privateness (N), estimate the client's readiness to be self-revealing and talk of highly personal matters. Low scorers tend to be open and forthright and to show ease in self-disclosure, a significant concern in coaching or counseling interactions. A score above 7 almost certainly indicates potential difficulty in speaking of personal matters; high scorers tend to be guarded, private, and hard to get to know.

Step 3

The third step involves estimating specific client motivational patterns. These patterns provide a broad sense of how the client is likely to react to the counselor in the sessions. The following are some useful cues for estimating motive patterns:

- Assess the client's conservatism or eagerness for change and self-improvement by considering the Openness to Change (Q1) score. A high-scoring client typically pushes for change; a low-scoring client tends to resist change.

- Assess the scores on the primary scales within global Tough-Mindedness to determine whether the client has a strongly emotional, intuitive, artistic temperament (A+, I+, M+, and Q1+) or a strongly detached, unsentimental, practical temperament (high scores on A-, I-, M-, and Q1-). Clients who are intuitive and emotional can tolerate a lot of ambiguity and are likely to respond well to abstract ideas and insights (M+), imaginative intuition and fantasy (I+), and original or innovative ideas (Q1+). For clients who are practical (A-, I-, M-, Q1-), emotions and the counseling relationship per se are less important than finding practical, no-nonsense solutions to problems. They typically respond well to clear procedures and concrete, logical suggestions.
- If scores on both Social Boldness (H+) and Liveliness (F+) are high, the client may have a strong social prominence motivation. Clients with this pattern expect and enjoy a lot of attention and positive feedback.
- If the client is warm (A+), emotionally sensitive (I+), or group-dependent (Q2-), he or she may be primarily affiliative or oriented toward emotional sensitivity and interpersonal nurturance. For such persons, the most important aspect of the therapeutic interaction is the establishment of a positive affective relationship. They will be interested in the therapist's compassion, empathy, and sensitivity to feelings, and they are likely to appreciate signs of caring, support, and direction from the professional. Low scorers (A-, I-) are likely to find such an approach too "touchy-feely" and to respect a more objective, detached, practical focus.
- If the client has a high score on Dominance (E+) in conjunction with high scores on Social Boldness (H+), Vigilance (L+), or Self-Reliance (Q2+), the client may have dominance or control as a primary motive. Such persons like to be in charge and have things their own way, and are not very open to advice from others. The professional might try to enlist the power of the dominance motive in the therapy enterprise (e.g., by asking, "When you behave that way, does it help you get what you want?") when discussing unproductive behavior. The realization that the ill-considered behavior is actually frustrating their goals can help to motivate change. Low scorers tend to be submissive (E-), shy (H-), dependent (Q2-), and to seek support and direction.

- If the scores on the primaries within global Self-Control are high, the client may have order as a primary motive. Such persons tend to pursue concrete tasks and well-defined goals in an organized, disciplined manner (Q3+, M-) and to follow rules and standards conscientiously (G+). They prefer sessions that are organized, focused, and proceed in a structured, systematic manner. If they trust the professional, they follow advice and put suggestions into practice.

Step 4

In preparation for client-counselor interaction, Step 4 involves evaluating the client's typical interpersonal style by consulting the patterns of primary scores within Extraversion and Independence global scales. The following patterns are among the most likely to present in a significant way in a counseling or consulting session:

- If Dominance (E) or Self-Reliance (Q2) is high, the client probably wants to do things his or her own way and may be resistant to advice or suggestions. This effect may be increased if L+ or Q1+ is present. Rather than get into a power struggle with such clients, professionals may do best at developing a collaborative relationship if they act as a consultant—someone off whom the client can bounce their ideas. An appropriate question to ask such a person is, "Well, what works best for you?"
- If the client is highly aloof (A-), self-reliant (Q2+), or suspicious (L+), he or she is likely to be withdrawn and to find close interaction unrewarding. Such clients are likely to have serious trust issues that may become the focus in extended counseling sessions.
- If the client is high on Warmth (A+) and low on Self-Reliance (Q2-), he or she is likely to have a strong need for companionship, support, and approval. If the pattern is pronounced, the client may seem dependent and needy.

Step 5

The final step in preparing for client-counselor interaction involves gaining a sense of the client's emotional resources and resilience. This step involves evaluating the primary scales that contribute to the global Anxiety scale or involve the concept of self-esteem:

- Average to above-average scores on Emotional Stability (C+) suggest that the client has better resources for dealing with difficult situations, feelings, and impulses and thus often does well in psychotherapy. However, extremely high scores (especially combined with a high Impression Management score or a very low O- score) may indicate that the individual is not open to admitting problems or anxieties. Low scores (C-) often indicate emotional reactivity and an inability in moderating volatile feelings or impulses. Low scorers may have difficulty talking objectively or productively about their problems. However, low scores can also be the result of transitory stress or situational problems.

- High scores on Apprehension (O+) indicate self-doubt and insecurity, and high scores on Tension (Q4) indicate a driven, easily frustrated style. Although they do indicate that the client is uncomfortable, high scores on Apprehension or Tension by themselves do not have such a pervasive effect on overall functioning as do low Emotional Stability (C-) scores.

- If the client is high on Apprehension (O+) and low on Extraversion traits (aloof, A-; serious, F-; shy, H-; self-reliant, Q2+), the client may shun social connections out of a sense of personal unworthiness or because they have developed negative expectations about relationships. Such persons often respond well to an attentive, supportive nondirective approach that gradually challenges their low self-worth or negative expectations.

- If clients show strong guilt (O+) plus a disregard of society's rules (G-), the individual may break rules and then feel guilty about it. For adolescents, this pattern can signal both current and future difficulty, and success is sometimes achieved in programs specifically designed to help them raise their Rule-Consciousness (G-) scores.

- If the client is emotionally reactive (C-) and either shy (H-), insecure (O+), or unrestrained (Q3-) as well, the client may show deficiencies in a sense of self-efficacy and also concrete deficiencies in taking action. Suggestions for activities that will help the person build a sense of self-efficacy are advised, such as taking music lessons, developing a hobby, caring for a pet, and participating in athletic activities. A behavioral self-management plan can be helpful, particularly if it involves training in breaking down tasks into achievable steps.

- If the client shows a combination of Dominance (E+), Social Boldness (H+), and tough rationality (I-) or self-assurance (O-), an archetypal male temperament is indicated. These individuals tend to be confident, fearless, forceful, and tough. They tend to project a "macho" image of invincibility. This often involves denial of sensitive or vulnerable feelings in oneself and others. Such persons are not prone to seek therapy, and prefer counseling interactions to be unemotional, factual, and to the point.

- If both global Anxiety and the primary Perfectionism (Q3) are high, the client probably experiences anxiety as painful but not paralyzing and should be self-disciplined and focused enough to take appropriate problem-solving steps. In this scoring pattern, the anxiety is bound by the high level of organized energy and focus signaled by the extreme score on Perfectionism. Persons with this pattern may respond well to reassurance and encouragement.

The preceding inferential statements are based on years of experience with the 16PF Questionnaire by several different practitioners. Conclusions were also tested in ratings by another group of practitioners (reported in the scale interactions section of chapter 3) and by a group of practitioners who work with adolescents. Overall, the pattern interpretations of 16PF variables received high marks in both adult and adolescent samples, receiving a *good* rating, which ranged from 65% of the time for some patterns to 100% of the time for others.

Using the 16PF Questionnaire to Anticipate Aspects of the Client's Personality That Could Hinder Self-Awareness, Progress, and Free Communication

In a counseling or consulting interaction, the client often displays set ways of perceiving the world that may represent specific resistances and misperceptions.

The following guidelines provide hypotheses about a client's potential resistances and misperceptions based on 16PF scores:

- If Rule-Consciousness (G+) and Perfectionism (Q3+) are both very high, the client may see the world according to unbending moral rules or unrealistically high standards. Effective communication and awareness may be blocked by attitudes and behaviors of rigid perfectionism, conformity, and exactitude.
- If Vigilance (L) is high along with global Anxiety, the client may believe that others are taking advantage of him or her or treating him or her unfairly. Effective communication may be blocked by attitudes of distrust, resentment, or passive resistance.
- If Social Boldness is high (H+) along with overall global Extraversion, the client may overvalue their own needs, feelings, and opinions and feel free to express them. Effective communication may be blocked by attitudes of exaggerated self-importance. If Anxiety is also low (particularly O-), the client may have the misperception that "only I am important" and block effective communication by attitudes and behaviors of exaggerated self-interest.
- If Extraversion is very low, the client may have the belief that "people are meaningless to me" or that "getting close to others may lead to control, manipulation, or abuse." Effective communication may be blocked by withdrawal and detachment.
- If Extraversion scores (especially A- and Q2+) are very low and Anxiety is very high, the client may misperceive his or her world as full of rejection and criticism, and he or she may block effective communication by hypersensitivity and expectations of rejection.
- If Independence is very low and Extraversion is low, the client may have an attitude of helplessness and may block effective communication by exaggerated compliance and submissiveness.
- If Tough-Mindedness is high (particularly I-) and Self-Control is low (particularly G- or Q3-), the client may have the attitude (common in adolescence) that "the rules aren't for me" and block effective communication by lying.

- Low scores on such impulse-control indicators as Rule-Consciousness (G-), Perfectionism (Q3-), and Emotional Stability (C-) are suggestive of acting-out problems and the concomitant denial.

- A flat profile, a set of 16PF scores with scores uniformly in the 5 to 6 range (except Reasoning, B), might lead to a hypothesis that the client does not have a clear sense of self. Sometimes this pattern follows a great trauma, either psychological or physical, which inhibits people from talking about themselves. For an adolescent, this type of profile sometimes indicates the presence of a terrible secret that interferes with communication.

- Sometimes a client's scores just don't fit, and the person revealed in the 16PF profile is far different from the person presented in other information sources such as biographical or referral information, projective tests, or structured ratings. The professional might hypothesize a terrible secret and concomitant denial. Timothy Leary (1957) discusses this kind of anomaly. His general conclusion is that such an inconsistency signals efforts on the client's part to manage anxiety, which the client is unwilling or unable to share.

Using the 16PF Questionnaire to Point Out Strengths and Weaknesses in the Client's Makeup

Scores on the five global scales and their contributing primaries can be used to form hypotheses about a client's general strengths and weaknesses.

Extraversion

High Scores

Potential strengths of high scorers (A+, F+, H+, N-, Q2-) include having strong social skills: being able to form strong, supportive nurturing relationships with others; having a trusting, compassionate, and generous outlook toward others and being helpful to them; being spontaneous, optimistic, and energetic; being a cooperative, supportive, and constructive team member; and being able to speak up boldly and confidently in meeting new people and in confronting people and problems. Potential weaknesses of extremely high scorers include being impulsive, unreliable, and inattentive to risks; being overly dependent on interpersonal contact, approval, and support; being too trusting and forthright in situations in which guardedness or tact are called for; and being overconfident, loud, or brash.

Low Scores

Potential strengths of low scorers (A-, F-, H-, N+, Q2+) include detached objectivity and interpersonal sophistication; the capacity for quiet, thoughtful introspection and concentration; a willingness to function and make decisions autonomously and independently; low impulsivity and emotionality; and a tendency to remove oneself from the immediacy of social activity to concentrate on other important matters. Potential weaknesses include a lack of sensitivity and supportiveness to others; an inability to reach out and form close, rewarding attachments; a lack of social skills in interacting effectively and persuasively in facing conflicts and opportunities; an inability to collaborate and function constructively on a team; and a lack of energy, spontaneity, and optimism. Extreme introversion can also be very painful.

Anxiety

High Scores

Potential strengths of high scorers (C-, L+, O+, Q4+) include alertness to potential problems or threats from the environment; motivation to accomplish, do well, and improve; sensitivity to the pain of others; and motivation to stay out of trouble. Potential weaknesses of extremely high scorers include vulnerability to emotional upset, self-doubt, and low self-esteem; less-than-effective cognitive functioning; immaturity and unreliability; avoidance of necessary risks that offer opportunities for growth; and tendency to be impatient, temperamental, or aggressive.

Low Scores

Potential strengths of low scorers (C+, L-, O-, Q4-) include calmness, resilience, and resourcefulness in the face of stress and frustration; self-confidence, poise, and tranquility; potential for leadership; efficient cognitive functioning; the ability to make mature, rational, reliable decisions; and a trusting forgiving nature. Potential weaknesses of low scorers include being overconfident, complacent, and remorseless ; lacking vigilance and wariness in the presence of a threatening environment; insensitivity to criticism and low motivation for self-improvement or achievement; and insensitivity or lack of empathy for others.

Tough-Mindedness

High Scores

Potential strengths of high scorers (I-, M-, Q1-, A-) include a capacity to make decisions based on logical, objective, unsentimental considerations; freedom from being swayed or overcome by feelings or needs; ability to stay focused on concrete, practical issues; favorable adjustment to tasks involving things rather than people; and adherence to established, traditional ways of doing things. Potential weaknesses include lack of awareness, sensitivity, or compassion for the feelings and needs of oneself and others; the possibility of ignoring human values in making plans, judgments, and decisions; lack of imagination, vision, or understanding of the big picture; resistance to change and innovation; and intolerance of ambiguity. Those at the extremely high end of this scale may be out of touch with their feelings, and they may have difficulty relating to people of an artistic or emotional nature.

Low Scores

Potential strengths of low scorers (I+, M+, Q1+, A+) include awareness of and sensitivity to the feelings and needs of self and others; creativity and an appreciation of music, art, and nature; openness to intuitive and innovative solutions to problems; strong imagination and an interest in ideas and big issues; and tolerance of ambiguity. Potential weaknesses include oversensitivity to people, feelings, and needs; an undue stress on subjective, artistic issues rather than objective facts in making decisions and plans; and a tendency to be impractical and absentminded. Low scorers are generally more prone to stress than are those at the high end on this scale.

Independence

High Scores

Potential strengths of high scorers (E+, H+, L+, Q1+) include a penchant for speaking up, taking charge, and leading a group; a willingness to shoulder responsibility, confront problems, and fearlessly persevere toward goals; an ability to think strategically in competitive situations; and a willingness to experiment with innovative and original approaches. Potential weaknesses include a propensity to be overbearing, controlling, or aggressive; a tendency to devalue the status quo and be argumentative or oppositional; a tendency to egotistical, thick-skinned, and insensitive to risks; a tendency to be suspicious, resentful, and dogmatic; and the tendency to use others for one's own gains.

Low Scores

Potential strengths of low scorers (E-, H-, L-, Q1-) include being an adaptable, obedient follower of authority; being humble, modest, and nonaggressive; being sensitive, considerate, and tactful about others' feelings; being trusting, unsuspecting, and forgiving of others; respecting established, traditional ways of doing things; and possessing cooperative group skills. Potential weaknesses include being unable to make one's needs and opinions known or to pursue aspirations; having a proclivity to be intimidated, pushed around, and taken advantage of by others; being too shy to meet new people or try new things; and being too set in one's ways.

Self-Control

High Scores

Potential strengths of high scorers (G+, Q3+, F-, M-) include awareness of the importance of following rules, regulations, and moral standards; reliability in meeting goals through careful, thorough, well-organized work; and an ability to diligently focus on concrete, practical, and arduous tasks. Potential weaknesses include the possibility of being so compulsive about rules and details that high scorers lose sight of the big picture, a propensity to offend others by rigidly insisting that things be done perfectly, and a tendency to take life and duties so seriously that they forget to have fun. Persons with extremely high scores sometimes insist on being right at the expense of being successful.

Low Scores

Potential strengths of low scorers (G-, Q3-, F+, M+) on this scale include being flexible, imaginative, or spontaneous in their approach to life; having a favorable adjustment to an artistic way of life; and having a relaxed, uninhibited, casual attitude that can put others at ease. Potential weaknesses include showing carelessness and disorganized, impractical, or irresponsible behavior; not planning or achieving goals; being impulsive, flighty, or unreliable; and having a tendency toward interpreting the rules their own way.

Using the 16PF Questionnaire to Suggest Areas for Further Exploration by the Client

Many possibilities exist for using a client's scores to understand important areas for further exploration, and as a jumping-off place for discussion. The discussion that follows concerns general guidelines on how to initiate and address the topic of extreme client scores and is intended to stimulate counselors to generate their own ideas in this regard.

Although the examples in this section focus on the challenges and limitations inherent in extreme scores, generally emphasizing client strengths more than weaknesses is most constructive. Adopting a cautious approach in regard to interpreting very high or very low scores is recommended. Such scores may indicate characteristics that are central to the client's personality, and suggesting changes in such characteristics can threaten the client's goodwill. Although some persons with extreme scores are open to hearing about ways to approach change and appreciate having the support, others are not.

A client with an extremely high score on Warmth (A+) is usually noted for compassion and attention to others. Such a person may be encouraged to recognize some disadvantage in this otherwise excellent quality in terms of overdependence on social contact, feedback, and approval; an inability to be alone; or an inability to be objective. For very low scores on Warmth (A-), a counselor might discuss whether the client experiences his or her detachment as a problem and wishes assistance in changing. The counselor might explore negative assumptions about getting close to others; however, changes on basic traits like Warmth can be slow to accomplish. Alternatively, a person sometimes can learn to adopt an attitude of benevolence as a substitute for interpersonal warmth; this can be accomplished by practicing wishing well to others, often without even verbalizing the sentiment.

Unless a client needs specific reassurance about intellectual capacities, avoid comments about the challenges indicated by a low score on Reasoning (B-). If further exploration is warranted because of a very low score, an intelligence test can be administered to verify the Reasoning score and to check for possible variances (e.g., between verbal and mathematical abilities). Knowing the reason for the low score can provide information on how to structure counseling sessions. For example, additional testing might confirm that the client has low intelligence or might indicate that the client was possibly distracted, unmotivated, or depressed at the time of the testing or has limited reading skills. For high scorers a general statement is often sufficient (e.g., "You seem to have enough intellectual ability for almost anything that interests you").

Clients with very low scores on Emotional Stability (C-) generally recognize that they are emotionally labile, react strongly to stress, and lack endurance. Their recognition of these usually makes them receptive to counseling, but they may react strongly to negative observations. Occasionally, people who are unaware of their instabilities score very high on this scale. Because they are out of touch with these vulnerabilities, such clients are unlikely to accept suggestions for further exploration in these areas or assistance for change. Extreme high scorers (C+) generally are concerned with presenting a picture of themselves as okay and their lives as completely fine. They may have trouble recognizing or accepting their problems or difficulties. Approaching their problems obliquely rather than directly can be advantageous.

A client's score on Dominance (E) can open many possible routes for exploration. High (E+) scorers tend to make broad statements about what most people think or feel, even though careful exploration may reveal otherwise. They may be unaware of others' reactions to their attempts at control or manipulation. More egalitarian methods of decision making may be worth exploring. A useful way to work with such persons is to enlist their dominance in the counseling work. Consider the example of a CEO with anger management problems: The counselor asked the CEO, "When you escalate some provocation into a fit of anger, do you get what you want?" This question not only appealed to the CEO's dominance but also was a springboard for teaching him how to handle escalations of anger. By learning to ask whether the rising anger he was feeling would achieve his purpose in a situation, the CEO became adept at short-circuiting escalations that would be ill serving. High scorers may also get into power struggles with the therapist or test limits in therapy.

Some very low scorers on Dominance (E-) seem at ease with a deferential, accommodating stance and are reluctant to be in charge of anyone. Such reluctance can become an issue when a client wants to advance in a job that requires supervision of others; he or she may learn to act like a boss but is unlikely to enjoy holding the reins of authority like a high (E+) scorer. It may be useful to explore low-scoring clients' fears about possible rejection or punishment if they disagree or stand up for themselves. Worthy of discussion are situations in which the client gets pushed into doing things that he or she does not want to do and ends up feeling badly treated by others.

High scorers on Liveliness (F+) may not realize how their energy and exuberance limits their ability to stay focused, achieve their goals, or be reflective. Exploration might also be helpful in understanding the draining effect that their animated, effusive style has on others, especially if their interest in projects or people is short-lived. Extreme low scorers (F-) may benefit from exploring reasons that they don't allow themselves to have more fun in life or act more spontaneously. Approaches to developing more social connections may be explored.

Very low scores on Rule-Consciousness (G-) are frequently accompanied by low levels of achievement in life, although the client may not see it as a problem. For example, bright adolescents can sometimes get by in high school even with poor study skills and work habits, but their irrational attitude of "Oh, it'll all work out" is an inadequate panacea for the pressures associated with college or a job. Low scorers may not have fully internalized society's rules about a range of things. Clients at the high end of the scale (G+) may have difficulty seeing that their highly correct behavior has any drawbacks. Nonetheless, being overly focused on conventional rules or being inflexible, preachy, or self-righteous can affect success in a variety of settings and may be an appropriate focus in counseling interactions.

People with very low scores on Social Boldness (H-) may be sensitive to rejection and have difficulty in socially demanding or challenging situations or in actively pursuing their interests or goals. Low (H-) scorers who are in occupations that typically exhibit high scores may be able to do the job, but they frequently experience discomfort. High scorers (H+) are seldom aware of areas for self-improvement. Particularly if clients are also high on self-assurance (O-), they may benefit from exploring the effects that their boldness or self-centeredness may be having on others.

High scorers on Sensitivity (I+) are more likely than low scorers to seek therapy or counseling, whereas the reverse is sometimes true for a consultation in an industrial setting. High Sensitivity scorers (I+) are attuned to emotional issues and eager for sympathy and support, whereas low Sensitivity scorers (I-) may lack awareness or understanding of other people and their emotional responses, leading to poor social skills and decision making at work. Moderating emotional hypersensitivity (I+) is difficult. One approach involves making high scorers aware of the difficulty of satisfying high levels of emotional needs. In addition, the sensitive person can learn skills of self-nurturance—how to attend to oneself with kindness. Generally, low scorers seek emotional support in sessions, and they may benefit from learning to balance their emotional approach with a concern for practical realities. Consultants working with executives with low (I-) sensitivity may point out the importance of leaders' understanding their people in all respects and that emotional responsiveness is one such respect. Low scorers are likely to need logical, objective reasons for learning the language of emotion, and they may have difficulty accepting their own vulnerable feelings.

Clients displaying high scores on Vigilance (L+) generally have trust issues and are wary about others' motivations. They may show a tendency to be suspicious, envious, resentful, and hostile; to hold grudges; or be passively aggressive. If a basic trust can be established with the client, the counselor can risk a comment on the difficulty of achieving any happiness while harboring such feelings (getting into arguments about the veracity of their suspicions should be avoided). If that comment is accepted and digested, the next step is to gauge the degree to which the client believes in their suspicious, distrustful feelings. If the client can acknowledge the irrationality and uselessness of the thoughts that accompany such feelings, the client can begin to work on letting go of the habit of pursuing their suspicious thoughts.

High scorers on Abstractedness (M+) may be unaware of the absentmindedness that results from their focus on abstract ideas. They may benefit from finding reliable ways to take care of practical realities. Low scorers (M-) may benefit from seeing how their practical and task-oriented focus sometimes results in their overlooking matters of bigger importance.

People with high scores on Privateness (N+) may benefit from exploring why they are so hesitant to reveal personal information even to friends and relatives. They can be encouraged to see that it is hard to have close or intimate relationship under these circumstances and that others may be alienated by finding out only after the fact about important events and decisions the client has made. People with low scores (N-) may find it helpful to explore how their lack of reserve affects them in situations that call for tact, formality, or guardedness about personal information.

Clients with high scores on Apprehension (O+) are prone to worrying, feelings of guilt and self-doubt, and pessimism. High scorers resist change but can yield to persistent, intelligent attempts to modify their belief system; they can be helped to see that their fears are usually based on false or irrational beliefs. The pangs of worry and guilt that burden high scorers are so unpleasant that usually they are eager to try to obtain relief. Clients with very low scores on this scale (O-) are generally unaware of any areas for self-improvement, and negative feedback may evoke defensive reactions. They may also be insensitive to real threats that arise around them.

Clients with high scores on Openness to Change (Q1+) may have difficulty accepting traditional, established ways of doing things or things that cannot be changed. If they are also dominant (E+), they may have trouble accepting instruction from authority figures. Low scorers (Q1-) may be so set in their ways that they avoid even positive changes. They may view anything new or untraditional as suspect or unworthy of attention.

Scores at either extreme of Self-Reliance (Q2) can merit attention from a counselor or consultant. At the high end are people who are so insistent on making independent decisions and maintaining their autonomy that they are virtually cut off from social feedback. They may have trouble working collaboratively with others and establishing close relationships. It may be useful to explore their fears about relying on others or asking for assistance. In contrast, those with very low scores are frequently too dependent on the companionship and support of others. It may be useful to explore the drawbacks of being too accommodating and dependent on others.

Clients with very high scores on Perfectionism (Q3+) have affirmed test items about being a conscientious, persistent worker, always on time, and so forth. Such idealistic standards can be problematic, especially if the high scorer believes that others should be perfectionists too. A high score may signal an insistence on personal perfection that is unattainable, burdensome, and not in the person's best interests. That is, the individual is so insistent on perfection that no allowance is made for relaxation or imperfections of any kind. Low scorers (Q3-) may have such a tolerance for disorder that they have not developed good habits for meeting their responsibilities or a strong, coherent way to organize their energy and life. They may have difficulty reaching their goals or using their abilities.

Clients with high scores on Tension (Q4+) are likely to feel tense, driven, and overwrought; this may be a transitory reaction to current stress, or it might be chronic. In addition to exploring the source of the tension, regular exercise, biofeedback, meditation, and other typical approaches to "Type A" personality traits may be helpful. Clients with low scores may benefit from exploring the effect that their relaxed state has on their drive, ambition, and motivation level.

COUPLES COUNSELING

In addition to its use in individual counseling situations, the 16PF Questionnaire also has application in specialized settings such as couples counseling. Typically, both partners complete the test and then review their own scores and their partner's scores. As noted by practitioners, the advantages of this approach are that it (a) provides clients with clear and reasonable knowledge about their own and their partner's basic personality traits in a positive, objective manner; (b) lowers costs by reducing the amount of therapist time needed to get to know the couple; (c) reduces the confusion and anxiety connected to the experience of self-revelation; and (d) reduces the complexity of an inherently complex situation and helps predict areas and styles of couple conflict.

Traditional psychological thinking about human attraction and pairing has been affected by at least three general principles:

- The principle of general adjustment, which is that psychologically healthy persons are more likely to be found in satisfying relationships
- The principle of similarity, which is that persons who are more similar are more likely to be found in satisfactory relationships
- The principle of complementarity, which is that people pair with those who differ from them to make up for their own weaknesses or lack of some characteristic

The first two principles are well supported by research. The third principle is supported by anecdotal evidence and theory but not by quantitative research.

Many psychologists who counsel couples often prefer to use a special version of the 16PF Questionnaire that produces the 16PF Couple's Counseling Report (CCR; see appendix). The results are supportive of the first two principles defined previously and provide useful information about which

16PF scales are most implicated in couple differences and dissatisfaction. With regard to the first principle, research findings indicate that persons most satisfied with their relationships differ from those least satisfied on the primary scales that contribute to the global Anxiety complex. The satisfied partners are higher on Emotional Stability (C+) and lower on Vigilance (L-), Apprehension (O-), and Tension (Q4-). The satisfied and dissatisfied partners also differ on Openness to Change (Q1), a scale that is not part of Anxiety. The general conclusion is that persons who are higher on Anxiety are prone to lower satisfaction in relationships.

The second principle, which states that persons who are more similar to their partners tend toward higher satisfaction in relationships, is supported by early 16PF research (Cattell & Nesselroade, 1967). Generally, partners who are more similar in their 16PF profiles are in more stable (and, by inference, more satisfactory) marriages. These findings with the 16PF are supported by a number of general studies on the similarity of married couples in physical characteristics, in demographic and sociological characteristics, and in personality and attitudes.

Even more specifically, recent research with the 16PF Fifth Edition has shown that differences between partners on certain primary scales are significantly related to couple dissatisfaction. Particularly implicated are Sensitivity (I), Abstractedness (M), Perfectionism (Q3), and Vigilance (L). Of somewhat lesser import in marital dissatisfaction are differences on Reasoning (B) and Emotional Stability (C).

Sensitivity (I), also an important scale in differentiating among occupations, has substantial influence on the values, interests, cognitive style, and preferences of partners. In fact, a significant difference in scores on this scale can indicate that the partners not only misjudge one another but also lack understanding for each other. One partner may focus on feelings and make judgments based on how people feel (I+), whereas the other may be more influenced by facts, costs, and logical issues (I-).

Differences on Abstractedness (M) also can create lack of understanding because of opposite perceptual styles: High scorers focus on abstract ideas and imagination whereas low scorers focus on concrete, literal issues. The second author notes that partners who are both high on Abstractedness entertain each other with their imaginings in a way that can be very binding. Such couples enjoy each other's company, have in-jokes, and sometimes even develop a kind of personal language.

Differences on Perfectionism (Q3) seem to operate in much the same way as differences on Sensitivity (I). The partner who scores higher on the scale often complains that the other is a loose cannon and behaves in ways that are unconscientious, disorganized, or unreliable. The partner who scores lower on the scale finds the other to be uptight, rigid, and too focused on details. Consequently, the partners have difficulty understanding each other.

When one partner scores several points higher than the other does on Vigilance (L), both are frequently unhappy because of it. The one with the higher score, troubled by an unreasoning tendency to suspicion, has difficulty trusting the other and indulging in simple enjoyment of the other. The one with the lower score, aware of the constant scrutiny of the other, grows weary of avoiding even innocent behavior that may be viewed as suspicious.

The preceding research findings indicate that marital dissatisfaction is related to partner differences on Scales I, L, M, and Q3 over a research sample of more than 300 couples. However, differences on other scales may be important in individual cases. For example, some practitioners note that large differences on Warmth (A), Self-Reliance (Q2), or Social Boldness (H) can indicate problems that a couple has over how much they should entertain, how sociable they should be as a couple, or how much they themselves should interact or do things together. A person scoring very high on scales A or H or low on Q2 always wants to be around people. If such a person is married to someone who scores in the Introverted direction on A and H, the couple will be pulled in opposite directions. The Extraverted partner, in order to satisfy his or her need for social contact, may decide to socialize without the other partner, who would rather spend some time alone, thus putting stress on the marriage.

In similar ways, pair differences on other scales can be used to objectify marital problems that are brought to a counseling situation. Partners may be helped by this means to develop a compassionate understanding of the differences between them and to see them merely as differences, devoid of the emotion-laden blaming that is often found in couple misunderstandings.

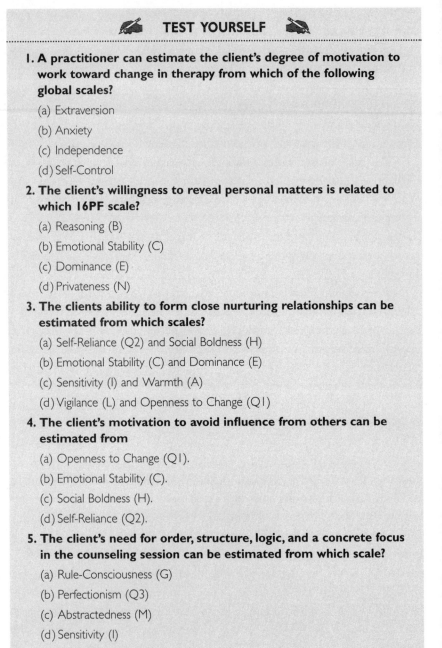

1. **A practitioner can estimate the client's degree of motivation to work toward change in therapy from which of the following global scales?**

   (a) Extraversion

   (b) Anxiety

   (c) Independence

   (d) Self-Control

2. **The client's willingness to reveal personal matters is related to which 16PF scale?**

   (a) Reasoning (B)

   (b) Emotional Stability (C)

   (c) Dominance (E)

   (d) Privateness (N)

3. **The clients ability to form close nurturing relationships can be estimated from which scales?**

   (a) Self-Reliance (Q2) and Social Boldness (H)

   (b) Emotional Stability (C) and Dominance (E)

   (c) Sensitivity (I) and Warmth (A)

   (d) Vigilance (L) and Openness to Change (Q1)

4. **The client's motivation to avoid influence from others can be estimated from**

   (a) Openness to Change (Q1).

   (b) Emotional Stability (C).

   (c) Social Boldness (H).

   (d) Self-Reliance (Q2).

5. **The client's need for order, structure, logic, and a concrete focus in the counseling session can be estimated from which scale?**

   (a) Rule-Consciousness (G)

   (b) Perfectionism (Q3)

   (c) Abstractedness (M)

   (d) Sensitivity (I)

   (e) all of the above

6. The client's preference for direction and instruction in the counseling session can be estimated from which scales:

(a) Dominance (E) and Self-Reliance (Q2)

(b) Reasoning (B) and Perfectionism (Q3)

(c) Social Boldness (H) and Privateness (N)

(d) Sensitivity (I) and Apprehensiveness (O)

7. A potential strength of high Anxiety that might be suggested for a client's consideration is that the client will be alert to potential problems. True or False?

8. A potential strength of low Tough-Mindedness that might be suggested for a client's consideration is awareness and sensitivity to the feelings and needs of others. True or False?

Answers: 1. b; 2. d; 3. c; 4. d; 5. e; 6. a; 7. True; 8. True

Seven

CAREER AND ORGANIZATIONAL APPLICATIONS

This chapter was cowritten by Jim Schuerger, Mary L. Kelly, and Scott Bedwell. Mary and Scott contributed the section on the predictive capacities of the 16PF Questionnaire in work settings. With the permission of the publisher, they adapted this technical information from the *16PF Select Manual* (Kelly, 1999) to make it relevant for all 16PF Questionnaire users, both experienced and novice.

CAREER CHOICE

How many of us know someone who is proficient at a job but is fundamentally unhappy in it? Consider the following anecdote, which involves a consultant working with an executive of a large retail company. While studying the 16PF scores of the female manager of one of the company's stores, the executive asked the consultant "What do you think of her as a manager?" The consultant noted that he would not have chosen her as a manager because her scores differed so much from typical manager scores, showing much more emotional Sensitivity (I+) and much less Independence and Dominance (E+). "But she's one of my best managers!" the executive responded. A few weeks after this discussion, the executive reported that the manager turned in her resignation, saying that she did not feel like a good fit in the job and wanted to pursue a career in social work.

This anecdote illustrates two points: (a) being proficient at a job is not the same as feeling happy in the job and (b) that people are more comfortable in a job when it is a good fit with their personality and skills. Feeling that a job is a good fit is an example of a broad principle that can be paraphrased in the following way: People like to be around other people when they feel similar to them; this is the "similarity principle" that is so important in mating,

221

selecting a job, choosing friends, and building a team. How to help people determine the kind of job in which they would be both proficient and a good fit is the topic of the first section of this chapter. The second section of this chapter considers fit from the employer's point of view, emphasizing how to choose employees best suited to particular positions.

A Good Fit to a Job

A variety of factors help determine whether a person can be a good fit to a job. These factors include but are not limited to ability, career interest, and personality. In terms of ability, for example, being a physicist requires more general intellectual ability than being a laborer. Furthermore, certain jobs require having more of a specific ability than others. For example, being an engineer requires more mathematical ability than being an English teacher. Having high ability for a job does not necessarily translate into having a high level of comfort in the job. People with high ability can feel out of place in a lower-ability job not only because they are unchallenged by the work but also because their coworkers often lack similar ability levels.

Another factor that determines job fit is career interest. Career interest can be measured by a person's responses to inventory items. For example, nearly 100 years ago, E. K. Strong discovered that persons in one occupation differ systematically from persons in other occupations in terms of their expressed interests. This finding is consistent with the similarity principle noted previously, and it constitutes the research basis for many interest inventories.

In addition to ability and interest, personality characteristics affect people's comfort level in a job. Personality characteristics that are particularly job related can be measured by the 16PF Questionnaire. For example, being comfortable talking to and interacting with new people is an important characteristic for a salesperson. The 16PF scale that taps being comfortable with new people is Social Boldness (H). Both experimental evidence and the experience of practitioners verify that having a successful sales career is difficult for people who score in the shy (H-) direction on this scale.

In a similar manner, a school counselor or physical therapist show a better fit with their jobs if they are higher on Warmth (A+) and Sensitivity (I+). On the other hand, a mechanic, electrician, or pilot show a better fit with their job skills and interests if they are not interpersonal in their focus (A-), if they think in a logical, objective manner (I-), and attend to practical, concrete issues (M-). Thus, comfort on the job is related to personality characteristics in many complex ways.

16PF SCORES AND CAREER COUNSELING

The 16PF as a measure of general personality characteristics can be useful in career counseling to address the issue of similarity of client and job as well as a number of other concerns. Interpreting a client's scores on the 16PF might include one or more of the following steps:

- Evaluate the 16PF profile to gain an overall view of the client's personality, including expectations for client-counselor interactions.
- Generate hypotheses about the client's general career-related behaviors.
- Generate hypotheses about the client's personality fit to various occupations in terms of personality.
- Integrate information from the 16PF profile with that from other relevant sources such as measures of ability, occupational interests, client history, and interview information.
- Generate hypotheses relevant to client's reason for seeking career counseling
  - If the purpose is to discover and explore career options, consider hypotheses about potential occupations.
  - If the client has already chosen an occupation, advance hypotheses about potential job matches or mismatches.
  - If the client is already in a job and cannot easily change, generate hypotheses about developmental possibilities.

Evaluate the 16PF Profile to Get an Overall View of the Client's Personality

The initial step of gaining a comprehensive view of the individual's personality is discussed in detail in chapter 4. Chapter 5 also provides information about developing expectations about the client-consultant interaction and how to facilitate that interaction.

Generate Hypotheses About General Career-Related Aspects of Behavior

Several common aspects of job behavior can be addressed using 16PF scores, including

- Leadership preference
- Preferred level of predictability and structure on the job
- Preference for working alone versus working with others
- Preferred manner of information-processing and solving problems

In helping to determine each of these aspects of behavior, several 16PF scales or scale interactions are relevant.

Being a Leader

Indication of leadership potential by scores on the 16PF is the subject of considerable research and practical experience, with the main findings being cited in *The 16PF Fifth Edition Administrator's Manual* (Russell & Karol, 2002) and *The 16PF Fifth Edition Technical Manual* (Conn & Rieke, 1994). A long history points to high Extraversion, low Anxiety, high Tough-Mindedness, high Independence, and high Self-Control as strong indicators of leadership potential among the global scales.

At the primary scale level, high Dominance (E+) is a main predictor of a tendency to seek influence over people and things. Within Extraversion, above-average scores on Warmth (A+), Liveliness (F+), and Social Boldness (H+) are indicators of an ease and facility with social interactions. Within Tough-Mindedness, high scores on Openness to Change (Q1+) indicate an interest in new ideas and approaches, and below-average scores on Sensitivity (I-) and Abstractedness (M-) suggest a tendency to be logical, objective, and practical in finding solutions. In the area of low Anxiety, leaders tend to be more self-assured and resilient (O-), more patient and able to handle frustration (Q4-), more trusting and cooperative (L-), and better at coping calmly and persistently with life's ups and downs. Leaders also tend to show above-average reasoning ability (B+).

Handling Predictability and Structure

Scores on the primary scales Rule-Consciousness (G) and Perfectionism (Q3) best indicate a client's attitude toward structure. People scoring on the high end of these scales (G+, Q3+) prefer a well-organized environment with clear guidelines, procedures, and goals. They believe in following rules and having things orderly. People scoring on the low end of these scales (G-, Q3-) often chafe at a highly structured, organized, restrictive environment, preferring one that rewards or at least tolerates some flexibility.

Preference for Working Alone Versus Working With Others

The chief indicator of this preference is the Extraversion global scale. High-scoring clients probably would not flourish in an environment that puts severe limits on social contact during the workday because they are essentially interested in people (A+) and companionship (Q2-), and because they enjoy the excitement, stimulation, and attention (H+, F+). On the other hand, clients who score low on Extraversion usually would find the demands of a high social-contact job more than they could handle. This difficulty can be particularly acute if they are aloof (A-), quiet (F-), shy (H-), or individualistic (Q2+). For such introverted persons, meeting new people is painful, and continuous demands that they do so can be aversive. Introverted people can learn to act in an extraverted way, but at a cost.

Preferred Manner of Managing Information and Solving Problems

In terms of 16PF scores, the Reasoning (B) score is a strong indicator of preferences in learning style and in processing information. High scorers tend to be quick thinkers and learners who are able to handle abstractions, whereas low scorers tend to be more deliberate learners who prefer dealing with concrete concerns. Scores on other primary scales can provide insight into other preferences for handling information and solving problems:

- Higher scores on Abstractedness (M+), Sensitivity (I+), and Openness to Change (Q1+) indicate an abstract, imaginative style that focuses on understanding meanings and patterns through intuitive and creative processes. Low scorers (I-, M-, Q1-) have a more grounded focus on immediate facts and practical realities and tend to use logical, objective thinking.
- A confident, objective, detached approach rather than one based on feelings or human values is suggested by lower scores on Warmth (A-), Sensitivity (I-), and Apprehension (O-).
- A decisive approach favoring closure rather than flexibility and spontaneity is suggested by higher scores on Rule-Consciousness (G) and Perfectionism (Q3) and a lower score on Abstractedness (M).

Generate Hypotheses About the Client's
Fit to Various Kinds of Occupations

In considering the fit of a client's personality to occupations, a professional can rely on his or her experience as well as on resources such as published occupational profiles and computer-generated 16PF reports (e.g., the Personal Career Development Profile or the Basic Interpretive Report). In addition, a common map of occupations, such as the Holland types, is invaluable in helping to organize the client's search for a suitable fit.

Information about specific jobs can be useful to clients who have narrowed down their choices, but such limited data are less useful to clients who are still exploring various occupational options. Fortunately, John Holland, a vocational counselor and researcher, addressed this need by creating a six-group typology. Holland describes his six types as a system of personality differences derived from occupational interests (Holland, 1997). A brief description of each type is presented in Rapid Reference 7.1.

The 6PF profiles scores of particular occupational groups can be productively sorted into their respective Holland types. The second author's occupational database contains more than 230 16PF job profiles with each profile representing a separate sample of persons in a particular occupation (Schuerga & Watterson, 1996). Below are summarized the typical 16PF score differences among the six Holland types.

The Realistic Type

The 16PF global scales that characterize this type are low scores on Anxiety, and high scores on Tough-Mindedness and Self-Control. These scores form a defining psychological pattern for the Realistic type of someone who is tough, calm, and task-oriented. Scores on the primary scales mirror this pattern for the Realistic occupations; these include being aloof (A-), unemotional (I-), practical (M-), confident (O-), calm (C+), rule-bound (G+), and self-disciplined (Q3+).

The Investigative Type

The global scale scores for this type generally are high on Independence, low on Extraversion and Anxiety, and medium to high on Tough-Mindedness. Scores on Self-Control are varied within the type but tend to be above average. Defining qualities for this type beyond high Reasoning (B+) include being aloof (A-), serious (F-), self-reliant (Q2+), logical and unemotional (I-),

≣Rapid Reference 7.1

The Six Holland Types

The *Realistic* type is characterized by an interest in orderly mechanical, manual, or outdoor activities. Persons who fit this type are more interested in tools, machines, and objects rather than people, and tend to take a tough, practical, no-nonsense approach to life. Typical occupations include carpenter, electrician, mechanic, and farmer.

The *Investigative* type is characterized by interests in science and mathematics and in problem solving and conceptual thinking. Persons in this type enjoy challenging work with ideas and symbols, can manage ambiguity, and do not care for repetitive tasks or work involving people and emotions. Occupational examples include scientist, computer analyst, and physician.

The *Artistic* type is characterized creative self expression and an interest in things of beauty as well as in the graphic, musical, literary, or performing arts. Persons of this type are not bothered by ambiguity, chafe at restraints, and tend to be nonconformist. Occupational examples include art teacher, writer, musician, or illustrator.

The *Social* type is characterized by an interest in helping or caring for others and encouraging them to live fuller, more satisfying lives. The quality of interpersonal relationships is very important for persons of this type. Typical occupations include counselor, teacher, nurse, or camp director.

The *Enterprising* type is characterized by an interest in organizing, persuading, or leading people; that is, this type's interest in others is characterized by dominance rather than by nurturance. Persons of this type value power and possessions. They are often ambitious, assertive, confident, and action-oriented rather than thought-oriented. Examples include marketing manager, salesman, executive, and attorney.

The *Conventional* type is characterized by an interest in accomplishing tasks or managing projects through organized, orderly, and efficient procedures. They are good at processing information, keeping detailed records, and operating computers and business machines. They tend to be conforming, to prefer clear instructions, and to dislike ambiguity. Occupational examples include accountant, payroll clerk, and credit investigator.

dominant (E+), innovative (Q1+), absorbed in ideas (M+), calm (C+), confident (O-), composed (Q4-), and self-disciplined (Q3+).

The Artistic Type

People in occupations of this type tend to score low on the global scales Tough-Mindedness and Extraversion, high on Independence, and medium on both Anxiety and Self-Control. The low Tough-Mindedness (in the receptive, creative direction) is a defining characteristic of the type. The low Extraversion and high Independence denote the artist's abilities to shut out other persons and to pursue their original, unique views. Although in the average range, Anxiety, is higher than for any other type, consistent with the stereotype of the neurotic, isolated artist. On the primary scales, this type tends to be bright (B+), detached (A-), individualistic (Q2+), adventurous (H+), dominant (E+), aesthetically sensitive (I+), imaginative (M+), innovative (Q1+), and nonconformist (G+).

The Social Type

Social occupations tend to have high scores on Extraversion, low scores on Tough-Mindedness and Anxiety, and above-average scores on Independence and Self-Control. On the 16PF primary scales, they tend to be warm (A+), outgoing (H+), genuine (N-), group-oriented (Q2-), emotionally sensitive (I+), calm (C+), trusting (L-), and open to change (Q1+). These scores suggest a concern for others that is sensitive, calm, and socially skilled.

The Enterprising Type

For this type, the overall 16PF pattern shows high scores on the primary scale Reasoning (B), high scores on the global scales Independence, Self-Control, and Extraversion, and low scores on Anxiety. This pattern emphasizes the bright, dominant, socially skilled, and task-focused qualities of the type. High Independence is a defining characteristic. On primary scales, this type tends to be dominant (E+), socially bold (H+), outgoing (A+), cheerful (F+), self-confident (O-), emotionally stable (C+), realistic (I-), and conscientious (G+, Q3+).

The Conventional Type

This type tends to score high on globals Self-Control and Tough-Mindedness, and below-average on globals Anxiety and Independence. Self-Control, a defining characteristic, captures the interest in organization, efficiency, and order that characterizes the type. On primary scales, this type tends to be rule-conscious (G+), logical and unsentimental (I-), focused on practical and concrete goals (M-), organized and self-disciplined (Q3+), and conventional (Q1-).

In summary, 16PF occupational profiles are generally consistent with Holland's type descriptions and with stereotypical perceptions. In spite of these reassuring score patterns, caution is necessary in interpreting a client's scores relative to these occupational types. Substantial differences are commonly found among the various occupations within any Holland type. Even within a specific occupation, persons will differ from one another in personality, depending on job functions and settings.

> ### CAUTION
>
> #### People in the Same Occupation Differ in Personality
>
> - Despite the existence of stable personality patterns in occupational types, a wide variety of scores can exist within a single occupation.
> - Avoid entering a counseling setting with fixed ideas about exactly where a client fits.

The 16PF patterns for Holland's types are presented here to help practitioners form hypotheses about the fit between a client's personality and occupational types. For more detailed 16PF occupational models, the *Handbook for the 16PF* (Cattell et al., 1992) remains an excellent resource. *The 16PF Fifth Edition Administrator's Manual* (Russell & Karol, 2002) does not present occupational profiles but does examine the relationship between the 16PF scales and the Holland types.

There are alternatives to comparing a client's scores with one of these profiles. For example, a practitioner could create a profile for a specific occupation based on a job. An even better alternative would be to empirically develop local profiles for common jobs. This method is most useful when a practitioner has worked for some time with a particular occupational group or a particular company. Another option would be to use a 16PF computerized interpretive report, such as the PCDP, which makes explicit comparisons between a client's profile and those of people in a large number of occupations.

Integrate 16PF Information With That From Other Sources

Most professionals depend on multiple sources of information in counseling clients about careers. Minimally, these sources usually include measures of a client's occupational interests, abilities, personality, and the client's work history. Whatever sources are selected, the accumulated information is most useful to the client when it is presented in an integrated manner.

If the information across several sources has consistent implications regarding occupational fit, it can reinforce the client's confidence in the counseling process and in the conclusions derived from the information. If the information leads in divergent directions, it can be a source of anxiety for the client. For example, a client may have an ability score below the typical level for an occupational area in which he or she is interested. Or a client might show an interest in management but be very low on Dominance (E), a defining characteristic for that kind of position. On a positive note, this divergence among information sources is important in its own right, a rich source for interpretation by the practitioner.

In a careful consideration of this topic, Lowman (1991) points out that little is known about cross-domain data relationships. He cites some early work on relationships between abilities and personality scales by Cattell (1987) and Cattell and Horn (1964), but he notes that there is "no theoretical or well-validated theoretical basis" for expectations in this matter. Thus, it remains a consideration for the professional's judgment. The interaction between career interests and 16PF scales discussed in this chapter represents generalizations that are supported not only by the authors' database and the test manuals, but also by published studies (e.g., Peraino & Willerman, 1983; Schuerger & Sfiligoj, 1998).

In spite of the lack of cross-domain information, evidence supports the predictive power of each domain separately. Lowman (1991) presents a chart that summarizes the known relationships in each domain. He also recommends several principles for integrating data sources in career counseling and provides guidelines for integrating materials across domains. The guidelines that follow are adapted from Lowman's work and supplemented by suggestions based on the authors' counseling experiences:

- Separately evaluate the data in each domain; that is, formulate hypotheses about the client's fit to various occupations from (a) interest data, (b) ability data, and (c) personality data. Consider each kind of data individually as though the others did not exist.
- Compare hypotheses across domains. If they are consistent, they suggest a clear career path.

- If the hypotheses are inconsistent across domains:
  - Interest and ability data should be given priority over personality data, reflecting the following maxim: "Motive for [substitute career interest here] wins."
  - Examine whether personality data indicate areas of special concentration within a field of interest. For example, if interests and ability data point to accounting, a client may be directed toward a consultative career in accounting if Extraversion is high or to a more "bean-counting" role in accounting if Extraversion is low.
  - Examine whether personality data indicate areas in which the client may need to learn compensatory behaviors. For example, if a person is high on interest in sales or management but low on the global scale Self-Control, the counselor may help the client forecast possible problems such as being late to meetings and missing deadlines. Then the counselor may suggest various ways to compensate for these anticipated problems, such as having a diligent assistant and using a personal electronic organizer.
  - If the ability data are inconsistent with interests, the client may need to find expression outside of the job. In such instances, personality data may help to clarify the reasons for the interests. For example, if a client shows interest in work below his or her ability level, personality characteristics that might weigh against high ambitions may need to be discussed.

Most clients present a mixed picture, with some personality scores consistent with their career interests and some inconsistent. Counselors need to alert clients to their level of consistency over the domains, and help clients not only explore the implications of any inconsistencies but also discover ways to compensate for them. Here is how a discussion about an inconsistency might be introduced in a counseling session:

Your score on [personality characteristic] is not very consistent with your interest score in [career interest]. You might find that if you get into [kind of work], you will feel different from other employees in [specific aspect] and may find your effectiveness is hampered in [some way]. Would you like to think of some ways in which you might compensate for this inconsistency?

A statement such as the preceding is most important when the personality scores are inconsistent with job-related interests or with a defining characteristic of an occupational type. Client patterns that are inconsistent are rare but need to be addressed when they do occur. The second author recalls a client who was a middle-aged man interested in obtaining a managerial position. His interests were in the area of Holland's Enterprising type but he had a low score on global Independence (4.5), well below what would be expected. A discussion of this client's scores began in the following manner:

> Your score on Independence is not very consistent with your interest in management or with your score on the Enterprising scale. If you get into management, you might find that you will feel different from other managers in that they will be more dominant and aggressive than you are. You may find that your effectiveness is hampered because you do not react to challenges as they do. You may want to think of some ways in which you can modify your attitudes or behavior to make it easier on yourself.

Generate Hypotheses Relevant to the Client's Reason for Seeking Career Counseling

Working with a high school or college student who has not moved toward a career goal is different from working with a 30-year-old who is uncomfortable in a job and wondering about a change. Some examples of how to help various types of clients understand their options are presented here.

A discussion of scores on the 16PF can help maximize options for a client who is confused about career possibilities, such as a college student. The counselor might begin by discussing the client's scores and the various kinds of occupations associated with those scores. The following are examples of statements that could be used to initiate a conversation about job implications relative to four of the 16PF global scores (excluding Anxiety):

- Extraversion is a measure of how interested you are in other persons and how effective you feel when you interact with others. A person high on this characteristic will often be seen as friendly, enthusiastic, socially visible, and group-oriented. Sales, management, and teaching are occupations that show high scores on this scale. A score below the average on this scale indicates a tendency towards Introversion. A person in the introverted direction is more comfortable with ideas, tasks, or things than with people. Artists, engineers, and technical workers tend to be introverted, with lower-than-average scores on this scale.

- Independence indicates a preference for being in charge or power-ful, such as being the leader of a group. Occupations with high scores on this characteristic are manager, doctor, and sales man-ager. Low scores on this characteristic show a preference for less visible activities and for group membership rather than group leadership. Among occupations with low scores are hands-on jobs such as mechanic or carpenter as well as jobs in clerical areas.

- Tough-Mindedness indicates a logical, pragmatic, no-nonsense approach to life. If you have a high score on this characteristic, you probably have an interest in things, such as machines and tools. Among occupations with high scores on this scale are mechanical jobs and some business positions that involve organi-zation and managing procedures. A low score indicates a prefer-ence for art, literature, and human relations. Typical occupations with low scores are those that are artistic as well as some in the helping professions such as nursing or counseling.

- Self-Control indicates how you answered questions about being conscientious or paying attention to detail and how well organized you are in your day-to-day activities. Students with higher scores on Self-Control often find it easier to get good grades than do those with low scores. People with high scores on this trait are in clerical occupations and detail-oriented jobs like computer programmer or dentist. Jobs with low scores include artist and psychologist.

For a client who is discontented in a job, the 16PF primary scores can help identify possible mismatches between the client's scores and typical scores for job incumbents. The following are just a few examples of the mismatches that counselors may encounter:

- If the client is in a managerial job (higher than first-line supervi-sor) and scores average or lower on Dominance (E) or Social Boldness (H), the client is likely to feel uncomfortable. Most other people at that level are on the high side of Dominance and Social Boldness and expect everyone else to be similar. High scorers display their ambitions and can be aggressive in advancing these ambitions. In short, they like to be in charge, and they want to get ahead. The client, being lower on these scales, does not espouse those ambitions in the same bold way. Many clients in this position take the aggression of their coworkers personally. Their hurt feelings can be interpreted as a weakness by their peers, who are accustomed to dealing with people who like challenges.

- If the client is in a sales job and scores low on Social Boldness (H), the client will almost certainly feel uncomfortable, especially if the score is 1 or 2. For such persons, initiating social interaction can be difficult, particularly if the other person is unknown or challenging. Sales agents with low (H-) scores dread going to work, calling on potential customers, and picking up the telephone to make prospecting calls or even callbacks.

- Sometimes clients who are low on Sensitivity (I) obtain jobs in the helping professions. They usually do so out of principle or because they want steady, low-risk work. Such persons lack the natural sympathy that is a defining characteristic of the helping professions. They may have difficult relationships with their peers, who typically will be considerate, aware of others' feelings, and vulnerable to having their own feelings hurt. Those low on Sensitivity can perform in the helping job, but theirs is a conscious effort versus the natural effort of their peers. Because of their unsentimental approach to problems, low (I-) people may be able to make some special contributions to their chosen helping profession, but they will need to be careful not to offend their peers.

- Most occupational profiles show scores that are at least high average on the global scale Self-Control; this is particularly true for jobs in the Realistic, Conventional, and Enterprising areas. If clients have below-average scores on this scale, they will find themselves in hot water on many jobs unless they take steps to compensate for their lack of careful work habits and attitudes. Simple coaching helps many, particularly if they are at least average on Emotional Stability (C). For others, use of organizing aids, such as a daily planner, can help rein in their tendencies.

Many clients who are seriously mismatched in their occupation will be most comfortable quitting that job and taking a new one that fits their interests, abilities, and personality. If quitting is not an option, the client can be encouraged to determine how to change the job, how to develop personal habits that will suit the job better, or how to cope with the emotional stress that accompanies the bad fit; these are all standard counseling options.

A Sample Career Counseling Case

Figure 7.1 presents a 16PF profile for Martha, an elementary school teacher who is in her 40s. Martha has never married and lives with her elderly parents. She decided to obtain career counseling because she has felt seriously dissatisfied with her work in the past few years. Her scores on the Holland types are all below 45 T score except for Social and Conventional, which are near 60 T score. These and her other career interest scores are consistent with her work as an elementary-school teacher. The discussion of career implications suggested by Martha's 16PF scores will follow the interpretation steps recommended earlier in this chapter.

Step 1

Evaluate the 16PF profile to gain an overall view of the client's personality, including expectations for client-counselor interactions.

Overall, Martha's 16PF profile presents a picture of a bright person (B = 9) who is extremely deferential (E = 1), shy (H = 2), serious (F = 2), private (N = 9), self-reliant (Q2 = 8), and conservative (Q1 = 1). She is quite tense (Q4 = 9) and also sensitive (I = 7). Although Martha is moderately caring (A = 5), she is extremely introverted and has an aversion to speaking about personal things (N = 9). She is a conscientious worker who carefully adheres to rules (G = 8).

Martha likely will find working with a counselor to be uncomfortable because of her shyness (H = 2) and her reticence to speak about personal matters (N = 9). She will expect the counselor to behave in a traditional professional manner (Q1 = 1). Expressing her needs and opinions when they differ from those of the counselor will prove to be hard for her (E = 1). Her difficulty in being assertive and outgoing (E-, F-, H-, Q2+) or open (N+, Q2+) suggests that she is most uncomfortable (Q4+) in her current work position, which probably induced her to try counseling.

RESPONSE STYLE (VALIDITY) INDICES

	Raw Score	Percentiles	
Impression Management	11	46%	within expected range
Infrequency	0	55%	within expected range
Acquiescence	52	28%	within expected range

PRIMARY FACTOR SCALES

Factor	Sten	Left Meaning	Standard Ten Score (STEN) 1 2 3 4 5 6 7 8 9 10	Right Meaning
A: Warmth	5	Reserved, Impersonal, Distant		Warm, Outgoing, Attentive to Others
B: Reasoning	9	Concrete		Abstract
C: Emotional Stability	4	Reactive, Emotionally Changeable		Emotionally Stable, Adaptive, Mature
E: Dominance	1	Deferential, Cooperative, Avoids Conflict		Dominant, Forceful, Assertive
F: Liveliness	2	Serious, Restrained, Careful		Lively, Animated, Spontaneous
G: Rule-Consciousness	8	Expedient, Nonconforming		Rule-Conscious, Dutiful
H: Social Boldness	2	Shy, Threat-Sensitive, Timid		Socially Bold, Venturesome, Thick-Skinned
I: Sensitivity	7	Utilitarian, Objective, Unsentimental		Sensitive, Aesthetic, Sentimental
L: Vigilance	4	Trusting, Unsuspecting, Accepting		Vigilant, Suspicious, Skeptical, Wary
M: Abstractedness	5	Grounded, Practical, Solution-Oriented		Abstracted, Imaginative, Idea-Oriented
N: Privateness	9	Forthright, Genuine, Artless		Private, Discreet, Non-Disclosing
O: Apprehension	5	Self-Assured, Unworried, Complacent		Apprehensive, Self-Doubting, Worried
Q₁: Openness to Change	1	Traditional, Attached to Familiar		Open to Change, Experimenting
Q₂: Self-Reliance	8	Group-Oriented, Affiliative		Self-Reliant, Solitary, Individualistic
Q₃: Perfectionism	6	Tolerates Disorder, Unexacting, Flexible		Perfectionistic, Organized, Self-Disciplined
Q₄: Tension	9	Relaxed, Placid, Patient		Tense, High Energy, Impatient, Driven

GLOBAL FACTOR SCALES

Factor	Sten	Left Meaning	Standard Ten Score (STEN) 1 2 3 4 5 6 7 8 9 10	Right Meaning
EX: Extraversion	1.8	Introverted, Socially Inhibited		Extraverted, Socially Participating
AX: Anxiety	6.8	Low Anxiety, Unperturbed		High Anxiety, Perturbable
TM: Tough-Mindedness	7.3	Receptive, Open-Minded, Intuitive		Tough-Minded, Resolute, Unempathic
IN: Independence	1.0	Accommodating, Agreeable, Selfless		Independent, Persuasive, Willful
SC: Self-Control	7.5	Unrestrained, Follows Urges		Self-Controlled, Inhibits Urges

Figure 7.1. 16PF profile for Martha, elementary school teacher.

Adapted with permission from Institute for Personality and Ability Testing, Inc. (1993). *16PF Fifth Edition Individual Record Form: Profile Sheet.* Champaign, IL: Author.

Step 2

Generate hypotheses about the client's general career-related aspects of behavior.

The 16PF results can help generate hypotheses in four general areas relating to work behavior: leadership, handling structure, preference for working alone or with others, and managing information and solving problems. In terms of suitability for leadership, Martha's 16PF scores are not a good fit. She does not have the standard pattern of global scale scores generally found among persons in a leadership capacity (i.e., high Independence, Extraversion, Tough-Mindedness, and low Anxiety). One relevant characteristic that she does have is high Self-Control. The latter characteristic coupled with her intelligence suggest that she might learn to cope in certain kinds of management positions, but she likely would feel very much out of place.

Her high score on Self-Control also suggests that she would lean strongly toward structure in any work situation and perhaps even try to impose structure on a loosely organized work situation. Her low Extraversion score indicates that she would prefer work in which she does not have to socialize much. This hypothesis is heavily supported by her very low scores on scales F (in the serious direction), H (in the shy direction), N (in the private direction), and by her high score on scale Q2 (in the self-reliant direction).

In terms of Martha's preferred manner of managing information and solving problems, a counselor would note first that she is intelligent (Reasoning = 9); that is, she is able to handle abstractions and tends to learn quickly. Her high scores on Rule-Consciousness (G) and average score on Abstractedness (M) and Perfectionism (Q3) suggest that she favors a decisive approach to solving problems, preferring closure to flexibility and spontaneity.

Step 3

Generate hypotheses about the client's fit to various occupations in terms of personality.

Step 4

Integrate information from the 16PF profile with that from other relevant sources, such as measures of ability and of occupational interests, client history, and interview impressions.

A counselor might begin developing hypotheses about Martha's fit to various occupations by examining her scores in regard to Holland types. The comparison shows that she has little in common with the Realistic type, which is characterized by high scores on Tough-Mindedness, or with the

Enterprising type, which is characterized by high scores on Extraversion and Independence. Martha is low on all of these scales. Although she shares the high Reasoning (B) and Introversion scores of persons in the Investigative type, she is low on Independence, which tends to be high in the Investigative type. Martha does have the high Self-Control of the Conventional type. She also has a high-average score on the primary scale Sensitivity (I), which is typical of the Social and Artistic types. This brief review indicates that Martha's personality profile bears the greater similarity to the Conventional and Social types, a finding that is consistent with her interest results.

Martha's high-average score on Anxiety is not helpful in distinguishing career possibilities because occupational profiles generally are low on Anxiety. Moreover, her very low scores on the primary scales Dominance (E) and Social Boldness (H) will limit her occupational choices. Persons for whom self-assertion is so aversive (E = 1) and who are so shy (H = 2), silent (F = 2), private (N = 9), and solitary (Q2 = 8) have difficulties in occupations that require much social interaction. Such extreme scores are quite rare. These low Extraversion and Independence scores in conjunction with her above-average Anxiety score indicate that Martha would likely be uncomfortable—even ineffective—in a management position.

Martha's score on Reasoning (B) presents a special interpretive problem. Such a high score, particularly if scores on mental ability measures have corroborated it, indicates a preference for an intellectually challenging career. Lowman (1991) addresses the implications of having a high ability score: "Abilities, if possessed, must actively be used or will result in dissatisfaction and a push for expression." (p. 193) In Martha's case, expression of her ability in a management position probably would be blocked by her low assertiveness. Moreover, expression of her ability in a standard Investigative career such as biologist or physicist would not be likely because of her low Independence. She is not only very conservative (Q1 = 1), unlike most profiles of scientists, but she is also low on personal assertiveness (E = 1). Her high intelligence probably would be expressed best in a Conventional or Social occupation with controlled personal contact, such as a backroom job. Otherwise, she would have to find expression for this characteristic outside of work.

Step 5
Keeping in mind the client's reason for seeking career counseling, generate hypotheses to match this reason.

> ## DON'T FORGET
>
> ### Guidelines for Interpreting a Client's 16PF Profile Relative to Career Counseling
>
> - Gain an overall view of the client's personality from the 16PF profile.
> - Resist overinterpreting 16PF scores.
> - Explore whether the scales on which the client's scores differ from those on the occupational model are essential or at least important for job function.
> - Discuss how the client's scores indicate job compatibility or incompatibility.
> - Alert the client to the possibility of a deficiency or excess on a characteristic, and begin the search for compensatory adjustments in action or attitude.

Martha's career history in elementary education and her measured career interests in the Conventional and Social types are consistent with the personality characteristics presented by her 16PF profile. Her job dissatisfaction most likely reflects her current general tension from personal or job-related stress.

EMPLOYEE SELECTION

Personality Predicts Performance

In addition to its utility in helping counseling clients find jobs that are a good fit for them, the 16PF Questionnaire can be useful to employers in finding effective employees. Demonstration of this fact begins with some general findings about personality characteristics and job performance.

During the late 1980s and early 1990s, the concept of five broad and very general personality characteristics (the Big Five) was introduced to the field of industrial and organizational psychology. In their widely cited 1991 article, Barrick and Mount reviewed the literature on the Big Five personality structure and conducted a meta-analysis on personality and job performance. Their analysis focused on the relationship between the Big Five personality dimensions and performance across various occupations, including professionals, police, managers, salespeople, and skilled and semiskilled employees. The results of the meta-analysis indicated that personality was predictive of both job and training performance across various occupations.

During this same period, three other meta-analytic studies also found a relationship between personality and job performance (Hough, Eaton, Dunnette, Kamp, & McCloy, 1990; Salgado, 1997; Tett, Jackson, & Rothstein, 1991). Although there was agreement across studies that personality measures are useful predictors of performance, some differences were found in the levels of validities across occupations. These differences probably can be attributed to different assumptions in the statistical procedures used in the various meta-analyses and to the different purposes of the studies (Barrick & Mount, 1998). Despite these differences, the general conclusion from the meta-analyses was that personality does predict job performance.

Incorporating Personality Into a Selection Process

Companies use various selection techniques to hire employees, such as cognitive ability tests, structured interviews, work samples, and biographical data (biodata) measures. Personality assessment adds a different type of information from that of the other techniques because it provides useful knowledge about interpersonal style, work habits, capacities for leadership and creativity, and traits that affect job performance.

The remainder of this discussion focuses on incorporating a personality measure within a selection system. The authors presume that the reader is knowledgeable about the issues surrounding the design and implementation of a selection system as well as the legal requirements associated with selecting employees. For valuable information about the issues involved in using psychological tests to select employees, the following resources are suggested: *Principles for the Validation and Use of Personnel Selection Procedures* (Society for Industrial and Organizational Psychology, 1987), *Standards for Educational and Psychological Testing* (American Educational Research Association [AERA], American Psychological Association [APA], & National Council on Measurement in Education [NCME], 1999), and *Uniform Guidelines on Employee Selection Procedures* (Equal Employment Opportunity Commission, Office of Personnel Management, Department of Justice, Department of Labor, & Department of the Treasury, 1979).

What Personality Dimensions Are Relevant?

This question actually consists of two related questions; one is embedded within the other. First, one needs to determine which specific personality dimensions are related to effective performance in a specific job and therefore should be included in the selection system. Second, the degree to which each personality dimension is important needs to be ascertained. In other words, is the nature of the relationship between the personality dimension and job performance linear or nonlinear? In a linear relationship, more of a personality trait is better (e.g., higher intelligence predicting higher academic performance). In a nonlinear relationship, both too little of a trait and too much of a trait may lead to poor performance (e.g., anxiety predicting ability test performance).

The job of safety manager can be used to provide a concrete example of how a linear relationship between a trait (e.g., Dominance, E) and job performance could be hypothesized. A safety manager would be most effective if he or she were willing to exert a large amount of influence to minimize unsafe practices in the work area—that is, if he or she demonstrated high Dominance (E+) characteristics, such as being assertive and persuasive, in fulfilling the job's expectations. In contrast, for other jobs (e.g., a creative design manager who works in a participative environment), a moderate level of Dominance might be related to effective performance; too low or too high a level of Dominance might result in less effective job performance. The following questions then arise: Is more always better? Or is a moderate level of a personality dimension optimal? Answering these questions requires a two-step process: (a) identify the conceptual link between personality dimensions and job performance and (b) verify the relationship with empirical evidence. The first step is accomplished by conducting a thorough job analysis, and the second step is typically done via a criterion-related validity study.

The results of a job analysis help identify the personality dimensions that relate to job performance. An in-depth understanding of the job also helps the selection expert develop hypotheses concerning the nature of the relationship between the dimensions and performance.

To identify relevant personality dimensions, the expert will need to use a job analytic method that includes personality predictors. For more information about personality-related job analysis methods, see Guion (1998) or Kelly (1999). After identifying the relevant dimensions, the selection expert gathers criterion-related validity evidence to confirm or disconfirm the relevancy of the dimensions and to clarify the nature of the relationship for those dimensions that are relevant.

Can Responses to the 16PF Questionnaire Be Faked?

Presenting a socially desirable image (or faking) on a personality test is a concern in a selection context. An argument can be made that job candidates are different from current employees because the test-taking motivations of the two groups are different. Candidates are answering the questions in order to obtain a job, whereas current employees usually do not have to worry about their images because they already have jobs. Although a socially desirable image may be presented on a personality test, this does not diminish the value of personality tests as being useful predictors of performance (Hough, 1998). In fact, Hough et al. (1990) conducted a study to examine the effect of faking or response distortion on criterion-related validity, and found that for the most part, validities remained stable even if the study participants distorted their responses.

The 16PF Impression Management (IM) scale provides information about the extent to which test takers are attempting to present a socially desirable persona. Scores on IM that are at or above the 95th percentile are high compared to the general population and therefore act as a red flag, warning of possible faking. The descriptor *possible* is applied because an extreme IM score does not necessarily indicate faking; some people actually see themselves in the favorable manner portrayed by their IM score. If the IM score of a candidate is elevated, the selection expert should try to determine whether it represents faking or a positive self-image, possibly by reviewing information on the candidate obtained from other sources (e.g., background data, other test results, interview). If the selection expert determines that the IM score indicates faking (and therefore invalid test results), he or she may want to discuss these qualities in detail during the interview, and possibly retest the candidate. Of course, retesting involves faith that valid results are obtainable.

Additional information about the Impression Management (IM) scale is presented in chapter 3. Two response-style indices—Acquiescence and Infrequency—are also indicators of invalid test results. These indices are discussed in chapter 3.

16PF Questionnaire and Performance: Criterion-Related Validity Evidence

IPAT, the publisher of the 16PF Questionnaire, has an ongoing process to collect criterion-related validity evidence from its customers. The collected data are entered into a database, summarized by occupation, and analyzed using meta-analytic techniques. To-date results of the meta-analyses indicate that some of the 16PF dimensions are highly predictive of performance in the three occupational areas of manager-executive, customer service, and protective services (police, security guard). The correlations indicate that effective managers and executives are emotionally stable (C+), outgoing (H+), trusting (L-), self-confident (O-), and open to new ideas and changes (Q1+). Capable customer service personnel are smart (B+), emotionally stable (C+), somewhat submissive (E-), serious (F-), objective (I-), and practical (M-). Competent protective service personnel are somewhat reserved (A-), energetic (F+), trusting (L-), self-confident (O-), and self-reliant (Q2+).

Thus, the job relevance of the 16PF scales has been established not only by broad meta-analyses covering a number of measures of personality but also by specific studies conducted by the test publisher. Two issues that may interest the reader are the degree to which 16PF scores show bias in selection and the degree to which subgroup differences occur in 16PF scores.

Does the 16PF Questionnaire Show Bias?

According to Guion (1998), *bias* "refers to systematic group differences in item responses, test scores, or other assessments for reasons unrelated to the trait being assessed" (p. 433). In other words, a personality test that is biased does not treat all groups to whom it may be administered in an equitable fashion, with the term *groups* referring to those protected under the law. For example, race, color, religion, gender, and national origin are all protected groups under the Civil Rights Act of 1964. If a test used in a selection system treats these groups and their subgroups differently, the selection system as a whole may be in violation of legal and professional standards.

Due to common misinterpretations of what *bias* means in a technical context, it has been replaced by the term *differential functioning* (Hambleton, Swaminathan, & Rogers, 1991). The latter term also was adopted due to sociopolitical reasons because *bias* tends to have negative connotations (Raju & Ellis, 2002). In today's testing nomenclature, differential functioning is said to exist when individuals from different groups or subgroups have a different likelihood of choosing a specific response to an item even though they have the same level of construct under consideration (Hulin, Drasgow, & Parsons, 1983; Lord, 1980). For example, suppose two individuals from different subgroups (e.g., male and female) are taking the same personality test. Further suppose that each has the same level of the quality Warmth (A+), but because of the way in which the Warmth scale items are phrased, the likelihood that each will respond true to the items is different. Therefore, the items would be demonstrating differential functioning for gender.

The preceding example of differential functioning focuses on responses to individual scale items. Some argue that investigations of differential functioning should be conducted for a test as a whole (Drasgow & Hulin, 1990; Raju & Ellis, 2002). To begin such an investigation, the items within each scale are summed to produce an index of differential functioning for each scale. Stating this step is simpler than accomplishing it because the direction of the differential functioning of the items within a scale may not be consistent; that is, some items may be easier for the first subgroup, whereas others are easier for the second subgroup. When the items displaying differential functioning are summed across the scales of the test, they may cancel each other out, with the result being close to zero (Raju, van der Linden, & Fleer, 1995). As a result, certain items within the test may demonstrate differential functioning, but the test as a whole will not.

Using the method described by Candell and Drasgow (1988) and Raju (Raju & Ellis, 2002; Raju et al., 1995), the IPAT research staff conducted an analysis to determine whether any of the 16PF Fifth Edition scales exhibit differential functioning for gender, race, and age subgroups. No differential functioning was evident at any of the 16 scale levels between males and females, Whites and non-White groups (African American and Hispanic), or age groups (people under the age of 40 and people 40 years of age and above).

Does the 16PF Questionnaire Show Group Differences?

In addition to examining whether a test functions differently for some groups, it is important to examine if the mean scores for subgroups (e.g., male versus female) are different. Mean differences are important in a selection context because of the potential for adverse impact. For example, an assessment instrument or system that results in differential selection rates for members of a protected group would have an adverse impact on that group (Guion, 1998). To define differential selection rates in this context, the "four-fifths rule" is often used. For example, if the proportion of females hired is less than 80% of the proportion of males hired on the basis of a particular assessment instrument, adverse impact exists for females on that instrument.

Each component in a selection system should be evaluated separately for evidence of adverse impact (Guion, 1998).

The presence of mean differences for subgroups is not directly related to the issue of differential functioning. Mean differences between subgroups can occur for a variety of reasons (Guion, 1998). Therefore, it is important to remember that differential functioning and mean differences are distinct phenomena; that is, the existence of one does not indicate the existence of the other (Reynolds, 1995).

Using the general population normative sample of 10,261 individuals, analyses on the basis of effect sizes were conducted to determine whether mean differences existed on 16PF scales between males and females, between Whites and non-White groups, and between people under 40 years of age and people 40 years of age and over (Maraist & Russell, 2002). Across the 16 scales, the results indicated very few meaningful differences between groups:

- Between males and females on Warmth (A), Sensitivity (I), and Apprehension (O), with females scoring higher than males on these scales
- Between Blacks and Whites on Reasoning (B) and Vigilance (L), with Blacks scoring lower on Reasoning and higher on Vigilance
- Between Hispanics and Whites on Reasoning (B), with Hispanics scoring lower on this scale
- Between people under 40 years of age and people 40 years of age and over on Liveliness (F) and Vigilance (L), with those 40 and over scoring lower on both scales

The finding that Blacks and Hispanics score lower than whites on the Reasoning (B) scale by one standard deviation and two thirds of one standard deviation, respectively, is similar to previous research on ability tests (Sackett et al., 2001).

A number of researchers have studied mean differences on personality scales between males and females as well as between minorities and nonminorities. The consensus is that for the most part, only minimal differences exist between the various subgroups on personality scales (cf., Hough, 1998; Hough & Ones, 2001; Salgado, Viswesvaran, & Ones, 2001).

A selection expert may determine that mean differences on certain scales of a personality instrument are adversely impacting a selection system. Often,

> # DON'T FORGET
>
> ## Key Points About the 16PF Questionnaire and the Selection Process
>
> - The 16PF Questionnaire is a measure of normal personality that is a useful tool in selection contexts for a wide variety of occupations.
> - Meta-analytic results show that 16PF scales are predictive of performance in a variety of jobs.
> - The selection expert should determine how to incorporate 16PF scores into the selection system, with the goal being to optimally predict effective behavior on the job.

eliminating scores on these scales from consideration in the hiring decision is advisable. When faced with this issue, the expert also needs to remember that adverse impact is not synonymous with illegal discrimination (Guion, 1998). Selection instruments that have proven validity may be legitimately used even if they result in adverse impact. The caveat is that the latter instruments may be used only as long as no better alternative instruments exist.

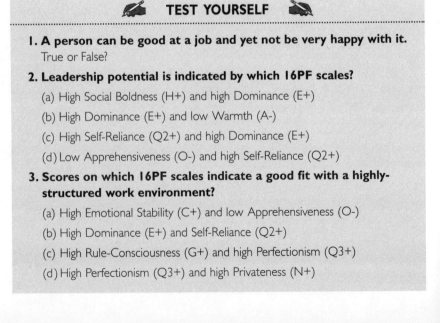

TEST YOURSELF

1. A person can be good at a job and yet not be very happy with it. True or False?

2. Leadership potential is indicated by which 16PF scales?

    (a) High Social Boldness (H+) and high Dominance (E+)

    (b) High Dominance (E+) and low Warmth (A-)

    (c) High Self-Reliance (Q2+) and high Dominance (E+)

    (d) Low Apprehensiveness (O-) and high Self-Reliance (Q2+)

3. Scores on which 16PF scales indicate a good fit with a highly-structured work environment?

    (a) High Emotional Stability (C+) and low Apprehensiveness (O-)

    (b) High Dominance (E+) and Self-Reliance (Q2+)

    (c) High Rule-Consciousness (G+) and high Perfectionism (Q3+)

    (d) High Perfectionism (Q3+) and high Privateness (N+)

4. An intuitive, creative approach to information processing and problem-solving is suggested by which 16PF scales?

(a) High Reasoning (B+) and high Self-Reliance (Q2+)

(b) High Dominance (E+) and high Social Boldness (H+)

(c) High Liveliness (F+) and high Tension (Q4+)

(d) High Sensitivity (I+) and high Openness to Change (Q1+)

5. Typical 16PF scores that predict performance in a sales job include

(a) below average scores on Apprehension (O-).

(b) above average scores on Social Boldness (H+).

(c) above average scores on Emotional Stability (C+).

(d) above average scores on Liveliness (F+).

(e) all of the above

6. For the Holland Enterprising type, which of the following are "defining characteristics?"

(a) Low scores on Anxiety primaries such as Apprehension (O-)

(b) High Extraversion primaries such as Social Boldness (H+)

(c) High Independence primaries such a Dominance (E+)

(d) All of the above

7. Personality tests can predict job performance. True or False?

Answers. 1. True; 2. a; 3. c; 4. d; 5. e; 6. d; 7. True.

Eight

ILLUSTRATIVE CASE REPORTS

Three cases are presented in this chapter; each is by a different author. Drs. H. B. and H. E. P. Cattell are responsible for the first case, which is followed by that of Dr. Schuerger. These two cases are from a clinical-counseling context. The third case is by Dr. David Watterson and illustrates the use of 16PF results in the process of leadership coaching. The three cases are considerably different in context and client, but all illustrate the use of the main elements of 16PF interpretation: response style indices, global scales, primary scales, scale interactions, predicted scores and other interpretive report content, and integration of all of these.

CHAD: A CASE STUDY

Step 1: Consider Context of Assessment

Figure 8.1 presents the 16PF profile of Chad, who was 23 years old at the time of therapy. He is the youngest of three sons in an educated, upper-middle-class family. Both parents had professional careers. When he sought therapy, Chad was still living at home and was unemployed. He presented as a pleasant, cheerful individual, but he was unconvincing in his assertion that he wanted psychotherapy to help in developing goals and in making a career choice. Later, it became clear that his parents had made participation in therapy a condition for his remaining in the family home and that his girlfriend was threatening to end their relationship if he did not find a decent job.

Although he was of at least average intelligence, Chad had dropped out of high school at age 16. His parents encouraged him to obtain a general equivalency diploma (GED) and to enroll in a junior college, but he dropped out before completing the first semester. Finally accepting that Chad was not academically inclined, his parents next attempted to interest him in a variety of careers. Despite his early enthusiasm for several, he never stayed in any one job or training program for more than 4 months, always citing boredom as his reason for quitting.

RESPONSE STYLE (VALIDITY) INDICES

	Raw Score	Percentiles	
Impression Management	14	64%	within expected range
Infrequency	3	80%	within expected range
Acquiescence	60	64%	within expected range

PRIMARY FACTOR SCALES

Factor	Sten	Left Meaning	Standard Ten Score (STEN)	Right Meaning
A: Warmth	4	Reserved, Impersonal, Distant		Warm, Outgoing, Attentive to Others
B: Reasoning	5	Concrete		Abstract
C: Emotional Stability	6	Reactive, Emotionally Changeable		Emotionally Stable, Adaptive, Mature
E: Dominance	4	Deferential, Cooperative, Avoids Conflict		Dominant, Forceful, Assertive
F: Liveliness	8	Serious, Restrained, Careful		Lively, Animated, Spontaneous
G: Rule-Consciousness	2	Expedient, Nonconforming		Rule-Conscious, Dutiful
H: Social Boldness	8	Shy, Threat-Sensitive, Timid		Socially Bold, Venturesome, Thick-Skinned
I: Sensitivity	5	Utilitarian, Objective, Unsentimental		Sensitive, Aesthetic, Sentimental
L: Vigilance	10	Trusting, Unsuspecting, Accepting		Vigilant, Suspicious, Skeptical, Wary
M: Abstractedness	5	Grounded, Practical, Solution-Oriented		Abstracted, Imaginative, Idea-Oriented
N: Privateness	7	Forthright, Genuine, Artless		Private, Discreet, Non-Disclosing
O: Apprehension	3	Self-Assured, Unworried, Complacent		Apprehensive, Self-Doubting, Worried
Q₁: Openness to Change	6	Traditional, Attached to Familiar		Open to Change, Experimenting
Q₂: Self-Reliance	3	Group-Oriented, Affiliative		Self-Reliant, Solitary, Individualistic
Q₃: Perfectionism	3	Tolerates Disorder, Unexacting, Flexible		Perfectionistic, Organized, Self-Disciplined
Q₄: Tension	6	Relaxed, Placid, Patient		Tense, High Energy, Impatient, Driven

GLOBAL FACTOR SCALES

Factor	Sten	Left Meaning	Standard Ten Score (STEN)	Right Meaning
EX: Extraversion	6.6	Introverted, Socially Inhibited		Extraverted, Socially Participating
AX: Anxiety	5.8	Low Anxiety, Unperturbed		High Anxiety, Perturbable
TM: Tough-Mindedness	6.0	Receptive, Open-Minded, Intuitive		Tough-Minded, Resolute, Unempathic
IN: Independence	6.4	Accommodating, Agreeable, Selfless		Independent, Persuasive, Willful
SC: Self-Control	2.7	Unrestrained, Follows Urges		Self-Controlled, Inhibits Urges

Figure 8.1. 16PF profile for Chad.

Adapted with permission from Institute for Personality and Ability Testing. (1993). *16PF Fifth Edition Individual Record Form: Profile Sheet.* Champaign, IL: Author.

Chad spent most of his time with a group of young men who seemed bonded together by their similar lifestyle. Most of their activities involved hanging out, partying, working on one another's cars, drag racing, and surfing. Some of these young men had had minor brushes with the law. Even within this group, Chad had obtained a reputation for being quite a "party animal."

Chad's parents blamed this group for their son's problems, saying that he was easily influenced. They felt that he had always relied on others to guide him and that he rarely made decisions independently. Chad's girlfriend, Mary, was an extremely goal-directed individual who saw Chad's lack of motivation differently. She believed that his motivational problems stemmed from his low self-esteem. Although she was frustrated by his aimless lifestyle, she was hesitant to leave him because she was worried about how he would get along without her.

After two or three clinical sessions, it became obvious that Chad did not really see his lack of career goals as a problem. He expressed confidence that his life would just unfold naturally and that what was most important was just enjoying each day. His only problem, he said, was the pressure being applied by his parents and girlfriend; however, he was formulating a plan to deal with this pressure. Because he was attracted to Mary's serious, responsible style, he was planning to look for a replacement who was similar to Mary but more relaxed and accepting of him. He also anticipated moving in with this new girlfriend, thus relieving him of the need to rely on his parents.

Step 2: Evaluate the Response Style (Validity) Indices

Because all of the validity indices are within expected limits, Chad apparently did not present a particularly positive or negative picture of himself, and he appeared to understand the questions and respond in a meaningful way to them.

Step 3: Evaluate the Global Scale Scores

Because Chad has only one extreme global factor (Self-Control) and one high-average global factor (Extraversion), his overall number of elevated global scores is within the average range and not unusual.

Chad's score on Self-Control is quite low, indicating that his level of internalized standards and controls is very low. Although some may perceive him as easygoing and flexible, he probably shows a significant lack of self-restraint and follows his own urges without the usual consideration for others' needs or for his own responsibilities.

Because Chad's Extraversion score is somewhat above average, social interaction appears to play a somewhat more important role in his life than in the average person's life.

Although global Anxiety, Independence, and Tough-Mindedness are all within the average range, Anxiety and Independence show some extreme but opposite scores among their contributing primary scales.

Step 4: Evaluate the Primary Scales in the Context of the Globals

Chad's overall profile shows seven elevated primary scales, which is in the high range. This suggests that his personality does contain some strongly defined characteristics and behavior patterns.

Extraversion

Chad's above-average score on global Extraversion is made up of three high scores plus two below-average scores on the contributing primary scales—a complicated combination. Beginning with the low Extraversion scores, his below-average score on Warmth (A-) suggests that he is somewhat aloof or detached and tends to keep some emotional distance between himself and others. His above-average score on Privateness (N+) denotes a similar tendency to be cautious and guarded about revealing personal information. These results are consistent with the clinician's experience of Chad in that he did not originally reveal his true motivation for seeking therapy, often did not reveal his true intentions to his parents or girlfriend, and generally tended to view people from the standpoint of what he could get from them.

On the other hand, his high score on Liveliness (F+) indicates that he brings a lot of enthusiasm to his interactions and that he is likely to be carefree and fun loving but also somewhat impulsive. His high score on Social Boldness (H+) further denotes someone who is sociable, talkative, and adventurous but possibly attention seeking and thick-skinned. Together, these two scores suggest someone whose social manner is enthusiastic and entertaining but who is often insensitive to others' feelings and reactions.

Chad's low score on Self-Reliance (Q2-) indicates that he feels a strong need for companionship and prefers to do most things with others rather than by himself.

Overall, his Extraversion scores suggest that he feels a strong need to socialize and to be around others but probably prefers to interact in a fun loving, superficial, attention-seeking manner rather than to develop deep, mutual relationships. These scores are consistent with the clinician's experience of Chad as a lively, sociable person who spends most of his time as part of a small group of peers pursuing stimulating activities together.

Independence

Chad's scores on the Independence subfactors further develop the picture of someone whose basic social relationships tend to be superficial and passive. Although his global Independence score is in the average range, the contributing primary scores are in opposite directions. His high score on Social Boldness (H+) indicates that he is gregarious and adventurous, but his high Vigilance (L+) score denotes mistrust of others. His below-average score on Dominance (E-) and his low score on Self-Reliance (Q2-) suggest that some general, underlying dependency needs may be present. Although no signs of suspiciousness surfaced in the clinical sessions or life history, his apparent tendency to be easily influenced by friends and to depend on his parents and girlfriend are consistent with the rest of these scores.

Self-Control

Chad's scores on the Self-Control primaries are consistently low, with three out of four in the poorly controlled direction. His high score on Liveliness (F+) suggests a carefree, spontaneous style that usually involves impulsivity and a lack of inhibition. Thus, he may be unreliable in following through on tasks and flighty in his focus. His very low score on Rule-Consciousness (G-) suggests that he has not internalized conventional standards of right and wrong and tends to be expedient rather than following established rules. Additionally, his low score on Perfectionism (Q3-) indicates a tendency to be disorganized and lacking in self-discipline. It suggests that he probably feels little compulsion to complete tasks conscientiously, to follow through on commitments, or to work toward long-term goals. Overall, these Self-Control primaries suggest that Chad is substantially lacking in internalized controls and standards and probably follows his own urges regardless of others' needs or his own responsibilities. These results are consistent with many aspects of his life history, including his lack of development of career goals, his lack of follow-through with previous jobs and training programs, and his laissez-faire attitude about life.

Anxiety

In the area of global Anxiety, Chad's average score is the result of combining extreme but opposite scores on two contributing primaries. His low score on Apprehension (O-) indicates that he experiences little worry or anxiety and strongly maintains an attitude of untroubled self-assurance. Although these characteristics probably make him resilient in stressful situations, he may seem self-satisfied or complacent to others and may not accept responsibility or blame even when it is appropriate. Although his high score on Vigilance (L+) indicates a tendency to be suspicious and guarded, this score was not supported by other clinical information, indicating a need for further assessment in this area. Taken together, these Anxiety factors suggest that Chad may use strong defenses like denial, which is consistent with his cheerful, thick-skinned interpersonal style. They are also consistent with his unworried, self-satisfied attitude about his current life situation.

Tough-Mindedness

All of Chad's Tough-Mindedness scores are in the average range except for his below-average score on Warmth (A-), which was already discussed in conjunction with Extraversion. His average scores in the areas of Sensitivity (I), Abstractedness (M), and Openness to Change (Q1) plus his average-range score on the Reasoning ability factor (B) are consistent with his self-presentation in the sessions and with his life history information, which shows no signs of particular aesthetic sensitivity, creative imagination, or intellectual curiosity. However, given Chad's tendency to avoid applying himself (especially academically), his actual reasoning ability may well be higher than measured.

Step 5: Consider Scale Interactions, Prediction Equations, Interpretive Report Content, and Comparison Profiles

Some of the information cited in this section is from the 16PF resource books and interpretive reports cited in Chapter 4 (Rapid References 4.1 and 4.2).

Chad's mixed scores on the Extraversion primaries present an interesting picture of his social needs. Karson and O'Dell (1976) describe extremely low scores on Warmth (A-) as often related to unrewarding or frustrating early relationships that lead to avoidance of close emotional connection with others. Although Chad's score on Warmth is not extremely low, this general meaning is a hypothesis worth investigating. His above-average score on Privateness (N+) further suggests an individual who is cautious about revealing personal information that might be used by others. The Cattell Comprehensive Personality Interpretation report (CCPI) states, "He tends to keep his reactions to himself and to carefully consider how much to say before speaking. Thus, overall, others may find him elusive or hard to really get to know."

The CCPI also notes that Chad's high scores on Social Boldness (H+) and Liveliness (F+) indicate someone whose social behavior is not only quite stimulating and entertaining but also superficial and attention seeking:

> Once the initial novelty of meeting someone new has worn off, he tends to lose interest in them. He is less emotionally attached to others than his engaging conversational manner would suggest. . . . He may be attention-seeking and may particularly enjoy the company of people who allow him to do more than his share of the talking. (CCPI)

These scores create a picture of someone who is cautious about close social relationships and who may have unmet needs for attention from others and for dependable companionship. His low score on Self-Reliance (Q2-), which may indicate some dependent features, further supports this picture. The Karson Clinical Report (KCR) states that

> When confronted with a situation that requires independent action, he often finds himself unable to act alone. His desire to do things with others may easily lead him to defer his personal agenda in favor of the group's. . . . His group orientation may be motivated by a desire to avoid weaknesses in areas of self-esteem and self-discipline. (KCR)

Chad's scores on the Independence primaries compound the conclusions from the Extraversion scales. His below-average score on Dominance (E-), especially in combination with his low score on Self-Reliance (Q2-), indicates a general tendency toward being compliant and passive. The CCPI states, "Since Chad relies heavily on other people's ideas and support, he may be easily swayed by others. . . . He may give in to others' wishes rather than have a disagreement." The CCPI also discusses the application of this score combination to intimate relationships:

> This suggests that his fear of abandonment may lead him to be yielding and conciliatory when he sees signs that his partner is pulling away . . . Because of the high value he places on togetherness, he may gloss over problems or deny that certain disagreements exist, thus promoting enmeshment between him and his partner. (CCPI)

The KCR states, "He does not always speak up when his needs and his point of view are ignored. This can lead to pockets of resentment, and he may express this resentment indirectly."

Chad's low scores on the Self-Control primaries complement the picture presented by his interpersonal scores. Regarding his low score on Rule-Consciousness (G-), the CCPI states, "He feels little compulsion to conform to societal rules and standards. . . . Nor is he inclined to experience guilt or self-reproach when he breaks rules or conventions." The KCR states that

> He shows so little regard for the rules of conduct associated with conventional standards of behavior that conforming to societal expectations may be difficult for him. Many of the tasks of living usually taken for granted may become optional in his mind. Other people, especially authority figures, may see him as unresponsive to their expectations. Activities that require a willingness to follow rules may make him feel too constricted to participate effectively. (KCR)

Regarding Chad's low score on Perfectionism (Q3-), the CCPI states, "He has low personal standards of achievement and probably is undisciplined and disorganized at times. He may not take pride in doing well or feel shame when he falls short of these standards." The KCR states, "His relative paucity of good habits to fall back on when necessary can leave him vulnerable to emotional distress." Chad's high score on Liveliness (F+) denotes a fun-loving, spontaneous style that also involves some impulsivity and unreliability. The KCR states, "Circumspection and reflection are not typical characteristics of his thinking. . . . He may jump to conclusions before considering all the facts."

Thus, Chad's overall behavior probably shows a lack of conscientiousness in meeting obligations and responsibilities, a lack of consideration for other people's needs, and a lack of development of personal long-term goals. This conclusion may be consistent with his Extraversion and Independence scores, in that theoretically individuals with unsatisfying early relationships may not identify closely with others—especially with authority figures—and thus may not internalize general standards and controls. Furthermore, Chad's lack of Self-Control may affect his ability to get his interpersonal needs met; people are less likely to affiliate with and support those who are irresponsible or unreliable.

Chad's scores on the Anxiety primaries, particularly his low Apprehension (O-) score, suggest an untroubled, self-assured style. This characteristic may make him confident and resilient in stressful situations, but it also may result from strong defenses. The CCPI states, "His self-esteem at present is above the optimal level for fairly appraising both his strengths and weaknesses. He may be defended against recognizing his own shortcomings." The PCDP adds, "He appears to have little need to explain his actions to himself or to other people." The CCPI reflects on the effect this trait has in relationships: "Chad does not take his fair share of responsibility and blame when things go wrong. Any problems between him and his partner may be exacerbated by his tendency to deny his role in them." The CCPI makes the following suggestions for the therapeutic process:

> Even constructive negative feedback is rarely used by Chad to gain self-understanding since it often exacerbates his defensiveness or triggers a flood of upsetting emotions. Thus, helping professionals should resist confronting his defense mechanisms prematurely or abruptly since they probably serve as protection for the low level of personal acceptance that underlies his confident veneer. Projecting blame onto others may be his standard way of guarding himself from recognizing his own faults and mistakes. Although it may be tempting to correct these projective distortions, they cannot be corrected simply by logical argument because they have a defensive role in guarding him against perceptions that might cause strong self-doubt. (CCPI)

Extremely high scores on Vigilance (L+) such as Chad's usually indicate a strong tendency to be distrustful and suspicious of others' intentions. However, because this trait was noticeably absent from the clinical interviews, further assessment in this area is needed.

Overall, these Anxiety factors suggest that Chad tends to use strong defenses like denial; this is consistent with his interpersonal profile, which depicts a cheerful, carefree, thick-skinned style with underlying dependency issues. His interpersonal needs plus his very low level of self-discipline or internalized standards may challenge his defenses. The KCR states that

> on a whole, his current average emotional adjustment seems to depend somewhat on his having found circumstances that do not overly challenge his defenses. Although his ego strength is adequate, he may not possess a reliable degree of self-control in difficult situations. To maintain his positive emotional adjustment, he will need to keep coming up with unique solutions to the demands made on him. (KCR)

Step 6: Integrate All Information in Relation to the Assessment Question

No excessive suspiciousness or other signs of Chad's extremely high Vigilance (L+) score were detected in his self-presentation or in his life history. His extreme Vigilance score was thus a signal to the clinician that there was more to Chad's story than was apparent. Although a high Vigilance score frequently indicates a tendency to be suspicious and distrustful of others' motives and to dwell on these suspicions, another possible meaning is the presence of a wary, hypervigilant orientation that is based on some real, present danger. Given Chad's lack of internalized social values and his peers' less-than-sterling characters, the clinician thought that something possibly was occurring in Chad's life about which he needed to be hypervigilant and defensive.

After several unsuccessful attempts to discover suspiciousness in Chad's behavior, the clinician confronted him with a conjecture about some kind of illegal activity. Chad was taken aback, thinking that the therapist had somehow learned his carefully guarded secret, and admitted that he and his friends had been growing and dealing marijuana for several years. He expressed no guilt or shame and said that in addition to earning easy money, he enjoyed the adrenaline rush associated with growing marijuana in the hills behind his parents' home and the need to be constantly on guard against discovery as a dealer. Like most marijuana dealers, Chad smoked on a daily basis, and this frequent and prolonged use probably contributed to his motivational problems.

Soon Chad's girlfriend left him, and his parents said he could no longer remain in their home. Because he had no place to live, he reluctantly followed the clinician's suggestion to enter a residential drug treatment program. Many aspects of this program meshed well with Chad's dynamics—participating in regular group meetings, gathering in fellowship with others recovering from chemical dependency, mentoring through sponsorship, and following a clear 12-step program. This environment uniquely accommodated Chad's needs for companionship, for external structure and direction from others, and for supportive figures, and he easily relinquished his "good-time" friends. The values and beliefs of the 12-step program provided a set of external standards and values around which to structure his life, compensating for his lack of development of his own internal ones.

Although Chad did not have the motivation to pursue long-term therapy, he functioned fairly well within the Narcotics Anonymous community. Follow-up indicated that he was attending meetings several times a week, was talking almost daily with his sponsor, and had adopted the higher-order values of the Narcotics Anonymous 12-step philosophy. However, he was still unemployed and receiving some assistance from his parents while he lived with people from Narcotics Anonymous. In fact, his animated, uninhibited style made him in great demand as a speaker at Narcotics Anonymous meetings, where he clearly enjoyed the limelight.

Although some may see Chad as merely transferring his dependency to Narcotics Anonymous, this association represented a substantial improvement in his overall quality of life. It moved him away from involvement in drugs and in criminal behavior, dependency on and conflict with his family, and limited relationships with others.

This case indicates how 16PF results can be useful in identifying aspects of an individual's functioning that would otherwise come to light only over an extended period of time (or not at all). In giving a comprehensive picture of Chad's personality, the 16PF results allowed the clinician to accurately assess his strengths and weaknesses and to work toward realistic options.

GORDON: A CASE STUDY

The presentation of Gordon's 16PF interpretation follows the six steps introduced in chapter 4:

1. Consider the context of the assessment.
2. Evaluate the response style (validity) indices.
3. Evaluate the global scale scores.
4. Evaluate the primary scales in the context of the globals.
5. Consider scale interactions, prediction equations, interpretive report content, and comparison profiles.
6. Integrate all information in relation to the assessment question.

Step 1: Consider Context of Assessment

Figure 8.2 presents 16PF scores for a client named Gordon. Gordon was seen in a counseling context and was self-referred. He was in his late thirties when he was seen, and he was recently married for the second time. His first marriage was very brief and had only lasted for a year and a few months, with no children. He had been working as a social worker when first seen, but he was convinced that he needed to get into some kind of work that "had a better future." He was particularly concerned with the money, but he also saw that he would probably burn out at the social work job, which he had entered because of his firmly held and idealistic social principles. He had been powerfully influenced during his college career by the lack of social justice in the world and felt compelled to work for social betterment. Although he did not feel any particular pressure from his new wife to change, he was struggling with the transition to married life and with a possible change of job.

Gordon had a bachelor's degree in psychology and had begun work for an advanced degree in social work but had quit it because he "just didn't like the field enough" to pursue advanced study, despite his idealism. He was from a working-class family of southern European origin and spoke of the importance of family in his life, not only out of principle but also in terms of emotional bonds. Despite his working-class background, he seemed inclined more to abstract, intellectual pursuits than to hands-on or procedural ones. Consistent with these inclinations, in the sessions he presented himself as thoughtful, imaginative, bright, and perceptive.

RESPONSE STYLE (VALIDITY) INDICES

	Raw Score	Percentiles	
Impression Management	8	22%	within expected range
Infrequency	1	55%	within expected range
Acquiescence	52	28%	within expected range

PRIMARY FACTOR SCALES

Factor	Sten	Left Meaning	Standard Ten Score (STEN) ⊢Average⊣ 1 2 3 4 5 6 7 8 9 10	Right Meaning
A: Warmth	2	Reserved, Impersonal, Distant		Warm, Outgoing, Attentive to Others
B: Reasoning	9	Concrete		Abstract
C: Emotional Stability	5	Reactive, Emotionally Changeable		Emotionally Stable, Adaptive, Mature
E: Dominance	8	Deferential, Cooperative, Avoids Conflict		Dominant, Forceful, Assertive
F: Liveliness	6	Serious, Restrained, Careful		Lively, Animated, Spontaneous
G: Rule-Consciousness	2	Expedient, Nonconforming		Rule-Conscious, Dutiful
H: Social Boldness	7	Shy, Threat-Sensitive, Timid		Socially Bold, Venturesome, Thick-Skinned
I: Sensitivity	5	Utilitarian, Objective, Unsentimental		Sensitive, Aesthetic, Sentimental
L: Vigilance	9	Trusting, Unsuspecting, Accepting		Vigilant, Suspicious, Skeptical, Wary
M: Abstractedness	6	Grounded, Practical, Solution-Oriented		Abstracted, Imaginative, Idea-Oriented
N: Privateness	4	Forthright, Genuine, Artless		Private, Discreet, Non-Disclosing
O: Apprehension	7	Self-Assured, Unworried, Complacent		Apprehensive, Self-Doubting, Worried
Q₁: Openness to Change	7	Traditional, Attached to Familiar		Open to Change, Experimenting
Q₂: Self-Reliance	9	Group-Oriented, Affiliative		Self-Reliant, Solitary, Individualistic
Q₃: Perfectionism	5	Tolerates Disorder, Unexacting, Flexible		Perfectionistic, Organized, Self-Disciplined
Q₄: Tension	8	Relaxed, Placid, Patient		Tense, High Energy, Impatient, Driven

GLOBAL FACTOR SCALES

Factor	Sten	Left Meaning	Standard Ten Score (STEN) ⊢Average⊣ 1 2 3 4 5 6 7 8 9 10	Right Meaning
EX: Extraversion	4.3	Introverted, Socially Inhibited		Extraverted, Socially Participating
AX: Anxiety	8.3	Low Anxiety, Unperturbed		High Anxiety, Perturbable
TM: Tough-Mindedness	5.6	Receptive, Open-Minded, Intuitive		Tough-Minded, Resolute, Unempathic
IN: Independence	8.6	Accommodating, Agreeable, Selfless		Independent, Persuasive, Willful
SC: Self-Control	3.6	Unrestrained, Follows Urges		Self-Controlled, Inhibits Urges

Figure 8.2. 16PF profile for Gordon.

Adapted with permission from Institute for Personality and Ability Testing. (1993). *16PF Fifth Edition Individual Record Form: Profile Sheet.* Champaign, IL: Author.

Gordon had never been in therapy as an adult, although he remembered being the object of some concern by family and school authorities when he was in grade school. "I think I spent some time with the school psychologist," he said. He believed that he had been somewhat depressed from time to time, but never so severely that he couldn't function. Currently the stresses of adjusting to his life changes and particularly to the prospect of changing jobs were affecting his mood, and he reported feeling depressed with a strong underlying tone of anger.

Step 2: Evaluate the Response Style (Validity) Indices

Gordon's indices (IM = 22nd percentile; INF = 55th percentile; ACQ = 28th percentile) are all within the normal range and are not remarkable. The score on IM is low enough to support the supposition that Gordon is in a mood to exaggerate his problems a bit(a common happening in a counseling setting.

Step 3: Evaluate the Global Scale Scores

Gordon has three elevated global scales: Anxiety (8.3) and Independence (8.6) are high, and Self-Control is low (3.6). In addition, Extraversion (4.3) is low-average, and Tough-Mindedness (5.6) is almost exactly average.

The most pronounced characteristics are Independence, Anxiety, and the low Self-Control. The high Anxiety score suggests that his level of adjustment was problematic at the time of testing, and the discomfort that he felt from it was probably what brought him to counseling. It was not clear the degree to which it was purely situational (related to life changes), or was a more lasting characteristic that was perhaps based on early life experiences. The high Independence suggests that he likes to be in charge and to have his say; it also suggests that he is ambitious and progressive. He would probably be uncomfortable working for a supervisor less intelligent than he (see Reasoning = 9), and he may very well get upset if he does not get what he wants. The low Self-Control suggests low internal behavior controls, a flexible attitude toward rules, and the possibility of getting in trouble with supervisors for these reasons. Gordon is low average overall on Extraversion, but it is worth noting that this score comes from averaging some very low scores with some average to above-average scores. In the next step, all of the global scores are discussed more elaborately in combination with their contributing primary scales.

Step 4: Evaluate the Primary Scales in the Context of the Globals

Gordon's Independence score, his highest global scale, is made up of scores on four primary scales, Dominance (8), Social Boldness (7), Vigilance (9), and Openness to Change (7). All of these scores are in the same direction, and two of them, Dominance and Vigilance, are quite high. The picture is consistent with and contributes to the notion that Independence is prominent in Gordon's life and may be a regnant characteristic, one that pervades his personality. It is likely that he is distrusting of others, as suggested by the high score on Vigilance (L+), and perhaps he may be cynical or have a chip on his shoulder. He may be easily offended or feel deprived of something or taken advantage of. This, combined with his high Dominance (E+) and above-average Boldness (H+) indicate that he is likely to be forceful, competitive, and stubborn in asserting his will. He will probably be somewhat acerbic in his efforts to influence others. Gordon's above-average score on Openness to Change (Q1+) suggests that a counselor can expect him to push for change in his own life and in his surroundings if he sees something that is not up to his standards.

Gordon's low-average Extraversion score represents an average among opposing primary scales: Warmth (2), Liveliness (6), Social Boldness (7), Privateness (4), and Self-Reliance (9). Two of them, Warmth (2) and Self-Reliance (9) are very much in the introverted direction. This is important because these two, sometimes called the motivational component of Extraversion, represent the warm-hearted affiliative drive and Gordon is low on these. This means that he is likely to have little inherent interest in other people and to be detached, cold, and individualistic in his lifestyle. Social Boldness (H+), is high average and represents Gordon's tendency toward social prominence. Privateness (N-) is low-average suggesting that Gordon is forthright and does not find it difficult to reveal private matters. Taken together, the Independence and Extraversion scales suggest that in social interactions, Gordon will push aggressively for his own ideas and interests and will show little concern, interest, or trust in others.

Gordon's high Anxiety score contains four primary scales, all of which are in the same direction: Emotional Stability (5), Vigilance (9), Apprehension (7), and Tension (8). Gordon's score on the Emotional Stability scale (C = 5) is average, which suggests that he has adequate coping resources. However, the other contributory scales are high (Vigilance, Tension) or high average (Apprehension). These traits, especially when combined with Gordon's dominance and social indifference, are likely to come across as impatience, distrust, and anger. This is consistent with the original impression of the interviewer. However, the average score on Emotional Stability is encouraging and suggests optimism about the outcome of the counseling; this score, along with the fact that the high scores on Anxiety are Tension, Apprehension, and Vigilance, make it more probable that the Anxiety is situational. The Apprehension score (7) adds the components of worry and self-doubt to the overall picture.

After Independence and Anxiety, the next most extreme global score is Self-Control (3.6), with its primary scales Liveliness (6), Rule-Consciousness (2), Abstractedness (6), and Perfectionism (5). All of these scales are in the average range except Rule-Consciousness, which is very low (G = 2). A counselor might hypothesize that the overall Self-Control would be average if Gordon showed more adherence to the ordinary rules of society.

The Tough-Mindedness scale is average: Warmth (2), Sensitivity (5), Abstractedness (6), and Openness to Change (7). Although Sensitivity and Abstractedness are average, Warmth (A = 2) is very much in the Tough-Minded direction, and Openness to Change (Q1 = 7) is high average in the opposite Receptive, open-minded direction. Thus, Gordon tends to be rather cool and aloof with people but is open to new ideas and new ways of doing things. The low Warmth (A) is consistent with some of his introverted qualities. His score on Openness to Change (Q1) along with his low Rule-Consciousness (G) and high Reasoning ability (B = 9) suggest that he may use his independent qualities to push for unconventional or innovative ideas.

In general, the most defining primary scores are the high scores on Reasoning (9), Vigilance (9), Self-Reliance (9), and Dominance (8), and the low Warmth (2) and Rule-Consciousness (2) scores. Gordon has presented himself as bright, aloof, distrustful, and not particularly respectful of society's expectations.

Step 5: Consider Scale Interactions, Prediction Equations, Interpretive Report Content, and Comparison Profiles

Gordon's profile matches that of several patterns from the Scale Interactions section in chapter 3. The reader is reminded that descriptions in the Scale Interactions section are best considered as sources of hypotheses for a practitioner. Two patterns (A- E+; A- Q2+) involve Gordon's very low score on Warmth (2). The first of these (A- E+) suggests that Gordon may present himself as stubborn and aggressive—wanting to have influence over others but without the Warmth that would soften his behavior. The second (A- Q2+) suggests that Gordon may be perceived as aloof, individualistic, and indifferent, possibly because of negative experiences with relationships.

Three other patterns are notable. Based on his very high Reasoning (9) and Vigilance (9), in company with the high score on Dominance (8) and the high average score on Openness to Change (7), the pattern (B+ E+ L+ Q1+) suggests a client with a high degree of intellectualized hostility, which may well show itself in angry or critical verbalizations. Another pattern taking rise from his low Rule-Consciousness and high Apprehension (G- O+), but also including his high score on Tension (Q4+), suggests that Gordon's presence in the counselor's office can be traced to transient distress coming from identity problems that are reflected in guilt about not conforming to society's common rules. Finally, a combination rooted in his very high scores on Vigilance and Self-Reliance (L+ Q2+) (but consistent with his low Warmth) links his withdrawal to his pervasive distrust of the motives and actions of others. H.B. Cattell (1989) interprets this pattern as a tendency to project one's own insecurities outward and blame others, a pattern common among adolescents.

In addition, information from the Personal Career Development Profile report (PCDP; see appendix) based on equations using Gordon's scores, are of particular interest. Gordon was found to score particularly high on Creative Potential, high on Formal Academic Interest, and very high on Authoritarian leadership and on Confrontive interaction style. These inferences can be seen to be consistent with other observations made from the primary and global scales and from the scale interactions.

Step 6: Integrate All Information in Relation to the Assessment Question

Gordon is struggling with life transitions and is seeing a counselor for help. Prior to meeting with Gordon, a counselor or therapist might note from his high Anxiety score that Gordon is probably experiencing significant discomfort and will be highly motivated to work hard in the counseling. Such proved to be the case. A second general consideration is the client's high score on Reasoning (B+), which suggests that Gordon will have significant intellectual resources and will be able to grasp subtleties of a counseling session.

The practitioner, noting the client's scores on Social Boldness (H+) and Privateness (N-) might anticipate no great hindrance for the client in speaking of personal matters but perhaps some difficulty in bonding and collaborating with the counselor because of the very low Warmth (A-) and high Self-Reliance (Q2+). As it turned out, the low Warmth did not present a large problem for the counselor-client interactions because Gordon did not need a warm relationship with the counselor; he only needed one in which he could feel that he was making progress on his problems. The counselor, who was in the low-average range on these scales himself, had no difficulty with Gordon's lack of natural warmth, finding it easy to respect Gordon's independent, self-directed, and principled approach to human relations.

In addition to a strong motive to alleviate the Anxiety, the counselor might hypothesize that Gordon would be strongly motivated toward dominance (E+), self-sufficiency (Q2+), Independence, and attention seeking (H+) in the sessions. It is essential for the professional to understand and respect Gordon's need for control and autonomy, and that it is difficult for a client such as Gordon to seek help or advice of any kind. A counselor should exercise great caution to not get into a power struggle with the client, who will prefer to see the counselor as an expert consultant who can help him solve some current problem.

In fact, with this approach, Gordon's dominance (E+), Independence, Self-Reliance (Q2+), and Social Boldness seemed to be expressed in the session more in terms of striving for excellence of some kind. Although Gordon did not get into power struggles in the sessions, it was always clear that he would make up his own mind about his life. In other words, autonomy more than dominance, proved to be a key element of counselor-client interaction during the sessions. The counselor found that Gordon could set his own pace and even provide a strong lead in terms of the method that was used during the counseling sessions. He wanted to talk and think things through without pressure, and just doing so allowed him to come to grips with his life-transition issues.

Noting Gordon's scores on the intellectualized hostility pattern (B+, E+, L+, Q1+), the counselor might expect that he might be hypercritical, impatient with the counselor's efforts, or actively hostile or resistant. However, with forethought on this issue, the therapist was able to avoid these problems. Although these characteristics were evident in the sessions, they were directed not toward the counselor but toward the foibles and failings of Gordon's bosses and coworkers and toward people who foster inequities in society.

Another pattern that did seem to influence counselor-client interaction in the sessions is one marked by high Self-Reliance and high Vigilance (L+, Q2+), suggesting a client who has withdrawn and is suspicious of others, interpreted by H. E. Cattell (1989) as a projection of the client's own insecurities onto others. This pattern and one other (G-, O+, Q1+), suggesting an identity problem centered on socially approved behavior, helped the counselor hypothesize that a focal point of Gordon's distress lay in his attempts to move from a somewhat naive, immature self-concept to a more adult, realistic one. In fact, when this hypothesis was presented to the client as an issue to be considered, it became the topic of lengthy and profitable conversations.

Gordon was very bright and did not value middle-class expectations as such. He was a person of great principle—one possible interpretation suggested for G-scores—and he could easily see hypocrisy and selfishness in the world. The lack of respect, distrust, resentment, and withdrawal (L+, Q1+, Q2+, A-) that accompanied these viewpoints supported his tendency to disregard society's rules (G-), but he couldn't be at ease with this attitude and felt guilty, frustrated, and self-doubting (O+, Q4+). He was experiencing a form of identity crisis, somewhat late in terms of the usual timetable—a crisis between the ideals and conflicts of his youth and the practical demands of making a living and providing for a family.

He was experiencing a conflict between his principles and the practical realities of life. The conflict came to be felt as a strong sense of insecurity, which added to his suspicions and hostility. He knew that to get what he wanted for his family, he had to get a different job and give up the social work position that he had entered because of his ideals. When he came to counseling, he was filled with resentment because of the necessity of this life change. He was uncomfortable with these feelings, and they eventually drove him to seek counseling. As all these issues came to a greater level of consciousness, he was able to accept the various sets of feelings and values that were influencing him and move on in a productive way.

An important aspect of the counseling was that Gordon's autonomy (Q2+) was respected and that he was able to address his issues on his own schedule. Because of this process, in which the counselor took a passive role, and because of Gordon's determination and intelligence (B+), he had more than one moment of enlightenment during the counseling, when he could see the issues clearly. He began to accept both aspects of himself—his idealism as well as his practical needs and wants. He began to accept life on its own terms, and he found he could give up blaming the world for a difficult choice he had to make. His anger and suspicion (L+) diminished, and with it his Anxiety also diminished. What had seemed to be an insoluble discrepancy between his ideals and his wants began to look more like a choice as he began to have more self-assurance.

Gradually, he found himself able to look for a different kind of work with a certain amount of excitement and pleasure. He realized that he did not have to sacrifice his ideals to take a higher paying job and that working for an ordinary business did not mean that he had to sell his soul.

Because he was bright, ambitious, and highly motivated, he found that he could readily get a job despite his anxiety and lack of warmth, and he began to get interested in the process of a job search. He selected information management as a field because of the intellectual challenge it posed and because of the opportunities for advancement it offered.

ERIC: AN EXECUTIVE COACHING CASE STUDY

The following case is written by Dr. David G. Watterson, Jr. and describes a leadership coaching process with a senior executive that Watterson completed. The 16PF Questionnaire is an excellent tool to use in the coaching process because it provides incisive, nonthreatening, constructive feedback to individuals about their personality style. One of the first steps in any coaching process is to heighten an individual's self-awareness, because being clear about strengths and weaknesses is a primary contributor to success in most areas of life. Goleman, Boyatzis, and McKee (2002) in their work on emotional intelligence (EI) and leadership have demonstrated this principle repeatedly. "In short, self-awareness facilitates both empathy and self-management, and these two, in combination, allow effective relationship management. EI leadership, then, builds up from a foundation of self-awareness." (p. 30)

When interpreting 16PF profiles in an occupational setting, the following five steps are often used: (1) consider all sources of information in understanding the assessment context; (2) evaluate 16PF global and primary scores, particularly in comparison to those of an appropriate occupational group; (3) evaluate particular 16PF primary scale interactions; (4) consider scores on research-based prediction equations; and (5) integrate all information into an action plan.

Step 1: Consider Context of Assessment

Eric was a senior vice president for an industrial supply company that was a wholly owned subsidiary of a larger corporation. His division made around $800 million in annual sales; the parent corporation made just under $4 billion in annual sales. At the time of the test administration, he was 46 years old, had been with the company for 17 years, and had been in the industry for his whole career (24 years) in distribution. He was feeling pressure to personally perform at a higher level in response to a request that he move into a more senior level within the larger corporation. He was viewed favorably for his contribution to increasing the business, but the organizational demands to be more of a leader and less of a hands-on manager were causing him concern. The company had expanded substantially in the last 5 years, and Eric's division was in a position for considerable growth and additional acquisitions.

In light of these circumstances, Eric had been sent to a well-known consulting firm for an independent assessment process, which included a 360-degree feedback instrument, an interview, and a number of cognitive measures. At that point, the present leadership coach was brought in to provide assistance in focusing his development. Although Eric was a bit apprehensive about this process, he was also excited to address some areas for development about which he had known for years.

Eric was interviewed and the 16PF Questionnaire administered. The results of the 360-degree tool that had been previously administered were also considered. They included very high scores for his thinking competencies, industry knowledge, drive for stakeholder success, and customer service. He was given lower ratings in the areas of empowering others, building organizational relationships, attracting and developing talent, and flexibility.

The results of the coach's interview with Eric fit with these 360-degree competencies. Eric had many years of experience and had become more knowledgeable during the organization's growth, had a high degree of thinking ability, and appeared driven to achieve and create positive results. At the same time, he was now at a point in his career at which some of his developmental areas were causing both him and the organization concern. The results of the 16PF assessment helped Eric to focus on his developmental issues.

Step 2: Evaluate 16PF Global and Primary Scores in Comparison to Appropriate Reference Groups

Figure 8.3 compares Eric's 16PF scores to those of a group of senior business leaders—the norm group for the 16PF Leadership Coaching Report (Watterson, 2002, pp. 25–26). Additional occupational profiles can be found in the 16PF resource books and 16PF reports presented in chapter 4 (Rapid References 4.1 and 4.2).

Comparing the individual to relevant group profiles highlights similarities and differences between the test taker's profile and the comparison profiles for particular organizational roles. Some differences are expected, depending on the type of industry and other extenuating circumstances surrounding the particular client. For example, in a more engineering-oriented business, Self-Control scores tend to be higher than in other executive groups. Similarly, in sales executive roles in the cosmetic industry, it is more important to be sensitive and aesthetically conscious (I+) than in other executive roles. The best frame of reference for a particular individual is a specific norm sample developed from that individual's company or setting. When an individual profile is compared to an occupational group, a difference of more than one sten point is worthy of notice; however, 1-point differences should be considered to be within the expected range.

Independence

In Figure 8.3, Eric's most distinguishing primary score difference from typical leaders is his considerable shyness (H-). There is a 5-point difference between Eric and typical senior executives, who are typically higher on Social Boldness. His low Social Boldness (H-) score significantly lowers his global Independence score (which is more than 2.5 stens below the average for the executive norm group) and also influences the nature of his Independence. Eric's other primary scales that contribute to global Independence—Dominance (E), Vigilance (L), and Openness to Change (Q1)—are all only

RESPONSE STYLE (VALIDITY) INDICES

	Raw Score	Percentiles	
Impression Management	12	50%	within expected range
Infrequency	2	71%	within expected range
Acquiescence	45	10%	within expected range

PRIMARY FACTOR SCALES

Factor	Sten	Left Meaning	Standard Ten Score (STEN) |-Average-| 1 2 3 4 5 6 7 8 9 10	Right Meaning
A: Warmth	5	Reserved, Impersonal, Distant		Warm, Outgoing, Attentive to Others
B: Reasoning	8	Concrete		Abstract
C: Emotional Stability	5	Reactive, Emotionally Changeable		Emotionally Stable, Adaptive, Mature
E: Dominance	6	Deferential, Cooperative, Avoids Conflict		Dominant, Forceful, Assertive
F: Liveliness	4	Serious, Restrained, Careful		Lively, Animated, Spontaneous
G: Rule-Consciousness	5	Expedient, Nonconforming		Rule-Conscious, Dutiful
H: Social Boldness	2	Shy, Threat-Sensitive, Timid		Socially Bold, Venturesome, Thick-Skinned
I: Sensitivity	5	Utilitarian, Objective, Unsentimental		Sensitive, Aesthetic, Sentimental
L: Vigilance	4	Trusting, Unsuspecting, Accepting		Vigilant, Suspicious, Skeptical, Wary
M: Abstractedness	5	Grounded, Practical, Solution-Oriented		Abstracted, Imaginative, Idea-Oriented
N: Privateness	7	Forthright, Genuine, Artless		Private, Discreet, Non-Disclosing
O: Apprehension	8	Self-Assured, Unworried, Complacent		Apprehensive, Self-Doubting, Worried
Q₁: Openness to Change	6	Traditional, Attached to Familiar		Open to Change, Experimenting
Q₂: Self-Reliance	6	Group-Oriented, Affiliative		Self-Reliant, Solitary, Individualistic
Q₃: Perfectionism	8	Tolerates Disorder, Unexacting, Flexible		Perfectionistic, Organized, Self-Disciplined
Q₄: Tension	8	Relaxed, Placid, Patient		Tense, High Energy, Impatient, Driven

GLOBAL FACTOR SCALES

Factor	Sten	Left Meaning	Standard Ten Score (STEN) |-Average-| 1 2 3 4 5 6 7 8 9 10	Right Meaning
EX: Extraversion	3.6	Introverted, Socially Inhibited		Extraverted, Socially Participating
AX: Anxiety	7.2	Low Anxiety, Unperturbed		High Anxiety, Perturbable
TM: Tough-Mindedness	5.8	Receptive, Open-Minded, Intuitive		Tough-Minded, Resolute, Unempathic
IN: Independence	4.6	Accommodating, Agreeable, Selfless		Independent, Persuasive, Willful
SC: Self-Control	6.7	Unrestrained, Follows Urges		Self-Controlled, Inhibits Urges

Key
...... = Target scores from Executive Group*
_____ = Eric Executive's scores
* See table 8.1 for the actual profile scores of the target Executive Group.

Figure 8.3. 16PF profile for Eric, executive.

Adapted with permission from Institute for Personality and Ability Testing. (1993). *16PF Fifth Edition Individual Record Form: Profile Sheet.* Champaign, IL: Author.

slightly lower than those of typical executives, so his strong shyness (H-) is the major contributor to his lower level of Independence. His shyness decreases his interest, motivation, and skills for interacting with others in a range of settings. Making presentations, pursuing new projects in an adventurous manner, and speaking up in regard to his vision and the general direction of the organization may be hard for him. For example, he may hesitate to make group presentations regarding business plans or outcomes of sales efforts or come across as lacking confidence when doing so. Additionally, such an extreme score on any scale (1, 2 or 9, 10) tends to have a pervasive effect across the entire personality.

Eric's scores on the other primary scores within Independence are generally within the target range for executives. He has average scores on assertiveness (E+) and openness to new ideas (Q1+), but his score on suspiciousness (L-) is in the below-average range. Thus, he has just an average interest in dominating or controlling others and in pushing for success and change, and he is more trusting and forgiving in his style rather than vigilant or competitive.

Anxiety

Anxiety is Eric's second most discrepant global dimension—he scores almost 2 points higher than the typical senior executive does. In terms of the primary scales that create this difference within the global, Eric tends to be much more apprehensive (a 4-point difference on O+) and much more tense (a 3-point difference on Q4+), whereas the other scales within Anxiety are more average. His high apprehensiveness (O+) results in a tendency to worry and to have higher levels of self-doubt than is productive. In addition, he experiences a high degree of tension (Q4+), which may cause him to appear driven and pressured and to experience stress physically. On the other hand, above average tension (Q4+) is important for providing energy in the drive for accomplishment, and Eric may use his higher degree of tension to drive his quest for achievement.

Eric's other Anxiety scores are closer to average: His general emotional balance tends to be average (C), and he is more trusting and forgiving than average (L-). These two scores represent assets because they indicate that there is not a great deal of suspiciousness or hostility (L-) and that he is not likely to be easily upset by negative events; rather, he is likely to bounce back from disappointments in an average period of time and show good coping skills (C+). Thus, overall, in the area of Resilience versus Anxiety, Eric's above-average score means that he is the kind of person who can be expected to function adequately in most situations but may have trouble under stress.

Overall, his resilience is lowered by his strong self-judgmental orientation and his high drive to perform.

Extraversion

On Extraversion, Eric's shyness (H-) again contributes to his significantly lower score. Other contributors to his low Extraversion are his tendency to be more quiet and serious (F is 2 points lower than that of the typical executive) and his tendency to be more private and unrevealing about his own thoughts and feelings (N is 2 points higher than that of other executives). These scores indicate that he is a rather shy, reserved, cautious individual who tends to be self-sufficient in his approach to his work and his life. Overall, he tends to socialize little and to develop few strong personal relationships. He prefers to work alone, hesitates to initiate and speak up in groups, and has fewer social skills to use with strangers. Overall, his Extraversion is strongly affected by his very shy nature, and he tends to keep private his perceived inadequacies. New people and new situations will be hard for him.

Tough-Mindedness

On this scale, Eric is quite similar to the typical senior executive. All his Tough-Mindedness scores are within the average range. He has a good balance in being moderately practical and tough-minded about work decisions (I, M) and at the same time responds with an average amount of empathy and openness to new ideas (I, Q1). He may not express these thoughts and feelings because of his reserve (F-, H-, N-), but they are there.

Self-Control

On the last global factor, Self-Control, Eric's score is also within 1 point of the typical executive's. On the primary scales that make up Self-Control, he shows a relatively good balance with the exception of being highly conscientious (Q3+), and somewhat more serious (F-). His tendency to be meticulous (Q3+) shows that he is organized and attentive to specific details, which may suggest a tendency toward perfectionism. This detail orientation has helped him to get a lot done in an accurate and precise manner. This drive to get things done correctly feeds his achievement orientation, drive, and desire to grow. The coach can capitalize on this strength in the coaching process. On the other hand, it also contributes to a strong drive to get overly involved in the smaller day-to-day details of running the operation, which is not conducive to high performance in a senior executive. This profile is typical for someone like Eric who came up through the ranks of the operations side of the business, where attention to detail was extremely important. However, when compared to that of more senior executives, his attention to detail is higher than may be optimum for a leader.

Evaluate Primary Scale Interactions

Additional meaning and insight can be gained by interpreting particular combinations of 16PF scores. These insights were developed through the interpretation of thousands of 16PF profiles, and many can be found in resource books, manuals, and reports such as those listed in chapter 4 (Rapid References 4.1 and 4.2).

In Eric's profile, his strong shyness (H-) combined with his tendency to be meticulous (Q3+) suggest an individual who has a high concern for wanting to appear correct and do the right thing in new social circumstances. People with these scores may hesitate to step out and be involved in new situations in which expectations are not clear. They may be uncomfortable not knowing the right thing to do, and this ambiguity may be difficult for them. For Eric, these scores are combined with the additional impact of being highly apprehensive (O+) and tense (Q4+). His tendency to worry and be insecure may contribute to his hesitancy about making mistakes or to his lack of confidence about how to handle new situations.

A further triple-score combination that builds on this same pair of traits is Eric's tendency to be shy (H-), private (N+), and perfectionistic (Q3+). This combination of shy, self-conscious Introversion with some degree of perfectionism indicates that he may hesitate to reveal much about himself because of a concern that his flaws and inadequacies will be revealed. Thus, he is likely to keep things to himself; this was very much a part of Eric's nature.

This combination of low Social Boldness (H-) and high Perfectionism (Q3+) is likely to be a focus in the coaching process. Important strategies will be to help Eric: (a) Develop an awareness of how he creates pressure for himself when presented with a new social situation, (b) develop skills to manage this social tension, and (c) practice in one or more group situations.

Another important scale combination involves the two primary scales that make up global Self-Control—Rule-Consciousness (G) and Perfectionism (Q3). The style of Self-Control can be quite different if the score on one of these scales is significantly higher than the other. When Perfectionism (Q3+) is 2 or more points higher than Rule-Consciousness (G), as it is for Eric, the individual may have a tendency to try to control situations through giving a high attention to planning all details. Because Rule-Consciousness (G) is lower than Q3, the person may have a certain degree of inattention and flexibility about rules and procedures and may not function according to regular routines and conventions. Instead, the individual will want to have control and knowledge of all the details.

This approach is typical of Eric, whose Perfectionism (Q3) score is more than 2 points higher than his Rule-Consciousness score (G). Eric likes to attend to many different parts of the business and to manage, plan, and know everything about how the business is performing. When the business was smaller, he was able to attend to all the details. As he has moved up in his role, he has passed the point at which it is appropriate to be attentive to all the details. With the business in a state of growth, he does not have all of the systems and routines in place to run the company's operations, so he is likely to become highly demanding of others and also quite stressed himself in trying to cover all this territory. Therefore, learning to delegate should be a key focus of his coaching process.

If these two scores had been reversed—a relatively higher Rule Consciousness (G+) score and a lower Perfectionism (Q3-) score—Eric would strictly follow regular routines and his challenge would have been to learn to be more flexible and less resistant to change and surprise. With this second type of over-control pattern, the individual has a tendency to adhere to set systems and procedures in order to control the situation. He or she is not as concerned about planning every detail but relies on conformity to rules and standards, which help things run smoothly because of systems being followed. However, with high Rule-Consciousness (G+) scores, flexibility and adaptability are limited, and the individual can be demanding and rigid about following set rules on procedures and standards.

A triple score combination that is relevant to Eric's profile is that of scores of 6 or higher on Openness to Change (Q1+), scores of 4 or lower on

Vigilance (L-), and scores of 6 or higher on Apprehension (O+). Generally, this combination denotes a higher likelihood that the person is quite self-critical; this combines the demand for rapid change, improvement, and development (Q1+) and directs it toward the self (L-). Because life and people often do not reach such demanding expectations, Eric may regard himself as coming up short, resulting in an even higher degree of self-doubt (O+). A relevant phrase in giving feedback to an individual like this is, "You tend to be your own most severe critic." The coaching strategy is to practice realizing expectations while using appropriate language (e.g., *I wanted to get that done* vs. *I should have gotten it done*).

Consider Scores on Research-Based Prediction Equations

A third interpretive approach is to look at research-based prediction equations that can be found in the resource books and interpretive reports in chapter 4 (Rapid References 4.1 and 4.2). These equations were derived from research using regression analyses to predict various criteria from 16PF scores. Equations have been developed to predict a wide variety of topics including achievement, leadership, creativity, interpersonal skills, empathy, self-esteem, and leisure interests (Conn & Rieke, 1994). Equations in various interpretive reports compare profiles statistically to an occupational group such as machine operator, accountant, or pilot. In Eric's situation, we can get a clearer picture of his abilities if we look at the equations related to the concepts of leadership, achievement, and creativity.

Several different 16PF equations have been developed for leadership based on different research samples; for discussions of these different equations, see chapter 9 of the *16PF Fifth Edition Technical Manual* (Conn & Rieke, 1994). For Eric, we used a special equation specifically developed from Eric's organization. The equation combines scores on abstract Reasoning (B+), Emotional Stability (C+), Dominance (E+), Liveliness (F+), Rule-Consciousness (G+), Social Boldness (H+), objectivity (I-), trust (L-), practicality (M-), self-assurance (O-), Openness to Change (Q1+), Perfectionism (Q3+), and low Tension (Q4-). On this equation Eric's score is 4.5, which is on the low side of average. Generally, the scores that lower his leadership score are his lower interpersonal scores (F-, H-, N+) and his higher Anxiety (O+, Q4+) scores. This information also helps to focus the coaching effort.

Eric's scores on the equation for achievement, however, is above average (7.2). This score supports the success that he has had as a competent learner and in developing strong business accomplishments. This equation capitalizes on Eric's intellectual ability (B+), his ability to be self-disciplined and organized (Q3+), and his average ability to be imaginative (M) and self-reliant (Q2+). His lower Extraversion and his shyness do not detract from his achievement capabilities or from his ability to learn. Some of his lack of interest in meeting new people and venturing forth, in fact, allows him to conscientiously pursue his learning activities so that he is able to focus on developing those competencies to a higher level.

The last equation that might be relevant to Eric's performance in a leadership role is his above-average creativity (6.5), which would allow him to be visionary and strategic as a leader. His score on creativity is not as high as his Achievement score, but it is certainly in the direction that would allow for moderate success. A number of his traits contribute to his above-average score on this equation: his high reasoning ability (B+), his seriousness and inward focus (H-, F-, N-), his objectivity (I-), his persistent self-discipline (Q3+), and his moderate-range scores on dominance (E) and openness to change (Q1).

By looking at scores on these equations, the coaching effort can gain some added clarification. They indicate that his leadership is highly supported by his abilities to be more creative and to drive to achieve, particularly in the areas of his learning and information acquisition; this is a strong contributing factor to Eric's success and to his overall approach. It leads to his high degree of product knowledge and business savvy as well as his desire to teach the same elements of the business to others. Numerous other equations can add perspective in guiding the coaching effort.

Integrating All Information Into an Action Plan

Overall, results indicate that Eric is a hardworking, bright, achievement-oriented, and driven person who has developed strong industry and business knowledge, high standards for getting things done right, and a history of creating results. As the business has grown, he has expanded his realm of responsibility, which includes having more and more people reporting to him. His results now depend less on what he can personally do and more on how well he leads others to create results; this has placed a much stronger emphasis on his ability to communicate and delegate. Thus, the focus of the coaching process is on communication and delegation and the personality characteristics related to these areas.

In this case in which effective leadership is the goal, the first step is to develop heightened self-awareness through constructive feedback. A useful tool in the feedback process is to read and discuss one of the computerized interpretive reports that contain hand-back materials, such as the Personal Career Development Profile report (PCDP) or the Leadership Coaching Report (LCR). These materials give the individual feedback in a comprehensive, objective, and independent fashion. Getting feedback from several different sources and through different kinds of interpretive styles is helpful to individuals. The next step in the coaching process involves selecting the parts of the report that are particularly important to the immediate situation and then developing an action plan.

In looking at developmental pathways for Eric and creating an action plan, one of the first areas on which to focus is that of gaining greater ease in social communication—overcoming his strong shyness (H+) and insecurity (O+) plus his general Introversion (F-, N+). Suggestions might include reading *Conversationally Speaking* (Garner, 1997), which focuses on opening conversations and maintaining them with ease, and *Your Perfect Right* (Alberti & Emmons, 2001), which focuses on assertiveness skills.

Even though Eric's Dominance (E) score is average, his resistance to being assertive is revealed in (a) his hesitancy to speak up or confront others (H+, O+) and his cautious, restrained nature (F-, H-, N+); (b) his tendency to be frustrated and self-blaming with missed expectations (Q4+, O+, Q3+, L-); and (c) his sense of inadequacy combined with his concern that he would be seen as failing (H+, O+, Q3+). One coaching strategy to address these issues would be to read *The 10 Dumbest Mistakes Smart People Make and How To Avoid Them* (Freeman & De Wolf, 1992) and practice the self-talk discussed in chapter 10 regarding the tyranny of *should* as well as concentrating on chapter 7 regarding perfectionism, inadequacy, and *not good enough*. Another strategy is to practice disclosing one thought, feeling, or idea each day.

In action areas, Eric focused on specific activities that he could delegate to others instead of doing himself. During the coaching process, a situation arose in which a national meeting that he would normally have attended himself became an opportunity for him to decide to send two of his direct reports. He also worked on changing his general way of handling the business by trying to ask more questions instead of telling people things. He continued to work on delegating more to others; he discovered that this benefited others' learning as well as freed his time for other projects. He made official announcements about the changes he was making, which also encouraged him to be less private and more open regarding his plans and his actions. He received more feedback about his ideas, which resulted in even better solutions. He also practiced introducing himself to others and starting conversations to combat his tendency to be reserved, and he took the opportunity to attend events at his children's school where he practiced new social skills such as introducing himself to many new people. Eric worked consistently on being more at ease in social circumstances and better at asserting himself. He made significant progress in these areas and is able to express his vision and be clear about his own expectations.

Over a 1.5-year period of time, Eric continued to work on his development. He attended a course on coaching skills in order to develop his social skills in talking and listening to others, and he also had all of his direct reports attend the same training so that they were all conscious of the steps involved in this process. In this way, everyone improved and supported each other as they all got better at these social skills. Late in the first year, he received individual coaching for his speaking skills and practiced by volunteering to be a speaker in the local Juvenile Diabetes Chapter. This gave him an opportunity to speak in front of strangers on a subject on which he was not an expert but had strong feelings (his daughter has juvenile diabetes). He joined Toastmasters International and when his travel permitted, he got the opportunity to speak on unfamiliar topics and introduce himself to strangers. He continued to read *Never Good Enough: How to Use Perfectionism to Your Advantage Without Ruining Your Life* (Basco, 2000) and now is quite skilled in attending to his own self-talk. He also attended a weekend experience to accelerate his own listening skills. He has continued to support a leadership developmental program for his organization, and he continues to look at his own development as he moves forward. Eric has subsequently been promoted to Executive Vice President in the parent company.

Appendix

Reports Generated From 16PF Scores

- *16PF Basic Interpretive Report (BIR):* A multipurpose report, the BIR is organized in a simple five-scale framework. Interpretive statements are provided for each of the five global scale scores and the contributing primary scale scores, which are outside the average range of the scores. Predicted scores and explanatory statements are given for 13 interpersonal and behavioral dimensions and for the six Holland occupational interest themes.
- *16PF Basic Score Report (BSR):* This report is an economical scores-only report that features the primary and global scale scores in a graphic representation. Predicted scores are given for 13 interpersonal and behavioral dimensions and for the six Holland occupational interest themes. Professionals who are experienced in interpreting 16PF results often use the BSR.
- *16PF Cattell Comprehensive Personality Interpretation (CCPI):* The CCPI is suitable in clinical, counseling, and consulting situations requiring an in-depth understanding of an individual's personality. In addition to a 16PF profile (scores for the primary and global scale scales), this report provides narrative interpretations in a wide variety of areas, including information processing style, interpersonal relationship issues, and implications of personality for work behavior and for the therapeutic relationship.
- *16PF Couple's Counseling Report (CCR):* The CCR enables the counselor to quickly identify some of the key relationship issues, and it provides possible implications of similarities and differences between the two people. This report examines the personality organization of two people and compares the two profiles. To supplement the personality profiles, an additional set of questions provides information about each individual's relationship history and relationship satisfaction ratings for 11 different areas.
- *16 PF Human Resource Development Report (HRDR):* In business and industrial/organizational settings, the HRDR helps assess leadership and management potential, and serves as an effective training tool in management development decisions. The report offers a narrative section that can be shared with the client at the professional's discretion plus score pages for the professional only. The score pages provide information about the 16 primary scales and the five global scales; they also provide predicted scores on leadership style, leadership potential, and creativity.

- *16PF Karson Clinical Report (KCR):* This report offers a simple, fast, and reliable method of gaining an immediate understanding of a client's enduring personality makeup by identifying personal strengths as well as potential weaknesses. Through an in-depth interpretation of normal personality scales from a clinical perspective, the KCR describes behavioral manifestations and propensities as well as in-depth personality dynamics.. This understanding helps the clinician quickly put the presenting problems into the context of the total personality and facilitates a more rapid development of treatment plans.

- *16PF Leadership Coaching Report (LCR):* The LCR is a workbook-style report of more than 40 pages that assesses problem-solving ability and five key personality dimensions. It compares the developing leader's personal behavioral style with that of successful leaders. The LCR then identifies the personal gifts and limits of the leadership participant and explains how these gifts and limits are likely to manifest themselves in leadership situations (i.e., how a strength in one situation may be a limitation in another). The report provides the developing leader with strategies to enhance his or her strengths and suggests developmental activities for the areas targeted for development. Professional coaches use the workbook to facilitate the development process by providing the leadership participant with knowledge of his or her leadership style and the framework for an individualized developmental action plan.

- *16PF Personal Career Development Profile (PCDP):* The PCDP is an effective tool for outplacement counseling, personnel development, career exploration, and personal growth. It features an easy-to-understand, client-friendly narrative section that helps people achieve personality insights as they relate to career interests. Also available is the Personal Career Development Profile Plus, which adds a practical set of self-analytical questions to help clients review their profile and develop action plans for career and personal growth.

- *16PF Protective Services Report (PSR):* The PSR provides score profiles for the 16 primary and five global normal personality scales as well as narrative about the individual's scores on four personality dimensions that are most relevant in protective services settings (i.e., Emotional Adjustment, Integrity-Control, Intellectual Efficiency, and Interpersonal Relations). Because this report focuses solely on normal personality, it is useful in development and both pre- and post-offer selection applications.

- *16PF Select Report (Select):* This report facilitates the selection of applicants who are most closely matched with the personality characteristics that are important for effective performance in a particular job, as defined by the professional. The report generates an Overall Model Similarity score, which represents the degree to which the applicant matches the prespecified model. The 16PF Select is a shortened version of the test and takes only 20 minutes to complete. Interpretive statements regarding the applicant's scores on 12 personality scales are provided.

- *16PF Teamwork Development Report (TDR):* The TDR describes implications of personality data for behavior in team settings. The report is useful for adults about to enter a teamwork environment or who are currently working within a team. It can be used for development of the individual team members, the team as a whole, or both. A sharable section is provided for each team member with statements describing the person's distinctive scores along with ideas for development based on the personality profile. The professional's section contains team summary information, individual team member score profiles, and predicted scores for Leadership, Adjustment, Creativity, and the six Holland occupational interest themes.

- *16PFworld.com Report:* This report is a concise narrative that is generated from administration of the 16PF Fifth Edition on the publisher's NetAssess service. (The NetAssess service offers the 16PF test in a number of languages, scoring with the appropriate national norms, an interpretive report in the test language, and instant translation of the report into any of the other available languages.) The 16PFworld.com Report includes interpretive statements for the five global factor scores and for each primary factor score that is outside the average range. The report also includes graphic profiles of sten scores on the five global and 16 primary personality factors, scores for the three response style indexes (Impression Management, Infrequency, and Acquiescence), item responses, and the raw score for each of the 16 primary factors.

References

Alberti, R., & Emmons, M. (2001). *Your perfect right: Assertiveness and equality in your life and relationships* (8th ed.). San Luis Obispo, CA: Impact.

Allport, G. W. (1961). *Pattern and growth in personality.* New York: Holt, Rinehart, and Winston.

Allport, G. W., & Odbert, H. S. (1936). *Trait names: A psycho-lexical study.* Psychological Monographs, 47 (171, Serial no. 211).

Altus, W. D. (1948). The validity of an abbreviated information test used in the Army. *Journal of Consulting Psychology, 12,* 270–275.

American Educational Research Association, American Psychological Association, & National Council on Measurement in Education. (1999). *Standards for educational and psychological testing.* Washington, DC: American Educational Research Association.

Aron, E. N. (1997). *The highly sensitive person: How to thrive when the world overwhelms you.* New York: Broadway Books.

Aron, E. N. (1999). High sensitivity as one source of fearfulness and shyness: Preliminary research and clinical implications. In L. A. Schmidt & J. Schulkin (Eds.), *Extreme fear, shyness and social phobia: Origins, biological mechanisms, and clinical outcomes. Series in affective science* (pp. 251–272). New York: Oxford University Press.

Ashton, M. C. (1998). Personality and job performance: The importance of narrow traits. *Journal of Organizational Behavior, 19*(3), 289–303.

Ashton, M. C., Jackson, D. N., Paunonen, S. V., Helmes, E., & Rothstein, M. G. (1995). The criterion validity of broad factor scales versus specific facet scales. *Journal of Research in Personality, 29,* 432–442.

Barbaranelli, C., & Caprara, G. B. (1996). How many dimensions to describe personality: A comparison of Cattell, Comrey, and the Big Five taxonomies of personality traits. *European Review of Applied Psychology, 46*(1), 15–24.

Barrick, M., & Mount, M. (1991). The big five personality dimensions and job performance: A meta-analysis. *Personnel Psychology, 44,* 1–26.

Barrick, M., & Mount, M. (1998). Five reasons why the "big five" article has been frequently cited. *Personnel Psychology, 51*(4), 849–857.

Bartram, D. (1995). The predictive validity of the EPI and the 16PF for military flying training. *Journal of Occupational & Organizational Psychology, 68*(3), 219–236.

Basco, M. R. (2000). *Never good enough: How to use perfectionism to your advantage without letting it ruin your life.* New York: Touchstone.

Beer, J. M. (2001). The influence of rearing order on personality: Data from biological adoptive siblings. *Dissertation Abstracts International, 61*(8), 4462B.

Cabrera, B.E. (2001). Lesbian gender identity. *Dissertation Abstracts International, 61*(8), 4462B.

Campbell, D., Hyne, S. A., & Nilsen, D. L. (1992). *Campbell Interest and Skill Survey.* Minneapolis, MN: National Computer Systems.

Candell, G. L. & Drasgow, F. (1988). An iterative procedure for linking metrics and assessing item bias in item response theory. *Applied Psychological Measurement, 15,* 78.

Cattell, H. B. (1989). *The 16PF: Personality in depth.* Champaign, IL: Institute for Personality and Ability Testing.

Cattell, H. B., & Cattell, H. E. P. (1997). *16PF Cattell Comprehensive Personality Interpretation manual.* Champaign, IL: Institute for Personality and Ability Testing.

Cattell, H. E. P. (1996). The original big-five: A historical perspective. *European Review of Applied Psychology, 46*(1), 5–14.

Cattell, R. B. (1943). The description of personality: Basic traits resolved into clusters. *Journal of Abnormal and Social Psychology, 38,* 476–506.

Cattell, R. B. (1946). *The description and measurement of personality.* New York: Harcourt, Brace, & World.

Cattell, R. B. (1957). *Personality and motivation structure and measurement.* New York: World Book.

Cattell, R. B. (1973). *Personality and mood by questionnaire.* San Francisco, CA: Jossey-Bass.

Cattell, R. B. (1979). *Personality and learning theory* (Vol. 1). New York: Springer.

Cattell, R. B. (1987). *Intelligence: Its structure, growth and measurement.* Amsterdam: North-Holland.

Cattell, R. B., Cattell, A. K., & Cattell, H. E. P. (1993). *Sixteen Personality Factor Fifth Edition Questionnaire.* Champaign, IL: Institute for Personality and Ability Testing.

Cattell, R. B., Cattell, A. K., Cattell, H. E. P., & Kelly, M. L. (1999). *16PF Select Questionnaire.* Champaign, IL: Institute for Personality and Ability Testing.

Cattell, R. B., Cattell, M. D., & Johns, E. (1984). *High School Personality Questionnaire.* Champaign, IL: Institute for Personality and Ability Testing.

Cattell, R. B., Eber, H. W., & Tatsuoka, M. M. (1992). *Handbook for the Sixteen Personality Factor Questionnaire* (Rev. ed.). Champaign, IL: Institute for Personality and Ability Testing.

Cattell, R. B., & Coan, R. W. (1976). *Early School Personality Questionnaire* (Rev. ed.). Champaign, IL: Institute for Personality and Ability Testing.

Cattell, R. B., & Horn, J. L. (1964) *Handbook and individual assessment manual for the Motivation Analysis Test*. Champaign IL: Institute for Personality and Ability Testing.

Cattell, R. B., & Krug, S. E. (1986). The number of factors in the 16PF: A review of the evidence with special emphasis on the methodological problems. *Educational and Psychological Measurement, 46*, 509–522.

Cattell, R. B., & Nesselroade, J. R. (1967). Likeness and completeness theories examined by sixteen personality factor measures on stably and unstably married couples. *Journal of Personality & Social Psychology, 7*(4), 351–361.

Chernyshenko, O., Stark, S., & Chan, K. Y. (2001). Investigating the hierarchical factor structure of the Fifth Edition of the 16PF: An application of the Schmid-Leiman orthogonalization procedure. *Educational and Psychological Measurement, 61*(2), 290–302.

Christiansen, N. D., Goffin, R. D., Johnston, N. G., & Rothstein, M. G. (1994). Correcting the 16PF for faking: Effects on criterion-related validity and individual hiring decisions. *Personnel Psychology, 47*(4), 847–860.

Conn, S. R., & Rieke, M. L. (1994). *16PF Fifth Edition Technical Manual*. Champaign, IL: Institute for Personality and Ability Testing.

Coopersmith, S. (1981). *Self-esteem inventories*. Palo Alto, CA: Consulting Psychologists Press.

Costa, P. T., & McCrae, R. R. (1976). Age differences in personality structure: A cluster analytic approach. *Journal of Gerontology, 31*, 564–570.

Costa, P. T., & McCrae, R. R. (1985). *The NEO Personality Inventory manual*. Odessa, FL: Psychological Assessment Resources.

Costa, P. T., & McCrae, R. R. (1992). *The Revised NEO personality inventory*. Odessa, FL: Psychological Assessment Resources.

Dee-Burnett, R., Johns, E. F., Russell, M. T., & Mead, A. D. (1997). *16PF Human Resource Development Report manual*. Champaign, IL: Institute for Personality and Ability Testing.

Digman, J. (1990). Personality structure: Emergence of the five-factor model. *Annual Review of Psychology, 41*, 417–440.

Drasgow, F., & Hulin, C. L. (1990). Item response theory. In M. D. Dunnette & L. M. Hough (Eds.), *Handbook of industrial and organizational psychology* (2nd ed., Vol. 1, pp. 577–636). Palo Alto, CA: Consulting Psychological Press.

Ellington, J., Smith, D. B, & Sackett, P. R. (2001). Investigating the influence of social desirability on personality factor structure. *Journal of Applied Psychology, 86*(1), 122–133.

Equal Employment Opportunity Commission, Office of Personnel Management, Department of Justice, Department of Labor, & Department of the Treasury. (1979). Uniform guidelines on employee selection procedures. *Federal Register, 43*, 38290–38315.

Farber, P. D. (1990). *Clinical use of the HSPQ.* Southeastern Psychological Association Workshop handout.

Franklin, E. C. (1983). A comparison among the sex-role orientation, self-esteem/ general adjustment, and personality profiles of men and women in male-dominated and female-dominated professions. (Unpublished doctoral dissertation, Kent State University).

Freeman, A., & De Wolf, R. (1992). *The 10 dumbest mistakes smart people make and how to avoid them: Simple and sure techniques for gaining greater control of your life.* New York: HarperCollins.

Garner, A. (1997). *Conversationally speaking: Tested new ways to increase your personal and social effectiveness.* Chicago: Contemporary Books.

Gerbing, D. W., & Tuley, M. R. (1991). The 16PF related to the five-factor model of personality: Multiple-indicator measurement versus the a priori scales. *Multivariate Behavioral Research, 26*(2), 271–289.

Goldberg, L. R. (1972). Parameters of personality inventory construction and utilization: A comparison of predictive strategies and tactics. *Multivariate Behavioral Research Monographs, 72*(2), 1–59.

Goldberg, L. R. (1993). The structure of phenotypic personality traits. *American Psychologist, 48,* 26–34.

Goldberg, L. R. (in press). The comparative validity of adult personality inventories: Applications of a consumer-testing framework. In S. R. Briggs, J. M. Cheek, & E. M. Donahue (Eds.), *Handbook of adult personality inventories.* New York: Plenum Press.

Goleman, D., Boyatzis, R., & McKee, A. (2002). *Primal leadership: Realizing the power of emotional intelligence.* Boston: Harvard Business School Press.

Gough, H. G. (1987). *California Psychological Inventory administrator's guide.* Palo Alto, CA: Consulting Psychologists Press.

Graham, J. R., & Lilly, R. S. (1984). *Psychological testing.* Englewood Cliffs, NJ: Prentice Hall.

Guastello, S. J. (1993). *The assessment of creative potential with the 16PF: Artists, musicians, research scientists, and engineers.* Champaign, IL: Institute of Personality and Ability Testing.

Guastello, S. J., & Rieke, M. L. (1993). *The 16PF and leadership: Summary of research findings 1954–1992.* Champaign, IL: Institute of Personality and Ability Testing.

Guion, R. M. (1998). *Assessment, measurement, and prediction for personnel decisions.* Mahwah, NJ: Lawrence Erlbaum.

Hambleton, R. K., Swaminathan, H., & Rogers, H. J. (1991). *Fundamentals of item response theory.* Newbury Park, CA: Sage.

Henderson, L., & Zimbardo, P. G. (2001). Shyness as a clinical condition: The Stanford Model. In W. R. Crozier & L. E. Alden (Eds.), *International handbook of social anxiety: Concepts, research and interventions relating to the self and shyness* (pp. 431–447). New York: Wiley.

Hofer, S. M., & Eber, H. W. (2002). Second-order factor structure of the Cattell Sixteen Personality Factor Inventory (16PF). In B. De Raad & M. Perugini (Eds.), *Big-five assessment* (pp. 397–404). Ashland, OH: Hogrefe & Huber.

Hofer, S. M., Horn, J. L., & Eber, H. W. (1997). A robust five-factor structure of the 16PF: Evidence from independent rotation and confirmatory factorial invariance procedures. *Personality and Individual Differences, 23*(2), 247–269.

Holland, J. L. (1997). *Making vocational choices: A theory of careers* (Rev. ed.). Englewood Cliffs, NJ: Prentice Hall.

Hough, L. (1998). Personality at work: Issues and evidence. In M. D. Hakel (Ed.), *Beyond multiple choice*. Malwah, NJ: Lawrence Erlbaum.

Hough, L., Eaton, N., Dunnette, M., Kamp, J., & McCloy, R. (1990). Criterion-related validities of personality constructs and the effect of response distortion of those validities. *Journal of Applied Psychology, 75*(5), 581–595.

Hough, L., & Ones, D. (2001). The structure, measurement, validity, and use of personality variables in industrial, work, and organizational psychology. In N. Anderson, D. S. Ones, H. K. Sinangil, & C. Viswesvaran (Eds.), *Handbook of industrial, work, and organizational psychology* (Vol. 1). Thousand Oaks, CA: Sage.

Hulin, C., Drasgow, F., & Parsons, C. (1983). *Item response theory: Application to psychological measurement*. Homewood, IL: Dow Jones-Irwin.

Institute for Personality and Ability Testing. (1973). *Measuring intelligence with the Culture Fair Tests: Manual for Scales 2 and 3*. Champaign, IL: Author.

Institute for Personality and Ability Testing, Inc. (1993). *16PF Fifth Edition Individual Record Form: Profile sheet*. Champaign, IL: Author.

Jackson, D. N. (1997). *Personality Research Form manual* (Rev. ed.). Port Huron, MI: Sigma Assessment Systems.

Jung, C. J. (1928). Psychological types. New York: Harcourt & Brace.

Karson, S., & Karson, M. (1998). *16PF Karson Clinical Report manual*. Champaign, IL: Institute for Personality and Ability Testing.

Karson, S., Karson, M., & O'Dell, J. W. (1997). *16PF interpretation in clinical practice: A guide to the Fifth Edition*. Champaign, IL: Institute for Personality and Ability Testing.

Karson, S., & O'Dell, J. W. (1976). *Guide to the clinical use of the 16PF*. Champaign, IL: Institute for Personality and Ability Testing.

Kaushik, T. (1995). An empirical investigation of the impression management scale of the 16PF 5th edition. (Unpublished master's thesis, Florida Institute of Technology, Melbourne).

Kelly, M. L. (1999). *16PF Select manual.* Champaign, IL: Institute for Personality and Ability Testing.

Kohlberg, L. (1964). Development of moral character and moral ideology. In M. L. Hoffman & L. W. Hoffman (Eds), *Review of child development research* (Vol. 1). New York: Russell Sage Foundation.

Krug, S. E. (1981). *Interpreting 16PF profiles.* Champaign, IL: Institute for Personality and Ability Testing.

Leary, T. (1957). *Interpersonal diagnosis of personality.* New York: Ronald Press.

Lord, W. (1997). *Personality in practice.* Windsor, Berkshire, England: NFER-Nelson.

Lord, W. (1999). *16PF5: Overcoming obstacles to interpretation.* Windsor, Berkshire, England: NFER-Nelson.

Lowman, R. L. (1991). *The clinical practice of career assessment.* Washington, DC: American Psychological Association.

Macgregor, C. J. (2000). Does personality matter: A comparison of student experiences in traditional and online classrooms. *Dissertation Abstracts International, 61*(5), 1696A.

Maraist, C. C., & Russell, M. T. (2002). *16PF Fifth Edition norm supplement: Release 2002.* Champaign, IL; Institute for Personality and Ability Testing.

Maslow, A. H. (1970). *Motivation and personality* (2nd ed.). New York: Harper & Row.

McAdams, D. P. (1990). *The person: An introduction to personality psychology.* New York: Harcourt Brace Jovanovich.

Mead, A. (1999). *Correlates of the 16PF Fifth Edition Reasoning scale.* Unpublished manuscript.

Mehrabian, A., & Steff, C. A. (1995). Basic temperament components of loneliness, shyness, and conformity. *Social Behavior and Personality, 23,* 253–264.

Mershon, B., & Gorsuch, R. L. (1988). Number of factors in the personality sphere: Does increase in factors increase predictability of real-life criteria? *Journal of Personality and Social Psychology, 55*(4), 675–680.

Meyer, R. G. (1989). *Clinician's handbook.* Boston: Allyn & Bacon.

Mogenet, J. L., & Rolland, J. P. (1995). *16PF5 de R. B. Cattell.* Paris: Les Editions du Centre de Psychologie Appliquée.

Motegi, M. (1982). *Japanese translation and adaptation of the 16PF.* Tokyo: Nihon Bunka Kagakusha.

Myers, I. B., McCaulley, M. H., Quenk, N. L., & Hammer, A. L. (1998). *MBTI manual: A guide to the development and use of the Myers-Briggs Type Indicator.* Palo Alto, CA: Consulting Psychologists Press.

Norman, W. T. (1963). Toward an adequate taxonomy of personality attributes: Replicated factor structure in peer nomination personality ratings. *Journal of Abnormal and Social Psychology, 66,* 574–583.

O'Connor, R. M, & Little, I. S. (in press). Revisiting the predictive validity of emotional intelligence: Self-report vs. ability-based measures. *Personality and Individual Differences, 3,* 29.

Ones, D. S., Chockalingam, V., & Schmidt, F. L. (1993). Comprehensive meta-analysis of integrity test validities: Findings and implications for personnel selection and theories of job performance. *Journal of Applied Psychology, 78,* 679–703.

Paunonen, S. (1993, August). *Sense, nonsense, and the Big Five factors of personality.* Paper presented at the meeting of the American Psychological Association, Toronto, Ontario.

Peraino, J. M., & Willerman, L. (1983). Personality correlates of occupational status according to Holland types. *Journal of Vocational Behavior, 22,* 268–277.

Piotrowski, C., & Keller, J. W. (1989). Psychological testing in outpatient mental health facilities: A national study. *Professional Psychology: Research and Practice, 20*(6), 423–425.

Pipher, C. M. (2002). *Construct validity of the 16PF and the NEO PI-R.* Unpublished manuscript.

Porter, R. B., & Cattell, R. B. (1975). *Children's Personality Questionnaire* (Rev. ed.). Champaign, IL: Institute for Personality and Ability Testing.

Prieto, J. M., Gouveia, V. V., & Fernandez, M. A. (1996). Evidence on the primary source-trait structure in the Spanish 16PF, 5th edition. *European Review of Applied Psychology, 46*(1), 33–43.

Quenk, N. L. (2000). *Essentials of Myers-Briggs Type Indicator assessment.* New York: Wiley.

Raju, N. S., & Ellis, B. B., (2002). Differential item and test functioning. In F. Drasgow & N. Schmitt (Eds.), *Measuring and analyzing behavior in organizations.* San Francisco, CA: Jossey-Bass.

Raju, N. S., van der Linden, W. J., & Fleer, P. F. (1995). IRT-based internal measures of differential functioning of items and tests. *Applied Psychological Measurement, 19*(4), 353–368.

Reynolds, C. R. (1995). Test bias and the assessment of intelligence and personality. In D. H. Saklofske & M. Zeidner (Eds.), *International handbook of personality and intelligence.* New York: Plenum.

Russell, M. T. (1995). *16PF Fifth Edition Couple's Counseling Report user's guide.* Champaign, IL: Institute for Personality and Ability Testing.

Russell, M. T. (1998). *16PF Fifth Edition Teamwork Development Report user's guide.* Champaign, IL: Institute for Personality and Ability Testing.

Russell, M. T., & Bedwell, S. (2003). *16PF Protective Services Report manual.* Champaign, IL: Institute for Personality and Ability Testing.

Russell, M. T., & Karol, D. (2002). *The 16PF Fifth Edition: Administrator's manual* (Rev. ed.). Champaign, IL: Institute for Personality and Ability Testing.

Sackett, P. R., Schmitt, N., Ellingson, J. E., & Kabin, M. B. (2001). High-stakes testing in employment, credentialing, and higher education: Prospects in a post-affirmative-action world. *American Psychologist, 56,* 302–318.

Salgado, J. (1997). The five factor model of personality and job performance in the European Community. *Journal of Applied Psychology, 82*(1), 30–43.

Salgado, J., Viswesvaran, C., & Ones, D. S. (2001). Predictors used for personnel selection: An overview of constructs, methods and techniques. In N. Anderson, D. S. Ones, H. K. Sinangil, & C. Viswesvaran (Eds.), *Handbook of industrial, work, and organizational psychology* (Vol. 1). Thousand Oaks, CA: Sage.

Schneewind, K. A., & Graf, J. (1998). *Der 16-Personlichkeits-Factoren-Test Revidierte Fassung Test-Manual.* Bern, Switzerland: Verlag Hans Huber.

Schuerger, J. M. (2001a). *16PF Adolescent Personality Questionnaire.* Champaign, IL: Institute for Personality and Ability Testing.

Schuerger, J. M. (2001b). *16PF Adolescent Personality Questionnaire manual.* Champaign, IL: Institute for Personality and Ability Testing.

Schuerger, J. M. (n. d.). Class notes for Psychology 517 and Psychology 523. Cleveland State University.

Schuerger, J. M., & Reigle, N. (1988). Personality and biographic data that characterize men who abuse their wives. *Journal of Clinical Psychology, 44,* 75–81.

Schuerger, J. M., & Sfiligoj, T. (1998) Holland codes and 16PF global factors: Sixty-nine samples. *Psychological Reports, 82,* 1299–1306.

Schuerger, J. M., & Watterson, D. G. (1996). *Occupational Patterns in the 16 Personality Factor Questionnaire* (Workshop handout). Chagrin Falls, OH: Watterson & Associates.

Schuerger, J. M., & Watterson, D. G. (1998). *Occupational interpretation of the 16 Personality Factor Questionnaire.* Cleveland, OH: Watterson & Associates.

Sherman, J. L., & Krug, S. E. (1977). Personality-somatic interactions: The research evidence. In S. E. Krug (Ed.), *Psychological assessment in medicine.* Champaign, IL: Institute for Personality and Ability Testing.

Society for Industrial and Organizational Psychology. (1987). *Principles for the validation and use of personnel selection procedures* (3rd ed.) College Park, MD: Author.

Sweney, A. B. (n.d.). *Interpretations guide for the 16PF.* Unpublished manuscript, Wichita State University, KS.

Tett, R., Jackson, D., & Rothstein, M. (1991). Personality measures as predictors of job performance: A meta-analytic review. *Personnel Psychology, 44,* 703–742.

Tsanadis, J. (2002). [An exploration of the relationship between personality, cognitive abilities, and emotional intelligence]. Unpublished raw data.

Tupes, E. C., & Christal, R. E. (1961). *Recurrent personality factors based on trait ratings* (Tech. Rep. Nos. 61–67). Lackland, TX: U. S. Air Force Aeronautical Systems Division.

Walter, V. (2000). *16PF Personal Career Development Profile: Technical and interpretive manual.* Champaign, IL: Institute for Personality and Ability Testing.

Watterson, D. G. (2002). *16PF Leadership Coaching Report manual.* Champaign, IL: Institute for Personality and Ability Testing.

Wiggins J. S., & Broughton, R. (1985). The interpersonal circle: A structural model for the integration of personality research. In R. Hogan & W. H. Jones (Eds.), *Perspectives in personality* (Vol. 1, pp. 1–47). Greenwich, CT: JAI Press.

Wonderlic Personnel Test. (1992). *Wonderlic Personnel Test & Scholastic Level Exam user's manual.* Libertyville, IL: Author.

Zimbardo, P. G. (1977). *Shyness: What it is, and what to do about it.* Reading, MA: Addison-Wesley.

Annotated Bibliography

MANUALS

Cattell, R. B., Eber, H. W., & Tatsuoka, M. M. (1992). Handbook for the Sixteen Personality Factor Questionnaire (rev. ed.). Champaign, IL: Institute for Personality and Ability Testing, Inc.

This older manual (for the fourth edition) contains important information. Written largely by the test author, it provides original information about the test design and development, its standardization, the meaning of the factors, and a wide range of reliability and validity information, including profiles for dozens of occupations.

Russell, M. T., & Karol, D. (2002). The 16PF Fifth Edition Administrator's manual Rev. ed.). Champaign, IL: Institute for Personality and Ability Testing, Inc.

This newer manual gives up-to-date information about the development of the 16PF Fifth Edition, its administration and scoring, scale meanings and profile interpretation, and reliability and validity information, including factor analytic studies, correlations with other tests, and criterion validity.

Conn, S. R., & Rieke, M. L. (1994). *16PF Fifth Edition technical manual.* Champaign, IL: Institute for Personality and Ability Testing, Inc.

This manual provides more in-depth technical information about the test development and validation process, including the primary scales, the global scales, the Reasoning (B) scale, and the response style indices. It gives more technical detail about the construction of the norm sample and describes various kinds of reliability and validity research, including factor analyses and prediction of criteria such as leadership, creativity, empathy, interpersonal skills, and the Holland occupational types.

INTERPRETIVE BOOKS

Cattell, H. B. (1989). *The 16PF: Personality in depth.* Champaign, IL: Institute for Personality and Ability Testing, Inc.

This book summarizes 10 years of research on the meaning of the 16PF scales conducted in the author's clinical practice. Cattell worked with three databases of clients, carefully recording observations of their behavior, such as their patterns of thinking, feeling, and interacting with others. She also recorded self-disclosures, psychosocial histories, mental status exams and clinical assessments, and therapist observations. This insightful book gives more detailed scale descriptions than any other book.

Karson, M., Karson, S., & O'Dell, J. W. (1997). *16PF interpretation in clinical practice: A guide to the Fifth Edition.* Champaign, IL: Institute for Personality and Ability Testing, Inc.

This book is extremely well written and contains expert, in-depth insight about a wide range of topics, including the general assessment process, strategies for profile interpretation and report writing, and the complexity of scale interactions. Written largely by Michael Karson, it provides a very contemporary and sophisticated perspective on the relevance of test results to treatment planning and therapeutic interaction, and presents over a dozen case studies that reflect current client problems and practice trends.

Lord, W. (1997). *Personality in practice.* Windsor, Berkshire (UK): NFER-Nelson Publishing Co.

Lord's book is aimed at practitioners, particularly industrial/organizational consultants, and begins with a thoughtful discussion of the differences between earlier editions and the Fifth Edition. The book goes on to discuss the meaning of the various scales and provides exceptionally tidy capsule summaries of them as well as the meaning of various scale combinations within each global factor. It also addresses cross-cultural usage of the test as well as specific issues in using the test in employee selection.

Lord, W. (1999). *16PF5: Overcoming obstacles to interpretation.* Windsor, Berkshire (UK): NFER-Nelson Publishing Co.

Whereas Lord's first book concentrates on the meaning of 16PF scales, this one focuses on understanding "the meaning of the profile in the context of a specific individual and a specific assessment issue." Lord makes use of her extensive experience with the test to address specific problems that interpreters often have, such as the potential for distortion in scores, the impact of personal values in understanding score meanings, the interpretation of difficult score combinations, and other problems. She closes the book with a couple of well-thought-out chapters on principles and suggestions for giving feedback to clients, including specific questions to ask interviewees to validate scores.

Schuerger, J. M., & Watterson, D. G. (1998). *Occupational interpretation of the 16 Personality Factor Questionnaire.* Cleveland, OH: Watterson & Associates, Inc.

This small book was constructed for use in 16PF workshops. In addition to providing scale descriptions that are particularly work-relevant, it gives detailed 16PF profiles for 60–70 different occupation groups. It describes the relevance of 16PF scores to the Holland Occupational themes and provides strategies for productively comparing client scores to these themes. It also describes various patterns of interaction among the scales.

Index

About the Authors

Heather E. P. Cattell, Ph.D., is the daughter of Raymond and Karen Cattell, and coauthored the fifth edition of the 16PF with them. Trained as a clinical psychologist, she has worked at clinics and hospitals in the San Francisco Bay area and has taught many courses at the undergraduate and graduate level. For the last 15 years she has worked on various projects at the Institute for Personality & Ability Testing (IPAT), including developing 16PF computer-based interpretive reports, international translations, workshops, and the new PsychEval Personality Questionnaire (updated CAQ).

James M. Schuerger, Ph.D., has worked for over 40 years as psychological researcher, teacher, and practitioner. He was first a teacher and counselor at the high school level, then a research assistant professor in Raymond Cattell's laboratory at the University of Illinois. He continues as teacher, counselor, and researcher at Cleveland State University, and he has taught under-graduate and graduate-level courses in psychological testing for more than 30 years. Dr. Schuerger has almost a hundred publications on topics in psycho-logical measurement and on the 16PF and its applications in particular, and he has conducted numerous professional workshops on the 16PF, often fea-turing occupational applications. He is the author of the Adolescent Personality Questionnaire and is currently developing a revision of the Children's Personality Questionnaire.

Acknowledgments

The authors would like to thank Mary Cattell, Ryan Ladd, and Judy O'Donnell for their dedicated and detailed editing. Without their generous and competent assistance, this book would not be the same. We would also like to thank Dave Watterson, Mary Lynn Kelly, Mary Russell, Scott Bedwell, Cathy Maraist, Jim Slaughter, and Kathi Keyes for their helpful ideas. Heather Cattell would also like to thank Jacqueline Miles and Cynthia Lust for their encouragement and support throughout this process. Most of all, we are indebted to the pioneering efforts of Ray and Karen Cattell in developing and nurturing the 16PF and to their absolute belief in the mea-surability of personality. Our fond thanks to all of these people.